CW00970534

THE
CULT
OF
THE BUDGERIGAR

OTHER BUDGERIGAR TITLES

Homing Budgerigars
Duke of Bedford

Inbreeding Budgerigars
Dr M D S Armour

World of Budgerigars
Cyril H Rogers
**This book covers in detail the development of the
different varieties and colours, and is essential
reading for those who are wanting an all-round
knowledge of the history and pioneers.**

The Budgerigar Book
Ernest Howson
Revised by James Blake

We have an extensive range of titles on poultry
breeds, poultry management, cage birds and various
rural activities.
Please send large SAE for catalogues.

THE

CULT

OF

THE BUDGERIGAR

W. Watmough, FZS

Past Chairman: Budgerigar Society

Revised by James Blake

**Illustrations based on colour
paintings by Eric Peake
& Frances Fry**

*The standard work dealing with every aspect of breeding,
management, and exhibition of budgerigars.*

Beech Publishing House
Station Yard
Elsted Marsh
Midhurst
West Sussex GU209 0JT

ISBN 1-85736-050-8

First published 1936

8th Edition, 2005

British Library Cataloguing-in-Publication Data

A catalogue record for this book is available

from the British Library.

Beech Publishing House
Station Yard
Elsted Marsh
Midhurst
West Sussex GU29 0JT

Printed and bound by Antony Rowe Ltd, Eastbourne

CONTENTS
Chapters

PUBLISHER'S FOREWORD

We have pleasure in presenting a new edition of the famous 'Cult' probably the best known of any book on budgerigars. The late William Watmough was the leader of those fanciers who established this fascinating bird in to the top ranks as a show bird, as well as being kept as pets by thousands.

The colours bred in captivity and their many variations, are far removed from the original green budgerigar introduced to the world by John Gould. The Budgerigar Society and its members have been responsible for the mammoth task of recording the standards and full details can be obtained from their office in Northampton or in one of the standard works on Budgerigars.

In recent times the standard colours have been painted by Eric Peake the renowned bird artist and what a difference this has made for the fancier who has had difficulty in determining what a particular variety looks like. This process started in 1980 and has been extended from that time.

One of the main differences seen in the 25 years or so, since the first painting, has been the change in the head and its parts. The cap and brow have changed thus improving the appearance of the head.

Birds have become more "streamlined" and the flights are quite rounded. However, the birds are still quite balanced which is an important requirement.

The question of TYPE and COLOUR is always controversial, but it is generally agreed that both aspects must be considered when a bird is being judged. A top class colour on a badly shaped bird is of little value and this principle needs to be applied at all times. The modern approach recognizes this important fact.

We hope this revised edition will continue to meet a need for those who require a guide on these fascinating birds.

Joseph Batty   January, 2005

Lutino Cock

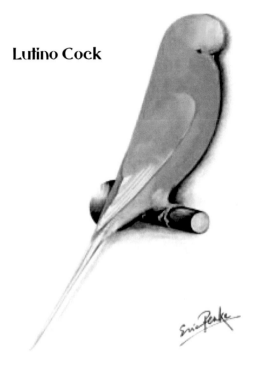

Yellow-wing
Dark Green

Light Green
Cock

Dominant
Blue Pied

Budgerigar Colours I

Grey Cock

Sky-Blue Cock

Opaline Light Green

Whitewing Cobalt

Budgerigar Colours II

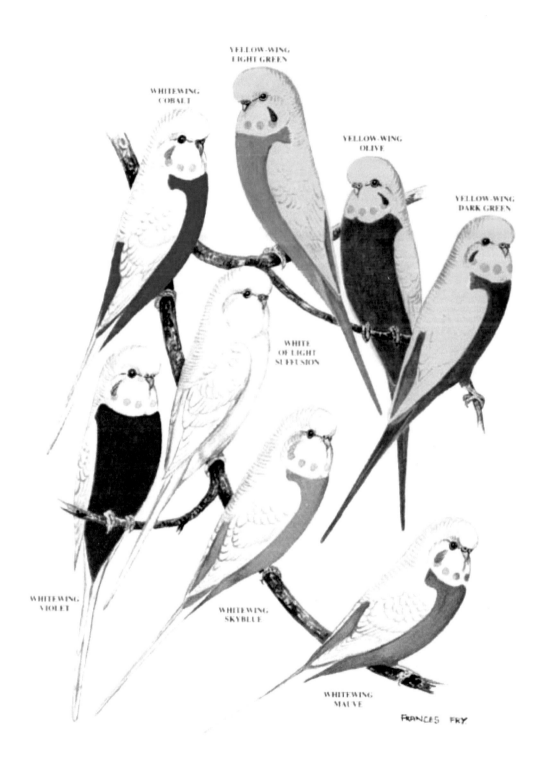

WHITEWING
COBALT

YELLOW-WING
LIGHT GREEN

YELLOW-WING
OLIVE

YELLOW-WING
DARK GREEN

WHITE
OF LIGHT
SUFFUSION

WHITEWING
VIOLET

WHITEWING
SKYBLUE

WHITEWING
MAUVE

FRANCES FRY

Budgerigar Colours III

ALBINO

FALLOW
LIGHT GREEN

GREYWING
LIGHT GREEN

LUTINO

YELLOW-
FACED
SKYBLUE

GREYWING
SKYBLUE

FALLOW
SKYBLUE

FRANCES FRY.

Budgerigar Colours IV

OPALINE
GREY GREEN

OPALINE
SKYBLUE

OPALINE
LIGHT GREEN

OPALINE
DARK
GREEN

OPALINE
COBALT

OPALINE
MAUVE

OPALINE
VIOLET

OPALINE
GREY

Budgerigar Colours V

CHAPTER 1
INTRODUCTION

The origin and discovery of the wild budgerigar are covered in Chapter 2. John Gould an Englishman made the discovery and proceeded to write about them. They were brought to this country in 1840, although they had been noted and mentioned in earlier publications.

Taking them up as cage and aviary birds was a slow process so, although they were being bred and sold, it was not until 1925 that the Budgerigar Society was formed. This was the landmark in its development because the society allowed the necessary publicity to be given and allowed its members to have a say in its form and, later, to be able to produce the multitude of colours from what had been a single colour species.

The number of budgerigars being shown immediately prior to 1925 was ten entries at a major show at the Crystal Palace, yet in 1938 in Bradford there were 1,570 exhibits and, after that the numbers grew so that in 1951 over 2, 000 birds were on show at Olympia, and the progress has continued, although at times numbers have declined and, clearly, something should be done to prevent the so-called animal rights movement from spoiling the hobby of keeping birds.*

These are not wild birds; they have been bred in captivity and prefer it that way. The present author has kept birds and allowed them outside, but they are always glad to be back and enjoy the comfort of a roomy aviary and top quality food and attention when required.

---

* The forced cancellation of the National Cage & Aviary Show in December, 2004, was a great disappointment to many dedicated fanciers and to those suppliers of goods to the cage bird fancy.

INTRODUCTORY

Many attempts have been made to design the ideal aviary for cage birds and much has been written on the subject. All responsible bird societies encourage the need for adequate space and proper food. There is generally no question of cruelty involved and, at the correctly run shows -- and most come into that category -- adequate space is given in the show cages. With budgerigars there is no problem because all the essential requirements are met without difficulty. The birds can open their wings and fly around in a normal and contented fashion.

Some fanciers give their birds a tremendous amount of room, almost as if they were in the wild, although, in fact, this is not required. The provision of plants and shrubs, nest boxes, landscaping of aviaries and many other features have also received attention and have been adopted.* Many birds are now better off than those in the wild !

From time to time there have been attempts made to allow budgerigars complete freedom, although whether this is now permitted under European regulations is questionable. One expert designed a special aviary to cope with free-flying birds and this was adapted by many fanciers.**

Despite difficulties which have been experienced the Fancy is still quite strong. Thousands of birds are shown each year, and many thousands are kept by enthusiasts simply as pets. Budgerigars are easily kept, they breed in a range of colours, and are not costly to purchase or to maintain. Obviously, top show birds will be expensive, but they represent many years of work and development so the newcomer buying the high class birds knows there is usually a ready market at a relatively high price; pet birds are not expensive.

The enthusiasm is almost world wide. Even in their country of origin, Australia, show birds are kept. They are also wide spread in America, New Zealand, Canada, South Africa and in European countries.

The *Colour Standards* issued by The Budgerigar Society are used throughout the World. Reference is made to them in books and in features by overseas societies. There is an official ringing system which helps to control the pedigree side of the Fancy. Every thing possible is done to encourage the growth of the Fancy and to improve the welfare of the Budgerigar.

Aviaries -- A Practical Handbook, Joseph Batty, BPH
** *Homing Budgerigars*, The Duke of Bedford, BPH

INTRODUCTORY

There is a good sale for surplus stock of pleasing quality. Those who breed on correct, up-to-date lines, and who produce youngsters good enough to be exhibited, or capable of themselves breeding winners, have usually no difficulty in finding customers, whilst for Budgerigars as pets there is a continuous demand, and the bird shops buy large quantities in order to supply this market.

I have never advised anyone to go in for Budgerigar keeping as a sole means of livelihood. It should primarily be viewed as a most enjoyable recreation for a true bird lover, although, of course, it will not be any the less appealing because of its possessing profit-making potentialities, or at least paying its way.

The biologist has in this Parakeet a subject *par excellence* for the purposes of genetic research, as will be appreciated by my readers as they peruse the more scientific chapters of this book. Wonderful work has already been done in applying the principles of inheritance to Budgerigar culture, and there is still vast scope for exploration by the scientist, the amateur scientist, and the experimentalist. Therefore it causes no surprise that these people have given to the Budgerigar progressively more and more attention.

A fascination is there provided by the possibility that in a nest there might be found a chick of a colour hitherto unknown in the species — a mutant. Fortunate is the breeder who is the first to produce an entirely new colour variety. His name will become immortal in the Fancy, and he will benefit financially because the selling value of birds of a colour never previously seen is very high.

All those good reasons which I have described as being responsible for the phenomenal progress which we have witnessed in my opinion provide in themselves a complete insurance for the welfare of this branch of the Cage Bird Fancy.

The Budgerigar Fancy is well organised. The shows are most capably managed, and the classifications provided are comprehensive and extensive. In almost all the districts in which bird fanciers reside there are ornithological or solely Budgerigar societies each of which organises members' shows and in th majority of cases one annual open show. Members' shows are excellent trial grounds for potential exhibits at the larger exhibitions. These societies also arrange for lectures, visits to large Budgerigar establishments, judging competitions, etc.

Then there is that great body, the Budgerigar Society. This was founded by a few enthusiasts who visualised the immense possibilities possessed by the Budgerigar as an exhibition bird. Optimistic as they no doubt were over fifty years ago I doubt if even they or any other person interested in this Parakeet at that time ever dreamt, even in their most inspired moments, that the edifice of which they were laying the foundations would grow to be the gigantic monument to their labours which the Society has become.

3

The work which this organisation has done and is doing is invaluable to the hobby, as I am sure my readers will be convinced when I enumerate, as I will now do, some of its activities.

It produces annually a year book containing information essential to the breeder and exhibitor. Four times per annum the Society publishes the *Budgerigar Bulletin*. This publication contains most instructive articles, both practical and scientific, letters on current topics, descriptions of all the latest developments, and news of the Society's activities.

Every member is given a code number which is engraved on the rings that he puts on his birds' legs. The parent body is doing a great work in assisting show promotion. It grants its patronage to a large number of shows and offers trophies and diplomas for competition. Once per annum it organises the big club show in England and sponsors one in Scotland. It makes arrangements for the special provision of Beginners' classes, Novice classes, Intermediate classes, and Champion classes.

It is the Budgerigar Society which sets the Standards of Excellence for the different colour varieties and produces pictures of the Ideal Cock and the

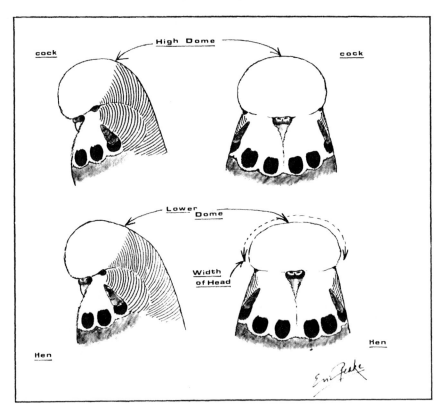

Ideal Hen and the Scale of Points, which indicates the relative importance of the exhibition properties. All these are kept throughly up to date.

The administration of the governing body is controlled by the General Council which elects the Executive Committee. The Council, which is responsible for high-level decisions, consists of representatives of the B.S, appointed by postal ballot of the members, and an equal number of representatives of the Area Societies. There is a President, President Elect, Vice-President, Chairman, and Vice-Chairman.

The British Area Societies affiliated to the Budgerigar Society are the following:-*

Lancashire, Cheshire and North Wales including the Isle of Man Budgerigar Society.
Lincolnshire and East Anglia Budgerigar and Foreign Bird Society.
London & Southern Counties Budgerigar Society.
Midland Budgerigar Association.
Northern Budgerigar Society.
South Midlands Budgerigar and Foreign Bird Society.
South Wales and Monmouthshire Budgerigar Society.
Western Counties Budgerigar and Foreign Bird Society.
Yorkshire Budgerigar Society.

These Area Societies do most valuable work within their own boundaries. They grant patronages to shows, organise club shows, issue Year Books and other publications, arrange for lectures and social functions.

In addition to the Area Societies the following Specialist Societies have associate membership with The Budgerigar Society:

Clearwing Budgerigar Breeders' Association
Crested Budgerigar Club.
Rare Colour & Variety Budgerigar Society.
Variegated Budgerigar Club.

These Societies look after the special interest and development of certain Colour forms on the same lines as the Area Societies.

The dove-tailing of the activities of the Area and Societies with those of the parent body provides one of the best small livestock national organisations that I have ever known.

In 1947 there was inaugurated by the Budgerigar Society, in co-operation with the Area Societies, a big Ring Cash Prize Scheme, which has been a tremendous success.

There is also affiliated to the Budgerigar Society a number of overseas clubs and societies. This is a development which is receiving great encouragement by the General Council. It is a step in the much-desired direction of making Budgerigar culture completely international in character. Eventually we hope to see a universal Ideal, Standard of

* **Since the administrative details are subject to change readers should contact the Budgerigar Society to ensure there have been no revisions.**

Excellence and Scales of Points, and progress is being made in this direction.

Much more could I say about the Budgerigar Society, because I am an enthusiastic supporter of it, but I think I have written sufficient to convince my readers that we have here a body which is fully alive to the best interests and the requirements of this branch of the Fancy.

In the August of 1954 there was organised in Harrogate, Yorkshire, the first World Budgerigar Convention. It was supported by manufacturers and merchants who cater for the requirements of breeders, the overseas press, Budgerigar clubs and societies in other lands, and individual fanciers in every country in which our delightful little Parakeet is cultivated.

Authorities gave papers on subjects important to the hobby; there was a film show; teams of experts answered questions; and there were many lively and constructive discussions. There was an exhibition, the *pièce de résistance* of which was a genetic tree which demonstrated the evolution from the original wild Light Green of Australia to the many varied and beautiful colours in which Budgerigars are now produced.

Other features included an Inter-Area Society Show, at which the British affiliated Area Societies entered birds, in competition for three silver challenge trophies, and trade displays, while the social side was not neglected. A large number of fanciers attended the event, including the representatives from America, Canada, South Africa, Australia, Sweden, Belgium, Denmark, Holland and Hong Kong.

The World Budgerigar Congress is now held on a regular basis. Recognised authorities give lectures, and there are illuminating Question and Answer sessions and discussions. The social events, consisting of a dinner dance and civic reception, are enjoyed by all who attend.

Numerous smaller clubs are ably catering for their members and the Fancy generally; many of these are affiliated to Area Societies.

To those who have been breeding Budgerigars for some years much that I have written in this introductory chapter will be old news, but to those who have recently started to keep these remarkable birds or who are at present contemplating doing so, I think the position of the Fancy to-day cannot fail to be highly encouraging.

CHAPTER 2

ORIGIN AND HISTORY

AUSTRALIAN ORIGINS

The wild Green Budgerigar *(Melopsittacus undulatus)*, from which wild ancestor all our present domesticated birds in their grand array of colour varieties are descended, is a native of Australia. It has had a variety of names — *Undulated Grass Parakeet, Zebra Parakeet, Zebra Grass Parakeet, Shell Parrot, Scallop Parrot, Warbling Grass Parakeet, Undulated Parrot, Canary Parrot* and *Betcherrygah* from which the now universal name Budgerigar is derived. The usual definition of Betcherrygah is "good bird," but it is stated on reliable authority that it is an old aboriginal dialect word meaning "good food."

According to eminent naturalists who have written descriptions of the Budgerigar's native habits, these birds are migratory, the movements of the flocks being governed by the food supply. They stay in one district so long as the plains are green and luxuriant, but as soon as scarcity of water dries up the herbage, away they go to the proximity of streams and to the northern parts of Australia where a rich supply of ripening and ripe grass seeds awaits them.

Favourite habitats are the Liverpool Plain in New South Wales, the Alexandrina and Wellington Lakes, and the country which is irrigated by the Murray River. One of the favoured breeding places is the mallee shrub. Undoubtedly their distribution in Australia is wide, as is clearly demonstrated by Mr. Neville W. Cayley (F.R.Z.S. New South Wales) in *Budgerigars in Bush and Aviary** in which he quotes records of the observation of these birds in flocks of many thousands in a large number of places separated from each other by vast distances.

---

* Neville W. Cayley, F.R.N.Z. (N.S.W.), *Budgerigars in Bush and Aviary* (Angus & Robertson Ltd., Sydney).

Mr. Allen Silver describes their habitat as "Australia generally, Gulf of Carpentaria and Port Denison on the East, through the interior to New South Wales, Victoria, and West and South-west Australia. Absent in Tasmania, seldom moving South of Melbourne and not normally a coastal bird. Type of country favoured — grass land and timber and salt bush flats."

It is said that during the course of their migration separate flocks become merged into one huge concourse, which accounts for the immense numbers which are to be seen flying together and which cover so large an area that at times they cause the light of the sun to be partially obscured.

Our winter is their breeding season in Southern Australia, at the end of which they migrate north. Eggs have, however, been observed in various months in different parts of the country, ranging from March to August, for instance.

In Dr. Karl Russ's book, *The Budgerigar,* there is quoted a description of the habits of these little Parakeets at breeding time in the mallee shrub from the pen of Mr. Adolf Engelhardt, which reads as follows:-

"The remarkable shape of the mallee is particularly favourable for the purpose of nesting. About eight stems grow out of the same roots to a height of about 36 ft. with white bark and scanty tops. Every hollow trunk, every knot-hole, in case of necessity even every suitable cavern in the roots is used for nesting, often by two or three couples together. In a few weeks things get quite lively. The ripe seeds of grass are perfectly suited to feeding the young. Anyone who happened to pass such a spot at this time would be able to catch hundreds of them easily in his own hands. In huge swarms they fly up from the grass when they hear anyone approaching. They perch in long rows on the bare twigs, amusing themselves by chirping songs and unsuspectingly they watch bloodthirsty man raise his gun to let fly a charge sufficient to bring down dozens at once. At last the available seeds are consumed. Perhaps there is also lack of water. The passion for travelling seizes the birds and leads them further. Their next aim is to reach the Alexandrina and Wellington Lakes, through both of which flows the Murray before it discharges itself into the sea. It is uncertain whether the morasses there provide them more abundantly with grass seeds or whether the proximity of fresh water attracts them; but this is the spot to which every year the bird catchers come in order to lay their snares and to catch many thousands. This, however, only applies to the years with abundant rainfall. But in other years, when the rainfall remains below the yearly average, Budgerigars seem to disappear completely. No doubt they then move to the far north where often, in the summer heat, violent thunder showers occur, which, as stated before, completely change a sandy desert in a short time into a grassy plain. All migrating parrots seem to know that by anticipation; for where nature has laid their table, they attend."

The number of chicks in the nests are four to six. Dead timber provides favourite sites. The holes in which the eggs are laid are from 6 in. to 1 ft. depth, with an entrance from 1½ in. to 2 in. in diameter. No nesting material is provided.

The flocks are not seen in the same places at the same seasons every year. In some years comparatively few birds are to be observed in a district. In other years they are there in thousands. They suffer seriously in abnormally hot weather. For instance, during the heat wave experienced in Australia during the early months of 1932 many thousands of Budgerigars succumbed.

These wild birds are Light Greens and answer to the description which I have given at the opening of Chapter 3. On isolated occasions Yellows have been seen. For instance, Mr. J.A. Keartland in remarks quoted in *Budgerigars in Bush and Aviary,* says:-

"While crossing the Great Desert of Western Australia I noticed two all-yellow birds flying with a flock on their way to water."

Mr. J.P. Rogers in *Emu,* Volume II, 1902, also reported the appearance of a Yellow amongst the wild birds and we are informed that Dark Greens have also been recorded, and there is a skin of a specimen of this colour in the Kensington Natural History Museum. It is clear, however, that very few variations from the Light Green have been observed amongst wild Budgerigars, though they may have mutated more frequently than we realise, the mutants having died young, probably being weaker than the Light Green, as is often the case with new mutants.

Mr. Cayley, author of *Budgerigars in Bush and Aviary,* describes paler forms as follows:-

"*Melopsittacus undulatus intermedius:* Differs from *M. undulatus* in its paler coloration especially on the neck and back, and darker on the head and underneath than *M.u. pallidiceps.* Type: Northern Territory (Alexandra).

"*Melopsittacus undulatus pallidiceps:* Differs from *M. undulatus* in its pallid coloration, especially noticeable on the head. Type: Port Torment, North-west Australia. Range: Western Australia."

Wild Light Greens

Some years before the war several fanciers in this country imported wild Light Greens for experimental purposes. These included the late J.W. Marsden and Major J.S.S. Clarke. Some of these birds were exhibited, not for competition but as an object of interest, at shows in this country. They were bright and level in colour, but for size and type, judged by modern standards, they were not comparable with the specimens staged at our shows.

Mr. Marsden at that time sent me the following note with regard to the wild Greens then in his aviaries:-

"They arrived from Australia in a box cage in perfect condition. They are as alike in appearance as peas in a pod. They reached me in the middle of December and I kept them in quarantine until 15th March when I put them in the breeding aviaries. I provided coconut husks and nest boxes. Two hens went to nest in the husks, four in the boxes. Most of them were sitting within two weeks. I lost one cock, so I mated his hen to a good White cock. The number of youngsters produced was quite satisfactory.

"I have had four pairs in one aviary, which consists of a 4 ft. by 5 ft. shelter and a 4 ft. by 12 ft. flight. There is one perch in the flight and one perch in the shelter. They are 12 to 13 feet apart, therefore they have a good distance to fly. There is also an elder bush four or five feet high in the flight. They clear this when they are flying.

"When one of the wild Greens had chicks about two weeks old the box was very dirty. I replaced this with another box of the same pattern. The hen would not go into it. I waited a long time and then found that the perch on the front was not exactly the same height as in the first box, so I attached the old front to the new box, which she at once entered.

"I wish there could be at every show one wild Green or a bird bred from a pair of wild Greens so that people could see the shade of colour.

"The wild birds in the flights have perfect wing carriage but some in cages cross their wings. This year I have bred two youngsters from the Australian Greens which are flightless and which I put down to bad feeding during the cold spell."

The first description of a Budgerigar was given by the naturalist Shaw (*Naturalists' Miscellany*, 1789-1813, and *Zoology of New Zealand*, 1794). Shaw originally used the definition *Psittacus undulatus*. It was Gould who adopted the generic name *Melopsittacus*.

It was not until 1840 that living Budgerigars were introduced into this country. In that year Gould, the famous explorer and investigator, brought to England a pair which had been bred by his brother-in-law, Charles Coxon, and at the same time published the first description of their habits *(The Birds of Australia* 1840-8).

According to Wagler in 1831 a single specimen was exhibited as a rarity in the Museum of the Linnæan Society in London.

Dr. Russ states that in Berlin Budgerigars bred for the first time in 1855. This occurred in the home of the Countess von Schwerin.

Russ asserted that the first pair of Budgerigars sold in England was bought by the wholesale merchant, Charles Jamrach, in London for £26 and sold by him to Dr. Butler of Woolwich for £27.

It is recorded that Mr. Joseph Abrahams was the first to breed the Yellow variety in England. This was in 1884 and they were bred from Yellows obtained from Belgium. The particular bird can now be seen at the Natural History Museum at Kensington, where it is described as "A Pale

Variety."

The late W. Swaysland is said to have exhibited Yellows as early as 1886.

Mr. R.J. Watts, writing in *The Budgerigar Bulletin* of June 1933, said: "The first record of the Yellow's appearance at an exhibition is given by Dr. W.T. Green in one of his books published something like fifty years ago in which he states that a bird of this colour was exhibited at the Alexandra Palace Show. My earliest experience with them began about the year 1908."

Dr. Russ gives the date of the first Yellow as about 1872. It is believed that they were bred in Belgium in that year.

Skyblues and Greywings

Skyblues (*vide* Mr. Silver) made their first appearance in 1881. The Van der Snickt report of 1881 mentions that the first bird of this colour was a cock, that it was paired to a Yellow hen, and that later another Skyblue (a hen) was obtained from the pair which bred the first Skyblue.

Mr. O. Millsum (whom I knew as a successful exhibitor of rabbits) was at one time aviary manager to Mr. Pauvvels of Everberg. He told me that the Skyblue Budgerigars exhibited by him on behalf of Mr. Pauvvels at the Horticultural Hall in November, 1910, and at the Crystal Palace in 1911, and which were the first Blues ever seen in England, were descended from stock birds owned by a Dutchman somewhere about 1885.

Dr. H..Steiner of Zurich tells us that Blue Budgerigars appeared for the first time in 1878 in Belgium, but they disappeared a few years later without leaving any trace.

Mr. Allen Silver says that the first White Budgerigar he remembers occurring in this country was bred by the late H.D. Astley in September, 1920, from a pair of Skyblues.

Yellows also appeared in Mr. Astley's collection of Blues and Greens.

Mr. Tom Goodwin exhibited a White for the first time at the Dulwich and Peckham Show held on 31st October, 1922.

The late J.W. Marsden stated that Olives were introduced into England from France by the late J.D. Hamlyn in 1918, that the first Apple Greens (Greywing Greens) were bred by Mrs. Ransome of Wimbledon in 1919, Cobalts by Mr. George Hedges in France in 1923, and Mauves a year later by the late Mrs. Dalton Burgess and Mme. Lecallier. Mr. Marsden has also informed me that Mr. Pelham Sutton was the first to breed Skyblues in England. These were from a pair of Skyblues and they were hatched in 1912. Mrs. Ransome's Greywing Green (she named it a "Jade") was, he says, bred from a blue bred Green hen purchased from him, and a bad coloured Yellow cock.

Mr. C.H. Rogers exhibited a Greywing Dark Green hen in 1925 at Cambridge. This bird has appeared in the nest of one of his Normal Olive Green hens and a Light Green cock. The pedigree of the Olive Green hen was not known but the Light Green was pure.

Mr. Silver, writing in the *Bulletin* of December, 1931, said:-

"The Green Greywing as we know it to-day seems on account of its variable external appearance to have arisen, as far as records go, in 1920, although I and several of my bird keeping acquaintances seem to have observed it in mixed consignments of Yellow-coloured birds.

"Mr. G.F. Hedges bred one in 1920 and 1921 apparently from blue coloured and yellow coloured parents. M. Blanchard says his father obtained this pair from two Green coloured birds previous to the war, and at the same time some Yellows. M. Blanchard calls them Jades.

"In 1925 in Germany they were referred to as May Green Budgerigars and previously here as Apple Greens.

"The first Skyblue Greywing I saw was shown by a Mr. Hedges as a Pearl in 1928. Mr. Arthur Lewis produced Greywing Cobalts about the same time (1927-8) when he sent Mr. Humphries wings of dead birds (pearls).

"Mrs. Wall of Marlborough, Wilts., who was particularly interested in this phase of the Budgerigar obtained Cobalt Greywings in 1929 and Mauve Greywings in 1931."

It has been stated that Greywing Greens (erstwhile described as Apple Greens) existed in Germany and Belgium as long ago as 1875.

M. Blanchard first observed the Dark Green in the summer of 1915 and the first Olive in the autumn of 1916. He obtained Cobalts in 1920 by crossing Blues and Olives together.

Again *vide* Mr. Silver's remarks in *The Budgerigar Bulletin*, Mr. G. Hedges, when in charge of the collection of Mme. Lecallier, bred Cobalts in 1923. In 1924 Mrs. Dalton Burgess bred Mauves from Cobalts.*

According to Mr. Allen Silver (*Budgerigar Bulletin*, December, 1931) "Bailley Maitre" alludes to the occurrence of a Lutino in approximately 1885. The next recorded instance seems to have been the two bred by the late Mr. C.P. Arthur of Melksham, who in his day was the largest breeder of Budgerigars in this country. These birds were claimed at a Cheltenham show and afterwards exhibited in London.

In a contribution which appeared in *Ornithologie und Wissenschaft* dated 15th August, 1933, by Dr. Hans Steiner the statement was made that in 1879 at least nine pink-eyed birds were in existence and that in 1881 a fancier bred no fewer than twenty-five. All were hens. Mrs. George Lait, of

---

* The late Harry Humphries (one-time secretary of the Budgerigar Society) sent to me the following comments: "Mr. G.F. Hedges was aviary attendant for Mme. Lecallier, after which he was aviary attendant for Mrs. Dalton Burgess until her death. It was his brother, Walter, who exhibited the 'Pearlwing' at the Crystal Palace Show. Mr. Arthur Lewis sent me two wings, both being from what we now style Grey-wing Cobalts. They were a most beautiful shade of grey on the wings, better by far than we usually see these days on the bench. He had no idea how they came. "They just came."

Grimsby, bred the first Yellowfaces. This was in 1937. They were exhibited by her for the first time at the "Yorkshire Observer" show in Bradford in 1938.

Between 1925 and 1928, Budgerigars became the fashion in Japan and very high prices were paid for specimens. The value of Skyblues rose to over £100 per pair and for Cobalts, Whites, and Mauves £150 and more per pair is said to have been paid by Japanese buyers.

A Budgerigar Boom

Although Budgerigar breeding proceeded apace, demand exceeded supply, and the value of birds of this species rose out of all proportion to their intrinsic merits. Small fortunes were made during this boom, which had no precedent in the avian world. The whole thing was abnormal and neither the demand from Japan nor the prices ruling could possibly be sustained, and with even greater rapidity than the movement had started so did it end.

With reference to the Japanese boom the late Harry Humphries wrote "The highest price ever obtained at any period was for a pair of Whites (we knew then only the one shade or suffusion — the present-day White Skyblue). They were sent out to a member of the Royal House of Japan, who paid a fabulous sum for them, and both birds were dead upon arrival.

"For a long while these Whites were decidedly delicate. The early Whites often changed hands at £100 per bird in this country. The peak period for prices was undoubtedly round about February 1927. Then the ruling prices were as follows: Skyblues £125 a pair, Cobalts and Mauves £175, Whites about the latter price, too — all for adult birds.

"The best price I knew to be obtained in this country for other than Whites was for a pair of Crystal Palace winning Cobalts that fetched £200. Apple Greens, round about 1926 and 1927, sold for about £20 a pair. The B.S. officially named these 'Jades' for a while — indeed until the Greywing became established."

Apropos the high prices paid by the Japanese, it must be appreciated that the large sums secured by breeders were not for high-class show specimens, but for quite ordinary birds in so far as type is concerned. Therefore, the figures cannot be properly compared with the very big prices paid during the war and since for Budgerigars of *outstanding* merit.

The late Mrs. Brown, of Morecambe, imported Whitewing Violets from Australia — to which country she was a frequent visitor — in the middle 'thirties. Mr. Fred Garvey and I both purchased some of these birds from her about 1939. But the Violet also appeared as a mutation in England about the same time.

Figure 2-1   Early Specimens of a Budgerigar in the Wild

CHAPTER 3

TYPE IN BUDGERIGARS

THE DESCRIPTION

In this and the chapter immediately succeeding it I describe the Budgerigar, its shape, its colour, and its markings, as the fancier desires to produce them, in accordance with the Standard of Excellence issued by the Budgerigar Society, and in order to win prizes at our shows.

Before proceeding to that, I think it will be interesting if I give here the naturalist's description of the wild Green Budgerigar from which all our beautiful colour varieties are descended. Therefore I reprint the following from *The Budgerigar* by Dr. Karl Russ:-

"*The Budgerigar (Melopsittacus undulatus,* Shaw).

"The Budgerigar is one of the smallest parrots, being about the size of the sparrow, with long, pointed wings and tail, pleasing green and yellow plumage, on the upper surface partly dark and undulated, with beautiful blue spots at the under side of the neck.

"Description of the adult male. — Forehead, top, straw-coloured; on the occiput, upper part of the neck, foreback and fore-shoulders, the feathers are characterised by regular black transverse undulations on a vividly greenish yellow ground. On the head, the dark transverse stripes are finer; at the back the dark stripes as well as the yellow stripes of the ground colour become broader. The lower part of the back, the rump, and upper part of the tail-coverts, are beautifully green. The parts around the cheeks and ears like the occiput show, in the upper part, very fine transverse undulations on a yellow ground.

"Several longer feathers, of a deep blue colour, descend from the cheeks and stand out sharply against the bright yellow throat where the plumage is lengthened into a beard; on both sides, two of these long feathers each show a roundish black spot at the point. The upper part of the throat is a fine yellow, remainder of under-surface a beautiful grass-green, tending to become yellowish; the small and medium wing coverts, a vividly greenish yellow with dark transverse stripes following the form of the feather in the shape of a half-circle, as on the fore-shoulder feathers. The last big feathers of the wing-coverts, the last secondaries, and the hind-shoulder feathers, are brownish black with a broad yellow border and similar narrower borders at both sides; the first big wing-coverts are a dim green with yellow borders like the others, with a blackish streak between the yellow border and the green colour. The remaining secondaries are, on the lace-half of the outer vane, a nice dark green with a yellow border, on the lace-half of the inner vane, blackish; the ground-half of the outer vane, a bright yellowish green, on the inner vane whitish yellow, which colour is continued as a narrow border till it reaches the tip. The light colour of the ground-half of the outer vane joins the broad yellow lace-edges of the large-coverts, forming a band which becomes broader.

The Primaries

"Primaries at the outer vane show a dark grey with a narrow yellow border except the first; interior vane, blackish from the second, with broad wedge-shaped yellowish spots in the centre, which produce on the under-surface a light transverse band, narrow in front, becoming broader at the back. The outer vanes from the fifth to the last show likewise a yellow-green spot, forming a band broadening backwards; lesser-coverts blue-green with dim whitish borders; anal feathers blue-green with broad yellowish borders; edge of the feathers a greenish yellow; under-surface of the feathers, a lighter green, the light designs are clearly noticeable; under wing-coverts yellowish green, partly white at the base with lighter green lace-half and broad yellow lace border; the two longer central tail feathers are dark blue at the base with a green-blue border; on the under-surface soot-coloured.

"The remaining tail feathers are a greener blue with broad lemon-coloured central spot over both vanes and a broad black border at the base of the interior vane, shading off to yellow, so that the tail on the outer as well as the inner side shows two broad slanting blackish-green bands and a brimstone-coloured one, the latter going at an acute angle from the edge to the centre. Under the small feathers there is a coating of down, clear white on the whole under-surface, light blue at the upper-surface, ash grey at the head and back; iris, pearl white or pale yellow surrounded by a broad bluish edge, bill greenish, horn-grey at the base, slightly dark with a vividly dark blue somewhat glossy cere; feet distinctly bluish, horn-coloured, sole white-grey, nails blackish.

"Adult Female. — Like the cock but more or less darkly undulated forehead, the blue spots on the cheek and the black ones on the beard, however, markedly smaller; cere of the bill from greenish yellow to brownish grey.

"Nesting plumage. — On the back a whitish grey fine down; forehead likewise, upper head and breast-sides when the feathers sprout already appear dark and show a vague transverse pencilling; the little blue spots on the cheeks are already present, but not the black ones.

"First plumage. — On the forehead, upper head and sides of the breast, a vague transverse undulation; fore-back vaguely olive-brown, hind-back and rump with indistinct yellowish transverse pencillings; under-surface dimly green. The entire colouring looks much paler than the plumage of the adult, the green and yellow dimmer, the brownish grey on the back, much more striking, bill black, eyes black, feet bluish-white (in the second week the bill becomes a lighter green-grey and the cere bluish white till flesh coloured)."

This description goes into a wealth of detail with much of which we practical breeders do not concern ourselves, and which is not referred to in the Budgerigar Society's Standard. Nevertheless, it must be appreciated that the quotation from Russ's book describes the Light Green Budgerigar as we know it to-day in its domesticated state; in fact, apart from colour variety differences it is descriptive of Budgerigars generally.

BUDGERIGAR SOCIETY DESCRIPTION

And now I come to that modern description of the shape of the exhibition Budgerigar, the Society's Standard, which reads:-

"*Condition* is essential. If a bird is not in condition it should never be considered for any award.

"*Type.* — Gracefully tapered from nape of neck to tip of tail, with an approximately straight back line, and a rather deep nicely curved chest.

"*Length.* — The ideal length is eight and a half inches from the crown of the head to the tip of the tail. Wings well braced, carried just above the cushion of the tail and not crossed. The ideal length of the wing is three and three-quarter inches from the butt to the tip of the longest primary flight, which must contain seven primary flight feathers fully grown and not broken. *No bird showng 'long-flighted' characteristics shall be eligible to take any award.*

"*Head.* — Large, round, wide and symmetrical when viewed from any angle; curvature of skull commencing at cere, to lift outward and upward, continuing over the top and to base of head in one graceful sweep, flecking on head is undesirable.

"*Beak.* set well into face.

"*Eye* to be bold and bright, and positioned well away from front, top and back skull.

"*Neck.* to be short and wide when viewed from either side or front.

"*Wings.* — Approximately two-fifths the total length of the bird, well braced, carried just above the cushion of the tail and not crossed.

17

"*Tail* to be straight and tight with two long tail feathers.

"*Position.* — Steady on the perch at an angle of thirty degrees from the vertical, looking fearless and natural.

"*Masks and spots.* — Masks to be clear, deep and wide, ornamented by four evenly spaced round throat spots, supported by two spots under the cheek patches, the size of the spots to be in proportion to the rest of the make-up of the bird as shown in the Ideals published by the Budgerigar Society. Spots can be either too large or too small. Birds that have had flash spots removed should be penalised.

"*Legs and Feet.* — Legs should be straight and strong, with two front and two rear toes and claws firmly gripping perch.

"*Markings* — Wavy markings on cheek, head, neck, back and wings to stand out clearly.

"*Colour.* — Clear and level and of an even shade."

Type is another word for shape, and shape, in my opinion, is the quality to which both breeders and judges should ever give the most attention.

Size is important, but not so important as type. Colour is important, but not so important as type. Markings are important, but not so important as type.

There is an old saying amongst horsey men that a good horse cannot be a bad colour. One cannot apply that literally to Budgerigars. A good Budgerigar can be a bad colour, so bad in fact, that to use an Irishism, it is not a good Budgerigar; but, my point is that *however good in colour and markings a bird may be, if it fails seriously in type it should not be able to compete successfully against specimens of good shape, reasonably good in colour and markings, which should beat it in spite of its excellence in colour and markings.* I hope I have made my meaning clear. To emphasise what I desire to impart I will put it in different phraseology:

In my estimation structural properties definitely come first and colour points second, but because I have written that, please do not get the false impression that I underestimate the value of colour and markings. I know full well that it is the superb colouring of the Budgerigar which is one of its greatest attractions. What I do say, however, is that the desired colour and markings must be on a well-formed body to make a Budgerigar worthy to be the recipient of high honours.

As to size, I do like *good* birds up to the size set by the Standard, viz., eight and a half inches from crown of head to tip of tail. Prior to October, 1951, the Standard said that a Budgerigar could not be too big. This was changed and now an over-size bird is at a disadvantage when exhibited. I don't like *bad* birds of the maximum size. Some big birds are very unshapely. They should not win prizes merely because of their size. On the other hand, a typical full sized one is better than a small one its equal in shape. To sum up,

Figure 3.1 Ideal Exhibition Budgerigar (Budgerigar Society)
This is slimmer than the modern, top class winners and the head is smaller
(see Colour Plates and page 234)

Figure 3.2 Ideal Exhibition Budgerigar Cock (Budgerigar Society)
This is slimmer than the modern, top class winners and the head is smaller
(see Colour Plates)

I prefer a good little one to a bad big one, but I give even greater preference to a *good* one well up to the ideal standard length.

What breeders have to aim for is reasonably large birds of the correct type, but never to achieve size at the expense of type, of which there is a great danger unless exceptional care is exercised in breeding.

Before I come to analyse the component parts of the Budgerigar which collectively constitute the shape of the bird as a whole, I want to emphasise the importance of that abstract quality usually described as balance, proportion, or the *tout ensemble,* but which words are inferior for the purpose to "symmetry," the dictionary meaning of which is "due proportion of the several parts of the body to each other: the union and conformity of the members of a work to the whole: harmony."

RESPONSIBILITY OF JUDGES

That definition conveys exactly what I desire to see in a high-class exhibition Budgerigar — perfect harmony between one property and another. So long as breeders and judges are faithful to the idea of the bird very good in *all* points in preference to the bird extravagantly good in some points but hopelessly bad in others, then there will be no danger of the Budgerigar becoming an ill-proportioned product such as some animals and birds have become as the result of crazes on the part of breeders and judges which have led to complete loss of beauty.

We who love the Budgerigar so much and who are so desirous of ensuring for it a bright future must ever fight against the risk of any particular property carrying too much weight in the minds of both judges and breeders. And it is the judges more than anyone else who have the matter in their hands. What they call for, exhibitors will strive to provide.

The Budgerigar Society is determined to make type the *sine qua non* which it should be, and that is why the General Council at its meeting in Blackpool on October 12th, 1951, changed the Standard, and fixed a maximum ideal length of eight and a half inches and a maximum wing length of three and three-quarter inches.

In recent years there has been observed the development of a kind of Budgerigar with excessively long tail and flights (thought to be the outcome of mutation) accompanied by a large head and (usually) large spots, though frequently with an undesirable body shape. Some judges were apparently favouring exhibits in this category, and head and spots and length and size were having too much influence on awards. Also some short-sighted breeders were, and still are, using these birds to improve head and spots and increase size, but at the expense of the all-round beauty of the species. This is a short-term rather than a long-term policy. Those who pursue it overlook the fact that the evil effects of using these abnormal Budgerigars will sooner or later be seen.

This was one reason for the change in the Standard, but there was another:-

There has arisen in the livestock world a great danger of size and development being achieved by the administration to birds and animals of drugs discovered by scientists, and while useful for certain utilitarian purposes, not intended to be used to "improve" show specimens. Steps had to be taken to avert the obvious dangers of the practice. Therefore, not only did the B.S. alter its Standard but it formulated a rule making it a penal offence to exhibit or sell Budgerigars to which an artificial growth promoting agent has been administered.

Head. — According to the Standard, the head should be round, and as a general statement this is undoubtedly correct. If, however, one took the point of a compass, placed it on the eye and drew a semi-circle, that would not absolutely convey a perfect Budgerigar's head. Such a bird would be inclined to appear rather lacking in fullness of frontal and back-skull, whereas there should be a pronounced rise of frontal and sufficient back-skull to prevent any appearance of the back outline of the head falling too rapidly to the neck. And yet there must be sufficient dome to avoid the appearance of flat-headedness which has been observable in many previous pictures of Budgerigars and which has been avoided in the Budgerigar Society's ideals reproduced on other pages. Personally I like to see a sufficiently high crown, its apparent height being increased by the eye being set well away from the top of the skull; and I want that high crown to be not only round in profile but also round when viewed from the front.

A big head is desirable. Many times in classes of Budgerigars at shows I have seen birds criticised for being small in head when actually they were larger in this property than some of their competitors that were not similarly blamed. The reason for this optical illusion was that the birds with apparently small heads had big bodies carrying much substance, whereas those with smaller heads but which *seemed* to be bigger had smaller bodies. The moral is obvious. If you have a big, well-built body you must have a good big head on top of it. Again it is all a case of proportion.

A not uncommon failing in heads, otherwise good, is lack of distance from the eye to the beak or gape. This gives a short-fronted, constricted appearance which is not pleasing. Given sufficient length between the two points named, and providing the general outline is otherwise correct, you have a sweep to the head which is most attractive.

Not only are shape and size of skull in themselves of paramount importance, but it is also very necessary that the head should be set correctly on the body. I realise that neck has a bearing on this desired conformity, and that a narrow neck can have much to do with the head not appearing to "sit" as it should on that part of the Budgerigar which comes below it.

Usually this incorrect combination to which I am calling attention is demonstrated by a distinct break in the back profile at a point in line with the spots. Sometimes the distance from a point level with the eye (the back-skull) to the top of the saddle is too short; and this again robs an otherwise high-class specimen of that finish in head, neck and body combined which is a characteristic of the outstanding individual.

Viewed from the front the head should be wide and the face should be full behind the wattle.

Budgerigars most satisfactory as regards body shape frequently fail in head. Those which excel in head by no means so often fail in body. Thus the importance of skull to the breeder is obvious.

Hens usually have lower domes and more bulging frontals than cocks. It is because of this structural difference in the two sexes that the Budgerigar Society issued a drawing of the ideal hen as a companion to the picture of the ideal cock.

The most prevalent faults in head are smallness, narrowness, pinched in face, and general snakiness — not infrequently all combined in the one mediocre specimen.

Beak and Cere. — Although the beak and cere of a Budgerigar are certainly properties of comparatively small importance, they do add their little bit to the general attractiveness of the bird if their formation is good.

The beak is hooked, and it should be strong in horn, nicely curved in outline, and correctly set into the face, so that it conforms to the general curvature of the skull. Thin beaks running to a sharp point in the upper mandible minimise the impression of strength which the head might otherwise give to the observer, and beaks which protrude, breaking the rotundity of the outline, are equally undesirable.

The horn of the beak should have a smooth, level surface, as distinct from a rough and corrugated one. Ridges on the upper mandible are not uncommon.

A blemish which completely bars a Budgerigar from being considered as an exhibition specimen, and which makes it valueless for selling, is an undershot beak. I shall deal more fully with this malformation when I write on the rearing of chicks.

The cere (that flesh substance at the base of the upper mandible) should not be too large, and it should be neat, smooth and heart-shaped. A rough cere springing up from the head is most unattractive. Ceres of this kind are often seen in very old birds.

In colour the cere should be bright blue in cocks, rich nut brown in hens. In chicks prior to the baby moult the cere is blue-white changing to blue or brown as sexual maturity is approched. In Lutinos and Albinos wattles are less deep in colour.

Cheeks. — The cheeks should appear to be full, not flat or pinched. Width of head will be almost inevitably accompanied by good width in an imaginary line drawn through from cheek to cheek.

Neck. — The neck should not be too long and it should be broad. A narrow neck is most objectionable. "Nipped in neck" is the term often employed to describe exhibits with this fault. As indicated in my remarks under the heading of "Head," the shape of the neck can be the cause of that undesirable break or angle at a point in line with the spots.

Body. — And now we come to that which as much as anything separates the high-class exhibition specimen from the very ordinary Budgerigar, viz., the outline of the body. We will take the back line first.

"An approximately straight back line," says the Standard, yet most pictures of Budgerigars show a gentle curve in the outline of the back. The back should be slightly rounded from side to side, but the line from nape of neck to the cushion of tail should not show curvature. To be more explicit, the back in profile from nape of neck to the tail should be nearer to being flat than being arched, consistent with the other important requirement, viz., *reasonably* rounded from side to side and with no signs of hollowness.

A pronounced curve in the back is definitely undesirable. It makes a bird what is known as "roach-backed." On the other hand, a very good bird whose stance approximates to the perpendicular without, of course, being actually in a completely upright position has something of a slight concave in the backline, which no experienced judge really treats as a fault.

Very important, in my opinion, is the line from the back of the head to the nape of the neck, its manner of joining with the line which goes from the nape to the tail, and the general curve at this point which gives to a Budgerigar that height of shoulder which so distinguishes the moderate bird from one capable of winning prizes in strong competition. A deep, gracefully curved neck line adds character to a Budgerigar. It cannot be obtained without the requisite width of neck. This line should also start at the correct place at the back of the head, which it will do if the head is correctly formed. If there is a lack of back-skull the neck line will commence in the wrong place, and the desired curve will not be there.

Even more important than the back and neck outlines is the breast line. This begins not immediately under the beak but a little lower down — roughly at the base of the bib. Thus just as behind there is a neck line and a back line, so in front there is a throat line and a breast line; but the throat line is naturally a very short one.

The breast is an all-important property in an exhibition Budgerigar. In profile it should present a graceful curve from the point beneath the throat above referred to until it joins the perfectly straight line of the tail. Where the throat line ceases and the breast line commences there is only a suggestion of break, no clearly marked indentation.

24

The chest should be wide and well rounded, and the body should be gradually and evenly tapered to the vent.

To return to a consideration of the profile, the foremost point should be, in my opinion, as shown in the pictures of ideals in this book. In many birds the foremost point is lower down, nearer to the legs. Such birds often have broad, deep, rounded chests, but they have an Aldermanic appearance, and even though they are to be preferred to the narrow, shallow-chested sort, they just lack that distinction which the more desirable outline gives.

Although the tapered body is required, the tapering must be so gradual that there is no rapid cutting away of the breast line between the legs and the vent. In other words, there must be a satisfactory depth and breadth of pelvis, and the outline must be carried right through without any sudden contraction at the stern, which at once gives an impression of weakness.

In some Budgerigars the outline from the legs until it joins the tail comes down too low, often accompanied by a fluffiness of feather — a sort of "down behind" appearance. It is frequently seen in birds which are too fat, and it is undesirable.

With a view to giving my readers a better idea as to the ideal curvature of the breast line, let me say that many are the Budgerigars which fall below exhibition requirements because imaginary lines drawn from nape of neck to base of mask, and from centre of back to front of chest, are not sufficently long. Birds of this class are too shallow in body, and they are nearly always narrow in chest as well. In short, they are too slim.

Now you can't have the correct breast line as described, however wide and deep the chest may be, unless your Budgerigar is sufficiently long sided; and if it has the correct length of side it will normally have the correct length of wing, viz., in the ratio of 3¾ in. to 8½ in. the ideal length. Broad-bodied birds lacking in length have a dumpy, or foreshortened, appearance.

In considering the outlines of a Budgerigar don't forget that it is essentially a creature of curves and that angularity is the antithesis to what is required.

And while realising that the breast must be deep, there must not be such a pronounced chest that the bird has a modified Pouter pigeon appearance, which always makes a Budgerigar look "heavy" and ugly.

Wings. — The wings, as indicated by the Standard, should be "well braced, carried just above the cushion of the tail and not crossed."

A very small crossing of the end primary flights, not more than about one-eighth of an inch, cannot be considered any serious blemish. It is when a bird really gets its flights crossed scissor fashion that it must be penalised in keen competition. This flight crossing is often caused by birds carrying their wings high up above their bodies instead of allowing them to rest gracefully above the tail.

Another fault of wing carriage, the very opposite of flight crossing but

25

even more objectionable, is drooping flights, the primary flights hanging down instead of being picked up smartly in the correct position. This is a prevailing fault in long tailed and long flighted birds. Good wing carriage makes a great difference to a Budgerigar's appearance, and it is an essential property if success at the shows is to be achieved.

Tail. — The tail does not carry a lot of weight with a judge when it is as it ought to be, but it handicaps a bird considerably if it is not set into the body in that straight line which is desired by the Standard. A drooping tail is often accompanied by a break in the back line at the rump, giving a cranked appearance which spoils the contour. An excessively long tail is a detriment in competition.

A Budgerigar when exhibited at a show mars its chances somewhat if its long tail feathers, instead of being whipped close together, are split, showing a gap between them. A minor point certainly, but one which really does disfigure a bird.

Legs and Feet. — The legs should be medium in length and the feet inclined to be small. They should be strong in bone. Thin, ultra-slender legs, sometimes due to a rickety condition, are undesirable.

Substance. — Earlier in this chapter I have written about size and its being of lesser importance than shape. Many people confuse the terms "size" and "substance" as the fancier interprets this word. A small bird can have substance and a big bird can lack it.

Substance, as livestock breeders speak of it, means almost in effect solidity. It is the opposite to weediness. It is the filling up in the correct manner of all that comes within the outline of a bird. It is a difficult term to describe but easy to illustrate with the living birds before one. Experienced breeders know exactly what it means and they all admire it.

Charm. — There is another quality more abstract than substance which a Budgerigar destined for the exhibition bench must possess if it is to have a big winning career. This is known as charm. It is very closely akin to that symmetry referred to earlier. In fact you cannot have charm without symmetry, and yet you can have a symmetrical bird which somehow lacks just that charm which so often distinguishes the super champion from the champion. It is a kind of personality which strikes you the moment you look at its possessor. You find it in humans, in dogs, in horses, in fact in all living things. It can never be completely present if it is unaccompanied by high condition.

Carriage. — The Standard stipulates that the bird should stand on a perch at an angle of 30 degrees from the vertical and should look fearless and natural. And so it should. It should be alert and full of *joie-de-vivre,* and yet it must be so trained that it does not climb and roll about in its enthusiasm to such an extent that the judge never gets an opportunity of properly examining it.

Another offender is that ill-trained Budgerigar which spends nearly all its time at a show in the bottom of a cage with its head pushed into one corner. This is usually due to lack of training and there is some hope if the bird is taken in hand.

I must give many more marks to the lively, alert Budgerigar than to a bird so "heavy" that he stands on the perch down on his hocks most of the time, easy to examine but not winning our praise, good though he may be in his separate show properties. We must retain in Budgerigars their natural liveliness, and, in my opinion, there is no particular difficulty in doing so with a bird so healthy, so agile, and so interested in all that goes on around him.

Many hens are not easy to train for show. When in high condition their maternal instinct is so strong that frequently they pass many fruitless hours when in a show cage apparently deceiving themselves into believing that the water pot is provided for them as a nesting box! Some hens show well, however, and both judges and breeders must strive to get hens as good in carriage as cocks and judge them by the same Standard, realising nevertheless that in mixed sex classes the hen does not always display herself to the best advantage in comparison with her opponents of the sterner sex. A fair-minded judge should make certain allowances in the case of hens when both sexes are competing together.

There is no worse fault in carriage than hoopiness; that is standing on the perch in such a manner that a line drawn from head to tail instead of being straight would be definitely curved. This particular fault frequently seems to be a combination of error in carriage and unshapeliness. A bird with a rather pronounced back curve ("roach-backed") develops this stance and usually, instead of holding its head up, gets into a more or less forward position.

Condition is of primary importance. Unless a Budgerigar is fit it should not be allowed to win prizes. In fact, unless a bird is in show condition it should never leave its aviary with the object of competing for honours.

A Budgerigar is in that state which is demanded by the Standard, and therefore by the judges, when it is a perfectly healthy specimen, proven by its tightness of feather, its brightness of eye, its alertness, its obvious joy in living, and its being neither too fat nor too thin but just carrying that amount of flesh which it should carry to display to the onlooker its beautiful lines.

It is steady in the cage, because it is well trained. It stands on the perch elegantly showing its beauty to all who pass along the aisles; it has not the sluggish almost immobile attitude of a bird less fit and, therefore, less sprightly.

Steadiness is essential, but this is a question of training which I shall come to later, and the bird can be steady and yet alert and never really quite still. The over-fat, ill-conditioned specimen is also steady, but it is a steadiness begotten of lethargy. The one form of steadiness is very easily

27

distinguishable from the other.

A highly-conditioned show specimen possesses that perfect fitness which distinguishes the trained athlete from the normal, healthy man; the trained race-horse from the horse ailing nothing and looking well pulling a trap through the streets — but not having that little bit of something extra, that "trained to the hour" look. Of course, we cannot get all our exhibits to be like this when we are showing them, but we want to have them as nearly perfect as possible. And we must realise that birds good in show properties put down in that ideal state which I have indicated are always difficult to beat. Obviously they make the most of themselves and they are the most likely to catch the judge's eye.

THE COLOUR VARIETIES & *STANDARDS*

The Budgerigar Society has issued recognized standards which must be used by fanciers and judges. These are quite essential because breeding for correct colour is one of the requirements for exhibiting.

As stated in earlier chapters, the physical characteristics are also essential so birds must not be judged on colour alone.

Chapter 4, which starts opposite, provides a guide to the main colours which were recognized at the time of the last edition of the book. Since then further modifications and more detailed explanations have been added and the fancier who intends to show should obtain the complete book of Standards from the Budgerigar Society.

CHAPTER 4

THE COLOUR VARIETIES

The Budgerigar Society has issued the following detailed descriptions of adults in the standardised varieties:-

Light Green — **Mask:** buttercup yellow, ornamented by six evenly spaced large round black throat spots, the outer two being partially covered at the base by cheek-patches. **Cheek patches:** violet. **General body colour:** back, rump, breast, flanks and underparts, bright grass green of a solid and even shade throughout. **Markings:** on cheeks, back of head, neck and wings, black and well defined on a buttercup ground. **Tail:** long feathers, bluish black.

Dark Green — As above but with a dark laurel green body colour. **Tail:** long feathers, darker in proportion.

Olive Green — As above but with a deep olive green body colour. **Tail:** long feathers, darker in proportion.

Grey Green — The Grey Green conforms to the standard of the Light Green except in the following details: **Cheek patches:** grey to slate. **General body colour:** dull mustard green. **Tail:** long feathers, black. (It should be noted that there are light, medium and dark shades of Grey Green).

Light Yellow — **Mask:** buttercup yellow. **Cheek patches:** silvery white to very pale pinkish violet. **General body colour:** back, rump, breast, flanks and underparts, deep buttercup yellow and as free from green suffusion as possible. **Primaries and tail:** lighter than body. **Eye:** black pupil with white iris.

Dark Yellow — Same as above but correspondingly deeper in colour.

Olive Yellow — As above but with a mustard body colour.

Grey Yellow — As above but with a dull mustard body colour. (It should be noted that there are light, medium and dark shades of Grey Yellow).

Skyblue — **Mask:** clear white, ornamented by six evenly spaced large round black throat spots, the outer two being partially covered at the base by cheek patches. **Cheek patches:** violet. **General body colour:** back, rump, breast, flanks and underparts, pure skyblue. **Markings:** on cheeks, back of head, neck and wings, black and well defined on a white ground. **Tail:** long feathers, bluish black.

Cobalt — As above but with a deep rich cobalt blue body colour. **Tail:** long feathers, darker in proportion.

Mauve — As above but with a purplish mauve body colour with a tendency to a pinkish tone. **Tail:** long feathers, darker in proportion.

Violet — As above but with a deep intense violet body colour. **Tail:** long feathers, darker in proportion.

Grey — **Mask:** white, ornamented by six evenly spaced large round black throat spots, the outer two being partially covered at the base by cheek patches. **Cheek patches:** grey-blue or slate. **General body colour:** back, rump, breast, flanks and underparts, solid grey. **Markings:** on cheeks, back of head, neck and wings, black and well defined on a white ground. **Tail:** long feathers, black. (It should be noted that there are light, medium and dark shades of Grey).

White — **Mask:** white. **General body colour:** back, rump, breast, flanks and underparts, white (suffused with the colour being masked). **Wings and tails:** white, bluish or light grey. (It should be noted that there are blue, cobalt, mauve, violet and grey shades in both light and dark suffusion).

Opaline Light Green — **Mask:** buttercup yellow, extending over back of head and merging into general body colour at a point level with the butt of wings where undulations should cease thus leaving a clear V effect between top of wings so desirable in this variety, to be ornamented by six evenly spaced large round black throat spots, the outer two being partially covered at the base by cheek patches. **Cheek patches:** violet. **General body colour:** mantle (including V area or saddle), back, rump, breast, flanks and underparts, bright grass green. **Wings:** to be the same colour as body. **Markings:** should be normal with a suffused opalescent effect. **Tail:** long feathers, not to be lighter than mantle.

Opaline Olive Green — As above but with an olive green body colour. **Tail:** long feathers, not to be lighter than mantle.

Opaline Olive Green – As above but with an olive green body colour. **Tail:** long feathers, not to be lighter than mantle.

Opaline Grey Green — As above but with a dull mustard green body colour. **Tail:** long feathers, not to be lighter than mantle. **Cheek patches:** grey to slate. (It should be noted that there are light, medium and dark shades of Opaline Grey Green).

Opaline Skyblue — **Mask:** white, extending over back of head and merging into general body colour at a point level with the butt of wings where undulations should cease thus leaving a clear V effect between the top of wings so desirable in this variety, to be ornamented by six evenly spaced large round black throat spots, the outer two being partially covered at the base by cheek patches. **Cheek patches:** violet. **General body**

colour: mantle (including V area or saddle), back, rump, breast, flanks and underparts, pure skyblue. **Wings:** to be the same colour as body. **Markings:** should be normal with a suffused opalescent effect. **Tail:** long feathers, not to be lighter than mantle.

Opaline Cobalt — As above but with a cobalt body colour. **Tail:** long feathers, not to be lighter than mantle.

Opaline Mauve — As above but with a mauve body colour. **Tail:** long feathers, not to be lighter than mantle.

Opaline Violet — As above but with a deep intense violet body colour. **Tail:** long feathers, not to be lighter than mantle.

Opaline Grey — As above but with a solid grey body colour. **Cheek patches:** grey to slate. **Tail:** long feathers, no lighter than mantle. (It should be noted that there are light, medium and dark shades of Opaline Grey).

Opaline White As for White but with a suggestion of Opaline characteristics.

Opaline Yellow: As for yellow but with a suggestion of Opaline characteristics.

Opaline Cinnamon Light Green — **Mask:** buttercup yellow, extending over back of head and merging into general body colour at a point level with butt of wings where undulations should cease, thus leaving a clear V effect between top of wings so desirable in this variety, to be ornamented by six evenly spaced large cinnamon brown throat spots; the outer two being partially covered at the base by cheek patches. **Cheek patches:** violet. **General body colour:** mantle (including V area or saddle), back, rump, breast, flanks and underparts, pale grass green. **Wings:** to be the same colour as body. **Markings:** should be normal cinnamon brown with a suffused opalescent effect. **Tail:** long feathers, not to be lighter than mantle.

Opaline Cinnamon Dark Green — As above but with a light laurel green body colour. **Tail:** long feathers, not to be lighter than mantle.

Opaline Cinnamon Olive Green — As above but with a light olive green body colour. **Tail:** long feathers, not to be lighter than mantle.

Opaline Cinnamon Grey — As above but with a pale green body colour. **Tail:** long feathers, not to be lighter than mantle. **Cheek-patches:** grey to slate. (It should be noted that there are light, medium and dark shades of Opaline Cinnamon Grey Green).

Opaline Cinnamon Skyblue — **Mask:** white, extending over back of head and merging into general body colour at a point level with butt of wings where undulations should cease, thus leaving a clear V effect between top of wings so desirable in this variety; to be ornamented by six evenly spaced large round cinnamon brown throat spots, the outer two being partially covered at the base by cheek-patches. **Cheek-patches:** violet.

31

General body colour: mantle, back, rump, breast, flanks and underparts, pale skyblue. **Markings:** should be normal cinnamon brown on pale blue ground with suffused opalescent effect. **Tail:** long feathers, not to be lighter than mantle.

Opaline Cinnamon Cobalt — As above but with pale cobalt body colour. **Tail:** long feathers, not to be lighter than mantle.

Opaline Cinnamon Mauve — As above but with pale mauve body colour. **Tail:** long feathers, not to be lighter than mantle.

Opaline Cinnamon Violet — As above but with pale violet body colour. **Tail:** long feathers, not to be lighter than mantle.

Opaline Cinnamon Grey — As above but with pale grey body colour. **Cheek patches:** grey to slate. **Tail:** long feathers, not to be lighter than mantle. (It should be noted that there are light, medium and dark shades of Opaline Cinnamon Grey).

Cinnamon Light Green — **Mask:** buttercup yellow, ornamented by six evenly spaced large round cinnamon brown throat spots the outer two being partially covered at the base by cheek patches. **Cheek patches:** violet. **General body colour:** back, rump, breast, flanks and underparts grass green, 50% or more of normal body colour. **Markings:** on cheeks, back of head, neck and wings, cinnamon brown on a yellow ground and distinct as in normal colour. **Tail:** long feathers, dark blue with brown quill.

Cinnamon Dark Green — As above but with a light laurel green body colour. **Tail:** long feathers, darker in proportion.

Cinnamon Grey Green — As above but with a pale grey green body colour. **Cheek patches:** grey to slate. **Tail:** long feathers, of a deep cinnamon shade. (It should be noted that there are light, medium and dark shades of Cinnamon Grey Green).

Cinnamon Skyblue — **Mask:** white, ornamented by six evenly spaced large round cinnamon brown throat spots, the outer two being partially covered at the base by cheek patches. **Cheek patches: violet. General body colour:** back, rump, breast, flanks and underparts skyblue, 50% or more of normal body colour. **Markings:** cheeks, back of head, neck and wings cinnamon brown on white ground and distinct as in normal colour. **Tail:** long feathers, blue with brown quill.

Cinnamon Cobalt — As above but with pale cobalt body colour. **Tail:** long feathers, cobalt with cinnamon shade.

Cinnamon Mauve — As above but with pale mauve body colour. **Tail:** long feathers, mauve with cinnamon shade.

Cinnamon Violet — As above but with pale violet body colour. **Tail:** long feathers, violet with cinnamon shade.

Cinnamon Grey — As above but with pale grey body colour. **Cheek patches:** pale grey. **Tail:** long feathers, pale grey with cinnamon shade.

THE COLOUR VARIETIES

(It should be noted that there are light, medium and dark shades of Cinnamon Grey).

Greywing Light Green — **Mask:** yellow, ornamented by six evenly spaced large round grey throat spots, the outer two being partially covered at the base by cheek patches. **Cheek patches:** pale violet. **General body colour:** back, rump, breast, flanks and underparts grass green, 50% or more of normal body colour. **Markings:** on cheek, back of head, neck and wings should be light grey and distinct as in normal colour. **Tail:** long feathers, grey with pale bluish tinge.

Greywing Dark Green — As above but with a light laurel green body colour. **Tail:** long feathers, darker in proportion.

Greywing Olive Green — As above but with a light olive green body colour. **Tail:** long feathers, darker in proportion.

Greywing Grey Green — As above but with a light mustard green body colour. **Cheek patches:** light grey. **Tail:** long feathers, dark grey. (It should be noted that there are light, medium and dark shades of Greywing Grey Green).

Greywing Skyblue — **Mask:** white, ornamented by six evenly spaced large round grey throat spots, the outer two being partially covered at the base by cheek patches. **Cheek patches:** light violet. **General body colour:** back, rump, breast, flanks and underparts sky blue, 50% or more of normal body colour. **Markings:** on cheek, back of head, neck and wings should be light grey and distinct as in normal colour. **Tail:** long feathers, greyish blue tinge.

Greywing Cobalt — As above but with a pale cobalt body colour. **Tail:** long feathers, darker in proportion.

Greywing Mauve: As above but with a pale mauve body colour. **Tail:** long feathers, darker in proportion.

Greywing Violet — As above but with a pale violet body colour. **Tail:** long feathers, darked in proportion.

Greywing Grey — As above but with a pale grey body colour. **Cheek patches:** pale grey. **Tail:** long feathers, dark grey. (It should be noted that there are light, medium and dark shades of Greywing Grey).

Opaline Greywing Light Green — **Mask:** yellow extending over back of head and merging into general body colour at a point level with butt of wings where undulations should cease leaving a definitie V effect between top of wings so desirable in this variety, to be ornamented by six evenly spaced large round grey throat spots, the outer two being partially covered at the base by cheek patches. **Cheek patches:** violet. **General body colour:** mantle (including V area or saddle), back, rump, breast, flanks and underparts, pale grass green. **Wings:** same colour as body. **Markings:** should be normal and light grey in colour with suffused opalescent effect. **Tail:** long feathers, smokey grey.

Opaline Greywing Dark Green — As above but with a light laurel green body colour. **Tail:** long feathers, darker in proportion.

Opaline Greywing Olive Green — As above but with a light olive green body colour. **Tail:** long feathers, darker in proportion.

Opaline Greywing Grey Green — As above but with a light mustard body colour. **Cheek patches:** light greys. **Tail:** long feathers, dark grey. (It should be noted that there are light, medium and dark shades of Opaline Greywing Grey Green).

Opaline Greywing Skyblue — **Mask:** white, extending over back of head and merging into general body colour at a point level with the butt of wings where undulations should cease leaving a definite clear V effect between top of wings so desirable in this variety, to be ornamented by six evenly spaced large round grey throat spots, the outer two being partially covered at the base by cheek patches. **Cheek patches:** violet. **General body colour:** mantle including V area or saddle), back, rump, breast, flanks and underparts, pale skyblue. **Wings:** same colour as body. **Markings:** should be normal and grey in colour with suffused opalescent effect. **Tail:** long feathers, grey.

Opaline Greywing Cobalt — As above but with pale cobalt body colour. **Tail:** darker in proportion.

Opaline Greywing Mauve — As above but with pale mauve body colour. **Tail:** darker in proportion.

Opaline Greywing Violet — As above but with pale violet body colour. **Tail:** darker in proportion.

Opaline Greywing Grey — As above but with pale grey body colour. **Cheek patches:** light grey. **Tail:** long feathers, grey. (It should be noted that there are light, medium and dark shades of Opaline Greywing Grey).

Yellow-Wing Light Green — **Mask:** buttercup yellow. **Cheek patches:** violet. **General body colour:** back, rump, breast, flanks and underparts, bright grass green. **Wings:** buttercup yellow, as free from markings as possible. **Tail:** long feathers, bluish.

Yellow-Wing Dark Green — As above but with dark laurel green body colour. **Tail:** long feathers, darker in proportion.

Yellow-Wing Olive Green — As above but with an olive green body colour. **Tail:** long feathers, darker in proportion.

Yellow-Wing Grey Green — This variety conforms to the standard for Yellow-wing Light Green except that general body colour should be dull mustard green. **Cheek patches:** grey to slate. **Tail:** long feathers, darker in proportion. (It should be noted that there are light, medium and dark shades of Yellow-wing Grey Green).

Whitewing Skyblue — **Mask:** white. **Cheek patches:** violet. **General body colour:** back, rump, breast, flanks and underparts, pure skyblue approximating to the normal variety. **Wings:** white, as free from markings as possible. **Tail:** long feathers, bluish.

Whitewing Cobalt — As above but with a cobalt body colour. **Tail:** long feathers, darker in proportion.

Whitewing Mauve — As above but with a mauve body colour. **Tail:** long feathers, darker in proportion.

Whitewing Violet — As above but with a violet body colour. **Tail:** long feathers, darker in proportion.

Whitewing Grey — As above but with a grey body colour. **Cheek patches:** grey-blue. **Tail:** long feathers, grey. (It should be noted that there are light, medium and dark shades of White Wing Grey).

Fallow Light Green — **Mask:** yellow, ornamented by six evenly spaced large round brown throat spots, the outer two being partially covered at the base by cheek patches. **Cheek patches:** violet. **General body colour:** back, rump, breast, flanks and underparts, yellowish green. **Markings:** on cheeks, back of head, neck and wings, medium brown on a yellow ground. **Eyes:** red or plum. **Tail:** long feathers, bluish grey.

Fallow Dark Green — As above but with a light laurel green body colour. **Tail:** long feathers, darker in proportion.

Fallow Olive Green — As above but with a light mustard olive green body colour. **Tail:** long feathers, darker in proportion.

Fallow Grey Green — As above but with a dull mustard green body colour. **Cheek patches:** grey to slate. **Tail:** long feathers, darker in proportion. (It should be noted that there are light, medium and dark shades of Fallow Grey Green).

Fallow Skyblue — **Mask:** white, ornamented by six evenly spaced large round brown throat spots, the outer two being partially covered at base by cheek patches. **Cheeck patches:** violet. **General body colour:** back, rump, breast, flanks and underparts, pale skyblue. **Markings:** on cheeks, back of head, neck and wings, medium brown on a white ground. **Eyes:** red or plum. **Tail:** long feathers, bluish grey.

Fallow Cobalt — As above but with a warm cobalt body colour. **Tail:** long feathers, darker in proportion.

Fallow Mauve — As above, but with a pale mauve body colour of a pinkish tone. **Tail:** long feathers, darker in proportion.

Fallow Violet — As above but with a pale violet body colour. **Tail:** long feathers, darker in proportion.

Note: An Opaline form of all shades of Yellow-wing and White-wing is recognized but these birds should only be shown in A.O.C. or Variety classes unless a separate class is scheduled: in no circumstances should they be shown in Yellow-wing or White-wing classes. When being judged, full consideration should be given to the quality of both the Opaline and the Clearwing characteristics.

Fallow Grey — As above but with a pale grey body colour. **Cheek patches:** grey to slate. **Tail:** long feathers, darker in proportion. (It should be noted that there are light, medium and dark shades of Fallow Grey). English and German forms are recognized; the German form having a white iris ring around the eye, the English form has none.

Lutino — Buttercup yellow throughout. **Eyes:** clear red with light iris ring. **Cheek patches:** silvery white. **Tail:** long feathers and primaries yellowish white.

Albino — White throughout. **Eyes:** clear red with light iris ring.

Yellow-Face — All varieties in the blue series except Pieds. **Mask:** yellow only, otherwise exactly as corresponding normal variety. Note: yellow-marked feathers in tail permissible.

PIEDS

Dominant Pied Light Green — **Mask:** buttercup yellow of an even tone, ornamented by six evenly spaced and clearly defined large round black throat spots, the outer two being partially covered at the base by cheek patches. **Cheek patches:** violet. **General body colour:** as the normal Light Green variety but broken with irregular patches of clear buttercup yellow or with a clear yellow band approximately half an inch wide round its middle just above the thighs. An all yellow or normal green coloured body should be penalised. Head patch is optional. (Note: all other things being equal, preference to be given, in accordance with the scale of show points, to birds showing the band.) **Wings:** colour and markings as the normal Light Green but having irregular patches of clear buttercup yellow or with part of the wing edges to shoulder but clear yellow on an otherwise normal marked wing. Completely clear wings should be penalized. Wing markings may be grizzled in appearance. All visible flight feathers should be clear yellow but odd dark flight feathers are not faults. **Tail:** the two long tail feathers may be clear yellow, marked or normal blue-black in colour. **Cere:** similar to that of the normal Light Green or a mixture of normal colour and fleshy pink. **Eyes:** dark with light iris ring. **Beak:** normal horn colour. **Feet and legs:** blue mottled as the normal Light Green, fleshy pink or a mixture of both.

Dominant Pied Dark Green — As above but with general body colour as for normal Dark Green.

Dominant Pied Olive Green — As above but with general body colour as for normal Olive Green.

Dominant Pied Grey Green — As above but with general body colour as for normal Grey Green. **Cheek patches:** grey-blue to slate. (It should be noted that there are light, medium and dark shades of Dominant Pied Grey Green).

Dominant Pied Skyblue — **Mask:** white, ornamented by six evenly spaced and clearly defined large round black throat spots, the outer two being partially covered at the base by cheek patches. **Cheek patches:** violet. **General body colour:** as the normal Skyblue variety but broken with irregular patches of white or with a clear white band approximately half an inch wide round its middle just above the thighs. An all-white or normal blue coloured body should be penalized. Head-patch is optional. (Note: all other things being equal, preference to be given, in accordance with the scale of show points, to birds showing the band). **Wings:** colour and markings as the normal Skyblue but having irregular patches of clear white on an otherwise normal marked wing. Completely clear wings should be penalized. Wing markings may be grizzled in appearance. All visible flight feathers should be clear white but odd dark feathers are not faults. **Tail:** the two long tail feathers may be clear white, marked or normal blue-black in colour. **Cere:** similar to that of normal Skyblue or a mixture of normal colour and fleshy pink. **Eyes:** dark with light iris ring. **Beak:** normal horn colour. **Feet and legs:** blue mottled as the normal Skyblue, fleshy pink or mixture of both.

Dominant Pied Cobalt — As above but with general body colour as for normal Cobalt.

Dominant Pied Mauve — As above but with general body colour as for normal Mauve.

Dominant Pied Violet — As above but with general body colour as for normal Violet.

Dominant Pied Grey — As above but with general body colour as for normal Grey. **Cheek patches:** grey-blue or slate. (It should be noted that there are light, medium and dark shades of Dominant Pied Grey). Note: an Opaline, Yellow-face and Cinnamon form of Dominant Pied is recognized but these should only be shown in Dominant Pied classes.

Clearflight Light Green — **Mask:** buttercup yellow of an even colour ornamented by six evenly spaced clearly defined large round black throat spots, the outer two being partially covered at the base by the cheek patches. **Cheek patches:** violet. **General body colour:** as the normal Light Green with the exception of one small patch approximately half an inch by five-eighths inch of clear buttercup yellow at the back of the head. Slight collar or extension of the bib, while undesirable, will not penalize. **Wings:** colour and markings as the normal Light Green but with seven visible flight feathers of clear yellow. Dark flights constitute a fault. **Tail:** the two long feathers should be clear yellow, dark tail feathers are a fault. **Cere:** similar to that of normal Light

Green. **Eyes:** dark with light iris ring. **Beak:** normal horn colour. **Feet and legs:** blue mottled or flesh coloured.

Clearflight Dark Green — As above but with general body colour as for normal Dark Green.

Clearflight Olive Green — As above but with general body colour as for normal Olive Green.

Clearflight Grey Green — As above but with general body colour as for normal Grey Green. **Cheek patches:** grey-blue or slate. (It should be noted that there are light, medium and dark shades of Pied (clear flighted) Grey Green).

Clearflight Skyblue — **Mask:** white, ornamented by six evenly spaced clearly defined large round black throat spots, the outer two being partially covered at the base by cheek patches. **Cheek patches:** violet. **General body colour:** as the normal Skyblue with the exception of one small patch approximately half-inch by five-eighths inch of pure white at the back of the head. Slight collar or extension of bib, while undesirable, will not penalize. **Wings:** as normal Skyblue but with seven visible flight feathers of pure white. Dark flights constitute a fault. **Tail:** the two long feathers should be pure white, marked or dark tail feathers are a fault. **Cere:** similar to that of normal Skyblue. **Eyes:** dark with light iris ring. **Beak:** normal horn colour. **Feet and legs:** bluish mottled or flesh colour.

Clearflight Cobalt — As above but with general body colour as for normal Cobalt.

Clearflight Mauve — As above but with general body colour as for normal Mauve.

Clearflight Violet — As above but with general body colour as for normal Violet.

Clearflight Grey — As above but with general body colour as for normal Grey. **Cheek patches:** grey-blue to slate. (It should be noted that there are light, medium and dark shades of Clearflight Grey).

Dark-Eyed Clear Yellow — **Cheek patches:** silvery white. **General body colour:** pure yellow throughout and free from any odd green feathers or green suffusion. **Wings:** pure yellow throughout, free from black or grizzled tickings or green suffusion. All flight feathers paler yellow than rump colour. **Tail:** as the flight feathers. **Cere:** fleshy pink in colour as in Lutinos. **Eyes:** dark without any light iris ring. **Beak:** orange coloured. **Feet and legs:** fleshy pink. (Note: the actual body colour varies in depth

Note: An Opaline, Yellow-face and Cinnamon form of Clearflight is recognized but these should only be shown in Clearflight classes. The non-head-spot type of Clearflight (described as Australian) with full body colour is recognized and should be exhibited in Clearflight classes where these are provided.

according to the genetical make-up, i.e. whether light, dark or olive green, etc).

Dark-Eyed Clear White — As above but with white body colour and free from any blue suffusion or odd blue feathers. **Flights and tail:** white. **Cere:** fleshy pink in colour as in Albinos.

(Note: a dominant form is also recognized having normal cere, eyes, beak, feet and legs, which may be exhibited with the above-mentioned types of dark-eyed yellows and/or whites where separate classes are scheduled for this variety. A yellow-faced form of dark-eyed clear is also recognized but these should only be shown in Dark-eyed Clear classes).

Recessive Pied Light Green — **Mask:** buttercup yellow of an even tone. **Throat spots:** as the normal Light Green variety, may be present from one to full number. **Cheek patches:** violet, silvery-white or a mixture of both. **General body colour:** irregular patches of clear buttercup yellow and bright grass green with the latter mainly on the lower chest, rump and underparts. Zebra markings on the top of the head and around the eyes are not faults. **Wings:** black undulations or polka-dot markings should not cover more than fifteen to twenty per cent of total area. All visible flight feathers should be clear yellow but odd dark flight feathers are not faults. **Cere:** fleshy pink in colour as in Lutinos. **Eyes:** dark without any light iris ring. **Beak:** orange coloured. **Feet and legs:** fleshy pink.

Recessive Pied Dark Green — As above but with a yellow and dark green body colour.

Recessive Pied Olive Green — As above but with a yellow and olive green body colour.

Recessive Pied Grey Green — As above but with a yellow and grey-green body colour. **Cheek patches:** grey-blue or slate, or a mixture of both. (It should be noted that there are light, medium and dark shades of Recessive Pied Grey Green).

Recessive Pied Skyblue — **Mask:** white. **Throat spots:** as the normal Skyblue variety, may be present from one to full number. **Cheek patches:** violet, silvery-white or a mixture of both. **General body colour:** irregular patches of white and bright skyblue with the latter mainly on the lower chest, rump and underparts. Zebra markings on top of head and around the eyes are not faults. **Wings:** black undulations or polka-dot markings should not cover more than fifteen to twenty per cent of total area. All visible flight feathers should be white but odd dark flight feathers are not faults. **Cere:** fleshy pink in colour as in Albinos. **Eyes:** dark without any light iris ring. **Beak:** orange coloured. **Feet and legs:** fleshy pink.

Recessive Pied Cobalt — As above but with a white and cobalt body colour.

Recessive Pied Mauve — As above but with a white and mauve body colour.

Recessive Pied Violet — As above but with a white and violet body colour.

Recessive Pied Grey — As above but with a white and grey body colour. **Cheek patches:** gey-blue or slate, or a mixture of both. (It should be noted that there are light, medium and dark forms of Recessive Pied Grey).

Note: an Opaline, Yellow-face and Cinnamon form of Recessive Pied is recognized but these should be shown only in Recessive Pied classes.

Lacewing Yellow — **Mask:** yellow, ornamented by six evenly spaced large round cinnamon throat spots, the outer two being partially covered at the base by cheek patches. **Cheek patches:** pale violet. **General body colour:** back, rump, breast, flanks and underparts, yellow. **Markings:** on cheeks, back of head, neck, mantle and wings, cinnamon brown on a yellow ground. **Eyes:** clear red with light iris rings. **Tail:** long feathers, cinnamon brown. Note: the depth of yellow of the body colour, etc., varies according to the normal counterpart being masked by the Lacewing character, i.e. the richest yellow is carried by the Lacewing Olive Green and the lightest by the Lacewing Light Green.

Lacewing White — **Mask:** white, ornamented by six evenly spaced large round cinnamon throat spots, the outer two being partially covered at the base by the cheek patches. **Cheek patches:** pale violet. **General body colour:** back, rump, breast, flanks and underparts, white. **Markings:** on cheeks, back of head, neck, mantle and wings, cinnamon brown on a white ground. **Eyes:** clear red with light iris rings. **Tail:** long feathers, cinnamon brown.

Note: the shade of white of the body colour etc., varies only slightly in tone according to the normal counterpart being masked by the lacewing character. (A yellow-faced form is recognized. Where no classes are scheduled for this variety it should be shown in any other colour classes).

CRESTED VARIETIES

Crested Light Green — **Head:** Ornamented with a Circular, Half Circular or Tufted type of Crest. (See note below). **Mask:** buttercup of an even tone ornamented on each side with three clearly defined round black spots, one of which appears at the base of each cheek patch. **Cheek patches:** violet. **General body colour:** back, rump, breast, flanks and underparts bright grass green of a solid and even shade throughout; markings on cheeks, back of head, neck and wings black and well defined on a buttercup ground. **Tail:** two long feathers blue-black.

Note: the above is the standard for the Light Green Crested form; all other colours will be on similar lines with change of colours where appropriate.

Circular Crest — This should be a flat round crest with the feathers radiating from the centre of the head.

Half-Circular Crest — This should be a half circle of feathers falling or raised in a fringe above the cere.

Tufted Crest — This should be an upright crest of feathers up to three eighths of an inch high rising just above the cere.

COLOUR *VERSUS* TYPE

Although, as I have explained in the preceding chapter, I consider type to be the first desideratum, this does not mean that I under-estimate the value of colour. I realise that however shapely a Budgerigar may be, if it fails considerably in colour or markings, it cannot be a valuable bird either for exhibition or breeding.

Referring to colour generally, and before commenting on particular colours, it is, I think, desirable to emphasise certain facts about body colouring which apply to all the varieties.

The colour should be bright and it should be level. Mottling or patchiness is most undesirable, although a bird absolutely even in colour on "the back, rump, breast, flanks, and underparts" (to quote from the Standard) is as yet an ideal rarely attained.

Unevenness or patchiness may be due to one of two causes. The first is where the colour varies in depth here and there, giving a shaded effect, but where, nevertheless, all the feathers are of the same colour denomination. An example is a Light Green uneven in colour on the breast but still not owning a feather which could be correctly termed dark green.

Now we come to the second and worse kind of patchiness, that where the uneven appearance is attributable to the presence of feathers carrying colour manifestly foreign to the colour variety in question. A notable example is the Mauve with cobalt patches.

Colours naturally vary in their brightness, and it is not possible for Mauves and Greys to sparkle in quite the same way as do, for instance, Light Greens, Cobalts and Violets. And yet all colours in adult birds in prime condition should convey an impression of scintillation.

Budgerigars possessing feather of fine texture have a satin finish to their plumage absent in the coarser-feathered birds, and this, apart from the actual colouring itself, undoubtedly adds brightness to the coloration generally.

Silky, close-fitting feather is, therefore, obviously a desirable property, and it should always be cultivated by breeders and encouraged by judges.

Budgerigars when in bloom often carry a sheen on their feathers. The desirability or otherwise of this has been frequently discussed, and opinions are divided as to whether it should or should not be favoured. No mention is made of it in the Budgerigar Society's Standard.

Personally, when judging, whilst I do not give birds possessing this sheen any particular preference, I do not on the other hand condemn them because of it.

This sheen — lustre it is also termed sometimes — is most observable in some Greens. Dr. Armour writing in *Cage Birds* a long time ago gave the best description I have read, and which I quote:

"In the Green we may have (in adult birds only as a rule) an inner area of brilliant green in each feather, the feather colour consisting of this inner area of green and a broad band of black with a marginal area, variable in width of bright clear yellow.

"It is the presence of this inner area of green in place of the usual black which gives the bloom to the wing plumage, and this appears with age, becoming more pronounced with each moult. This bloom shows itself on the back of the head and nape of the neck in a lovely greenish sheen mixed with the black striations.

"In Blues, Cobalts, and to a less extent in Mauves, we have this characteristic, the green inner area being replaced in their case by bright blue and the edging being either of very pale blue or pure white.

"I have seen only one specimen in which the white edging on the feathers was replaced by definite bright blue, and this bird I consider the most beautiful I have ever viewed.

Differences in sex are shown in the plumage of hens being generally duller in colour, the wings being definitely less brilliant than in the cocks. *Many look on excessive bloom as being faulty, but I consider that this is one of the great sexual differences which should be maintained as far as possible and enhanced by the breeding of birds carrying a good deal of inner colour in the wing plumage.*

"A bird of three or four years with pronounced bloom stands quite apart from his less brilliant brother, and it is to be hoped that that which is now considered by many a fault may become one of the principal show points in the exhibition Budgerigar."

I have quoted at length here from Dr. Armour because he, more than any other fancier of my acquaintance, was an enthusiastic admirer of this sheen. Personally, although I do not attach to it so much importance as did the Doctor, and cannot see it becoming one of the Budgerigar's principal show points as he would have liked it to become, I do not agree with those who would actually severely handicap a bird in judging because of the possession of this property.

The Budgerigar Society's Standard definition of the respective colours all refer to adult birds, and it is adult plumage which we visualise as we discuss colour. Judging the colour merits of chicks which have not had their first moult calls for different consideration. Just as these unmoulted young Budgerigars are duller in markings than are the older birds, so also are they less bright and less deep in colour. Consequently, their colour values must be calculated by comparison with other youngsters of similar age, and not adults.

Experience alone teaches a fancier to be able to tell accurately whether a baby will mature into a bird excelling or deficient in colour.

Light Greens. The Light Green is, of course, the common ancestor of all the other colours. Some years ago there were more Light Greens excelling in type, colour and markings than there were birds of any other colour, but the improvement in type which has been effected in some other varieties has deprived the Light Green of much of its former pre-eminence.

Evenness and freedom from patchiness, as in all the other colours, is, of course, required in Light Greens, and the colour should be the rich bright grass green called for by the Standard, and no other.

A Light Green can be so light that there is almost a suggestion of yellow about its body colouring.

On the other hand, a few so-called Light Greens are so dark that it is difficult when they are staged at a show to decide whether they are in the correct class or whether they should have competed against the Dark Greens. Similarly, we occasionally see birds in the Dark Green class lighter in colour than some of the exhibits entered in the Light Green class. Not much harm is done, however, because birds so coloured have no chance whatever of winning prizes under capable judges.

The yellow parts of a Light Green should be bright and approximating to the colour of a good Light Yellow, making a beautiful contrast with the intensely black markings.

Blue shading on the thighs and underparts spoils many Greens; and a general dullness about the colouring is another colour fault.

VALUE OF LIGHT GREEN

Through the years of the development of the Budgerigar Fancy the Light Green had proved to be so valuable as a cross for the retention and improvement of size, type, and stamina in the other colours, that the really pure Light Green became a *rara avis*.

Breeders then became imbued with the idea of establishing families of pure Light Greens by mating Light Greens to Light Greens only, and certainly some top class birds were bred in this way. Although many Greens which have led their classes have not been pure, and the purity cult was perhaps something of a fetish.

For reasons which I will explain in my remarks about breeding Light Greens in Chapter 12, this colour is now being out-crossed to other colours more extensively than was the case during the war and for a few years afterwards. This has been done not only with the object of improving other varieties, as in the old days, but to improve fertility in some of the best strains of Light Greens, which were beginning to fail in this respect. The Light Green's popularity remains constant. It continues to be a general favourite, and it provides intense competition at the leading shows.

Dark Greens. — The Dark Green is attractive as a show bird and has proved valuable for certain colour crosses. (See Chapter 12).

A good Dark Green, bright and level in colour, and of that laurel tone which the best judges favour, is very pleasing. It must, however, be a real Dark Green, not one of those dark Light Greens which I have referred to earlier in this chapter. In recent years there has been a steady improvement in the quality and numbers of Dark Greens exhibited. Many of these are genetically Violet Dark Greens produced during the course of efforts to breed good Violets.

Olives. — I find that people either greatly admire the Olive, or it makes no appeal to them whatever, and its popularity is not what it was in pre-war days, although more have been seen in the last two years than for a long time, and one might say there is a slight revival. I think that to some extent the wane in its popularity can be attributed to the development of the Grey Green — a bird of similar body colour which, though it is of a lighter shade, is generally much more level. In the old days we found that Olives were valuable on occasions for crossing with Mauves and sometimes with Cobalts, in addition, of course, as a mate to other Olives where Olive production was the only objective.

In Olives it is difficult to obtain both depth and evenness of colour in the same bird. So frequently when level in colour they lack depth, and similarly, when deep in tone they lack evenness.

In the perfect Olive there would, of course, be no green colouring at all, yet comparatively few are free from it, especially on the rump, the flanks, and towards the tail; and in a great number of cases when the sun shines on the birds, laurel green flecks on the breast are also to be seen.

Light Yellows. — When the Pure Yellow Red Eyes (Lutinos) commenced to increase in popularity there were many who said that the normal black-eyed Light Yellow would almost pass into oblivion. And there was a period when it seemed as though these gloomy prophecies were justified, but when I wrote the Third Edition of the *Cult of the Budgerigar,* there were signs of a renaissance in the variety, which, alas, has not materialised to any great extent, though there are still a few fanciers who are breeding Light Yellows in earnest. Many years ago it was discovered that a good Light Yellow was invaluable as an out-cross to the Lutino, and I am sure our Red-eyed

Yellows would not be as good as they now are if the Light Yellow had not been utilised in their cultivation; but now, alas, there are not available the very good Light Yellows necessary for such crossing.

Dark Yellow. − I consider the definition "Dark Yellow" as being of more value as a genetical term than as a practical colour description.

Many Budgerigars which are genetically Light Yellows are deeper in body colour than some birds which genetically are Dark Yellows, viz., birds which have one dark factor in their genetic formula. Dark Yellows are usually rather heavily pencilled and suffused with dark green. They are not really show birds unless they are free from marking and suffusion.

Olive Yellows. − This is a colour variety which does not appeal greatly to all fanciers. Personally, I think a good Olive Yellow is a really attractive exhibition specimen. To-day it is very exceptional to see one either at a show or in an aviary. Certainly if numbers of them could be bred with that mustard yellow colour referred to in the Standard as being ideal, they would be more popular than they are to-day, even though never so fashionable as some varieties. It is many years since I saw a really good one, though there was a day when Olive Yellows of good size, type and colour were frequently staged in the A.O.C. classes.

Skyblues. − The Standard says that the body colour must be "pure sky blue," which is quite to the point and admits of no argument. But what *is* controversial is depth of colour, and judges do not all think alike on this important point. A few birds which have achieved considerable success under some judges have been put down in their classes by other judges for the reason that in their opinion they were actually too deep in colour.

We all criticise the Skyblue which is too light − or "washy" − but only a minority condemn the Skyblue which is a little too dark, providing it is free from a cobalt tinge.

In giving judgement on the point disputed by the controversialists I would lean towards the darker coloured birds, conditional on there being a complete absence of cobalt, and whilst not losing sight of the fact that there can be a Skyblue too dark to conform to what most judges visualise as the ideal. That bird would, of course, have to be suitably penalised when it was in competition with more normal specimens.

For breeding purposes I am still more emphatic in my preference for the "too-dark" shade when compared with the "too-light" shade. In breeding it is easier to lose depth of colour than it is to gain it, which is a sufficient reason for this assertion.

Blues too dark for competition in Skyblue classes are regularly produced from Violet-breeding pairs. These are Violet-Blues, many of which are not easy to distinguish from Cobalts.

The Skyblue is an example of the truth that one does not find so often grounds for criticism of body colour in those varieties (the Skyblue is one of them) which do not carry a dark factor, as one does in those which have one dark factor (e.g., the Cobalt) and, more so, those with two dark factors (e.g., the Mauve).

Cobalts. — Many are the colour variations in this exceedingly attractive variety, but I think it can safely be said, broadly speaking, that there are two distinct main shades, viz., the bright, deep, real cobalt colour of the paint box and a Cobalt which has an obvious skyblue cast about it.

The two are quite distinctive, and a bird of the more desirable shade, if level in colour, sufficiently well marked and good in type, will secure the honours almost invariably. It must be admitted that frequently the best coloured Cobalts are smaller and of less substance than their inferior coloured rivals.

The ideal colour for a Cobalt is certainly much nearer in shade to the colour desired in the Violet than to the colour of the Skyblue, and yet there is — and should be — an obvious difference between Cobalts and Violets. Nevertheless I should be talking with my tongue in cheek if I were not to admit that prior to the coming of the Violet and its recognition as a new variety, if one had been exhibited in a Cobalt class, it would have been hailed as a Cobalt excelling in colour! It is difficult to carry tints in one's mind, but I am not at all sure that a few of the best coloured Cobalts of many years ago were not Violets as we know them to-day. I remember two noted Cobalt cocks exhibited by Mrs. Liddell which, if I am not very much at fault, were as nearly like our best Violets as makes no matter.

The show Violet (the one referred to in the Standard definition) like the Cobalt, has one dark factor. In spite of the fact that its genetic constitution at first gave the scientists many headaches, as I explain in my chapter, "Colour Production", practical fanciers should have no fears as regards Violet breeding, which is really a simple proposition.

VARIETIES OF VIOLET

In addition to the true Violet (Violet Cobalt) mostly known as Visual Violets, there are Violet Mauves and Violet Blues which are most valuable for breeding Visual Violets. Green coloured birds can also carry the Violet character and can be used in a Violet breeding plan as I will explain in Chapter 12.

The true Visual Violet is a most beautifully coloured bird. Non Fanciers looking at one quickly express admiration as, of course, do Budgerigar breeders. As the shades of colour carried by ordinary Cobalts vary in their depth and brightness so do those carried by visual Violets. This is because visual Violets are in fact Cobalts with the addition of one or two Violet characters in their genetical make-up.

Mauves. — The colour of the Mauve is a problem. Few and far between are the birds whose colouring anywhere approaches the ideal described by

‚the Standard — "purplish mauve with a tendency to a pinkish tone."

The principal colour faults in this attractive variety are leaden and cobalt or violet patches on the breast. Many are the Mauves, which if they are uneven are made so by cobalt or violet flecking. Others more even in colour have a cobalt tint running right through the mauve. More level these birds certainly are, but they are not really of the right shade of colour.

Violet breeders, who wisely use Mauves in their breeding teams, produce some Mauves well up to exhibition standard; in fact, I have noticed that some of them are better in colour than the normal Mauves, having more of that desirable pinkish tone. The value of the Mauve in a Violet-breeding family has caused an increase in its popularity. And some of the Mauves exhibited are of excellent type, which superiority is not always recognised as it should be in "Cobalt or Mauve" classes. The two varieties almost invariably have to compete against each other.

Whites of Light Suffusion. — White Skyblues, White Cobalts, White Mauves, White Greys and White Violets are birds white in plumage but suffused with one of the colours named.

For competition the nearer to the pure white the more desirable is the bird and the greater its chances of winning prizes. Some of the Whites which were leading the Light Suffusion classes in the years immediately preceding the war were so extraordinarily free from colour that it was often exceedingly difficult, except in a powerful light, to define the colour of the suffusion.

These colours in their Cinnamon form are of a much more pure white shade.

The interest in this variety has declined so much since the late nineteen forties that specimens are rarely seen even at the largest exhibitions of Budgerigars.

Whitewings. — Prior to the establishment of the Whitewing the White of deep suffusion was a recognised feature of our shows, and some specimens were of magnificent type and of good size. Generally speaking they were superior to the Whites of light suffusion in these properties. Depth of suffusion was no handicap to them in competition, in which respect they stood, of course, in a different category from lightly suffused Whites.

The arrival of the Whitewing "killed" the D.S. White as a show bird, for as soon as Whitewings of reasonably good type began to be exhibited the ordinary D.S. White had little or no chance of winning prizes, because in colour distribution the Whitewing was in every way superior.

The Standard says that the body colour must approximate to the Normal variety, and that the wings must be pure white. The body colours of Whitewings are skyblue, cobalt, mauve, grey and violet.

Yellow-wing Greens. — Yellow-wings are the Yellow form of the Whitewing, and there are some who consider that the two should be treated as one variety, under the embracing term "Clearwing." Then we should have Clearwing White Blues, etc., and Clearwing Light Greens, etc. The term "Clearwing" is regularly used by fanciers, even though it does not appear in the Standard.

The Standard is the same for both Whitewings and Yellow-wings, except as regards body and wing colour. A Yellow-wing with a clear yellow wing and a green body colour of normal density, is a very striking Budgerigar.

Greywings. — This variety is so named because the markings are grey, whereas, of course, the markings in the normal colours are black.

The Greywing is a beautiful variety of delicate tints. It has a beauty all of its own, and it is surprising indeed that at the time of writing it is not so popular as it was a few years before the war and earlier. I hope that some day we shall see a revival in Greywings.

Those who now essay to breed winning Greywings should bear well in mind that the markings should be grey "half-way between black and zero" (as the Standard expresses it) and not black or bordering on black. In pre-war days many winning Greywings were definitely too heavily marked, and often judges unwisely encouraged them. Truly a Greywing must be a Greywing, or it belies its name.

And then it is not desirable for the body colour of a Greywing to approximate to that of the corresponding Normal. It should be equally as bright and just as level, but definitely lighter.

The faults in colour which have to be overcome in the Normal colour varieties arise similarly in the Greywings, and, as will be understood from the Standard, the colour ideals are the same for the Greywings as the Normals except as regards depth.

The delicate tinting of the Greywing throughout is one of its greatest charms, and which alone provides the strongest possible argument against the recognition of Greywings which are so dark in body colouring and markings that they are not far removed from the Normals.

If we retain the Greywing as a "'tween shade" it will ever appeal to those who admire colours sweetly blended in preference to brighter tones contrasting greatly.

In Australia there is cultivated the full body-coloured Greywing — a bird which should actually possess the body colour of the Normal with the grey markings of our own Greywings. This bird has not been standardised by the Budgerigar Society, and if exhibited over here they would have to compete in the Any Other Colour class.

The genetic constitution of the full body-coloured Greywing is that of the Whitewing, except, to put it simply, the former has the factor of wing markings and the latter has not.

The colours in which Greywings can be produced are indicated in the Standard printed earlier in this chapter.

CHARACTERISTICS OF CINNAMONS

Cinnamons. — In appearance the Cinnamon differs primarily from the Normals and Greywings in that its markings are cinnamon-brown instead of black or grey.

The Cinnamon varieties, as the Standard indicates, correspond with the Normal varieties of the same body colouring. There is also a lighter form corresponding with the Greywings of the same body colouring.

A peculiarity of the Cinnamon is that it is born with pink eyes. As soon as the chick is hatched the pink eyes are observable through the skin. When the eyes open their colour has become ruby. Within seven to ten days they are of the normal colour. No matter what the colour of the Cinnamon its down when a baby is white, the skin is bright pink, and where any feathers appear the feather shafts assume a dark brown shade. The feet are a bright pink and the beak is orange. Cinnamons are usually very silky in feather.

The Cinnamon is one of the sex-linked varieties to which reference is made in Chapter 16.

CINNAMON WHITES AND YELLOWS

In my opinion, when crossing Whites with Cinnamonwings with a view to diminishing suffusion, it is most desirable to select lightly suffused Whites for the purpose. The experience of breeders has been that the first cross between a normal White cock and a Cinnamon White hen produces Whites quite normal in appearance. The normal White cocks so bred and which will be split Cinnamon should be mated to Cinnamon White hens. This mating usually gives Cinnamon White cocks and hens which are almost pale in colour. That is what I have been told on good authority but I have no personal experience of the matings described.

Soon after the Cinnamon appeared in numbers in this country there was ventilated the theory that it would prove to be a valuable outcross for the Light Yellow. It was asserted that owing to the absence of black melanin in the Cinnamon, Yellows more pure in colour than the old Yellows would be evolved. A number of breeders set to work on these lines, and some very good coloured Cinnamon Yellows were bred.

Be this as it may, it might well be that those set out to improve Light Yellows in shape, in which they have so sadly deteriorated, might be well advised to found a strain of Cinnamon Light Yellows, even if improvement in type were accompanied by some loss in depth and brightness of colour.

Apropos the reference to the utility of the Cinnamon for the breeding of almost pure Whites, I will refer to a history-making Budgerigar which was bred by Miss J. and Mr. G.N. Hughes in 1931.

This was a White Blue hen with faint cinnamon ticking on her otherwise pure white wings. As a youngster she won 1st and special best Budgerigar Kingston, 2nd Reading, and 1st and specials Slough; and in 1932, 1st East Ham, 1st Kingston Pair Show, 2nd Crystal Palace, and 1st Slough Pair Show only times exhibited.

This hen was bred from a pair of Greens/blue. Miss Hughes and her brother vouch for the fact that the parents were not split white. Therefore, theoretically a White should not have appeared, and in any case, in view of her unusual colouring, it is clear that the Cinnamon White Blue hen was a mutant. Had she lived she could have been the foundation dam of a new series of Whites, but, unfortunately, she died without issue, and, to make matters worse, her father did not live to become the sire of other youngsters. Up to the age of six weeks this hen had pink eyes.

Miss Hughes and her brother later in-bred with the mother and other relatives of the Cinnamon White Blue hen, but did not succeed in producing another bird with her colouring.

In 1931 Mr. A.D. Simms, of Potter's Bar, mated *inter se* Dark Greens bred from an Olive and a bird which appeared to be an ordinary Greywing Green. From the Dark Green × Dark Green mating eight Cinnamon hens in both Light Green and Dark Green appeared. Two of the Dark Greens passed to the ownership of Mr. G.F. Porter, of Codicote, who founded a family of Cinnamons therefrom, and who bred a wonderful Cinnamon White hen, which was practical proof of the potentialities of this new colour variety as an aid to purifying the colour of Whites.

Mrs. A. Collier also produced Cinnamons in 1933 from stock which, I have been given to understand, she obtained from Mr. Porter, and she had the honour of being the first to breed a Cinnamon Mauve.

R.J. Watts and C.H. Rogers both then of Cambridge, had Cinnamons and split Cinnamons from the Simms mutation which they used for experimental breeding. It was not long before R.J. Watts produced the first examples of Cinnamon Light Yellows and C.H. Rogers the first Cinnamon Greywing Greens or Light Cinnamons as they were first called.

In February, 1933, Cinnamons also appeared in the aviaries of Mr. G. Hepburn, of Peterhead. His first youngsters of this colour variety were Cinnamon Light Greens bred from a pair of Normal Light Greens, purchased from a dealer in Aberdeen. The Light Green cock was close ringed and had apparently been bred by Mr. Banham, of London. Mr. Hepburn was unable to trace any relationship whatever between these Light Greens and the birds from which Mr. Simms bred Cinnamons.

Albinos and Lutinos. — These red-eyed birds are named in the Standard as Pure Yellow Red-Eye and Pure White Red-Eye, but fanciers always speak of them as Lutinos and Albinos respectively.

The Albino is the albinistic form of the "blue" series — Skyblues,

Cobalts, Mauves, Whites, etc. The Lutino is the albinistic form of the "yellow" series — Greens, Yellows, etc.

In view of the snow-white beauty of the Albino it is strange that they have never achieved other than small popularity, whereas the Lutino is bred extensively. I think they provide scope for anyone who will give serious attention to them.

There is also a Yellow-faced of the Albinos which are often called Creams or Lemons.

THE FIRST ALBINO

The history of the Albino is interesting. An Albino was bred in Germany in 1932 and in the same year a hen appeared in the aviaries of Mr. F.J. Mulliss, of Horsham, from the mating Blue cock × Green/blue hen. Mr. Mulliss bred a number of normal coloured youngsters from her but never an Albino. She was, of course, a mutant.

There is an interesting story concerning Mr. Mulliss's hen. It appears that the season before this Albino was born its Green/blue dam was badly mauled in a fight, being bitten on the head, with the result that all the feathers came off except a fringe in front, and later she became bare all over her chest. After treatment her feathers grew again except on her head.

Mr. Elliott raised the question as to whether this shock had some effect on the reproductive organs of the bird which was responsible for the appearance of the Albino. Of course, this possibility remains unproved but I cannot subscribe to the theory. The German hen bred other Albinos.

An Albino has red eyes and is pure white in plumage, there being absolutely no markings and little suffusion. The feet are pale pink and the beak is very light in colour. An Albino is genetically a normal bird devoid of pigment as in all cases of Albinism in animal or bird life. Thus although Albinos when they are produced in numbers will be alike in appearance, their genetic constitution will vary according to their parentage. This is well understood by the scientists. For instance, Professor R.C. Punnett, F.R.S., in *Mendelism* (Macmillan) says:-

"Though Albinos, whether mice, rabbits, rats, or other animals, breed true to albinism, and though albinism behaves as a simple recessive to colour, yet Albinos may be of many different sorts. There are, in fact, just as many kinds of Albinos as there are coloured forms — neither more nor less.

"And all these different kinds of Albinos may breed together, transmitting the various colour factors according to the Mendelian scheme of inheritance, and yet the visible result will be nothing but Albinos."

No doubt this is correct, but the Albino Budgerigar, as already indicated, cannot mask Normal birds in the "yellow" series. It is the Lutino which does that. Not only do these albinistic birds mask ordinary colours, but they mask any recessive factors these normal birds may carry. As examples, a Lutino may be a masked Light Green/blue, and an Albino a masked Skyblue/white.

Albinos are sex-linked, though there was a non-linked family, and a White Fallow (rarely seen) does not differ from other Pure White Red-eyes externally. The Pure Yellow Red-eye is a bird pure yellow in colour with a light-coloured beak, pink legs and feet, and red eye. The cere is also lighter in colour than in the Normals.

The remarks I have made above about the genetic constitution of the Albino apply equally to the Lutino, except that the latter retains yellow pigment, whereas the Albino is void of pigment. This assertion, however, needs qualifying to the extent that Albinos often display — particularly in the underparts — a faint blue sheen, and Lutinos a faint green sheen. Both are exhibition faults.

The Lutino is dominant to the Albino, so we have Lutinos/albino, but never Albinos/lutino. Lutinos are sex-linked, though there were some strains which were non-linked, and a Yellow Fallow is similar in appearance to a Lutino.

At one time the opinion was expressed that the Lutino might prove a valuable aid to the production of Normal Light Yellows devoid of suffusion, but this theory was exploded long ago. Actually, it could never stand the test of close scrutiny. For instance, if we mate a Lutino masking Light Yellow to a Light Yellow, how can we expect better results than if we mated two good coloured Light Yellows? In fact we shall produce *more* suffusion from Lutino (Light Yellow) × Light Yellow if the Lutino is masking a Light Yellow with much green suffusion.

PROOF FROM BREEDERS

These statements are proved every season by Lutino breeders who mate some of their red-eyed birds to Normal Light Yellows. The Yellow/lutino cocks and ordinary Yellow hens produced always display more green than do Light Yellows bred in the orthodox way.

But even though red-eyed Yellows have not, and never can, assist the Light Yellow breeder, the Light Yellow has proved invaluable to the Lutino breeder, as I think I shall prove in Chapter 12.

Just as the Lutino cannot assist in Yellow production, so the Albino cannot help us to obtain better Whites of light suffusion.

The advance made by the Lutino in type and size, to say nothing of colour, during the last twenty years or so is most creditable to breeders. No longer do we see so many specimens which are "nipped in neck" exhibited at the leading shows, nor so many with mean hands and slim bodies, which were prevailing faults before the war. Some of the best Budgerigars staged are to be seen in the red-eyed classes.

Fallows. — The Fallow has never achieved any degree of popularity, and only occasionally are specimens seen in the Any Other Colour classes. As the Standard indicates, it is bred with all the Normal body colours. Then there is a light form of Fallow corresponding with the Greywing series, and there are Fallow Yellows and Fallow Whites. The markings are dark brown and the eye is red. The body colour is lighter than normal. The Fallow is not sex-linked.

The Fallow was reported from California, U.S.A., in 1931. In December, 1932, Mr. Shräpel and Mr. Kurt Kokemüller purchased Fallows which had been bred by Mr. Schumann, of Magdeburg. Mr. Kokemüller described these birds in *Der Wellensittich,* Hanover, on 26th January, 1934, and this article was translated by Mr. F.S. Elliott and published in March, 1934.

An interesting note on Fallow varieties appeared in *The Budgerigar Bulletin* of June, 1935. In the course of an article headed "The Material Foundations of the Various Colour Varieties of the Budgerigar and their Genetic Significance," Dr. H. Steiner, of Zurich, said:-

"As regards Fallow Budgerigars, I should like to begin by giving an historical note. The yellow birds with brown undulation markings and dark red eyes, which were bred by Mr. Schumann, of Magdeburg, in 1932, do not appear to have been the first occurrence of this mutation. Before this, in the year 1929, a Swiss fancier, Mr. Augustin, of Biel, bred a brown Budgerigar which according to the description given to me must have been a Fallow. It came from a mating Olive × Greywing Green. Like Mr. Schumann's birds this was also a cock, i.e., the opposite of the genuine Cinnamons which appeared first as hens. It was exhibited at a bird show in Biel in 1929, and purchased by a well-known fancier, Mr. Zaugg, of Solothurn, who had to hand it over to the municipal aviary of Solothurn in 1930 for a short time to be looked after, and unfortunately, this bird died there in the summer of 1930 without leaving any progeny."

Mr. Kokemüeller expressed the opinion that the Fallow was not due, as in the case of the Albino, to the absence of one of the two pigment-forming factors (the agents for the formation of the black colour) but that it was only a question of an alteration of one of these factors; that it was a form of dilution, that is to say, of an equal reduction of the melanin, and that therefore it was better to describe it as the Fallow Budgerigar rather than Cinnamon. Fallows were first imported into Britain about 1933.

It is recognised that there are two types of Fallow, the German which had an eye iris and the British which has a solid red eye colour.

Opalines. — When the first edition of *The Cult of the Budgerigar* was printed in 1935 the name Opaline was unknown in the nomenclature of our hobby. Some birds of this variety had been bred, however, providing an interesting story I shall tell later.

It only needed the appearance of a few Opalines at our shows for them to attract special attention. Their popularity was soon assured. The improvement in type was rapid. In fact, they made headway in the early years of their cultivation amongst the newest varieties.

A characteristic of Opalines even in their pristine days was the size of their spots and the rotundity of their heads. Now we see at our shows splendid Opalines. In fact, it is often asserted that there are more high class Opalines than there are birds of any other colour.

The Opaline's coloration is unlike that of any other variety of Budgerigar. The striations from the crown of the head to the base of the neck are much more narrow than in the Normals, Greywings, etc. This gives them a kind of grizzled appearance.

The ground colour on the wings is not yellow in the "green" series, but green; not white in the "blue," etc. series but the same colour as the body, though usually of a lighter shade. The "V", saddle or mantle at the top of the back should be as clear as possible, whereas, of course, in the Normals it is striated. The amount of black and of ground colour on the wings should be equal to be ideal.

Opalines are bred in all the recognised colours, and there sometimes occur Opaline Yellows and Opaline Whites. The Opaline is a sex-linked variety (see Chapter XVI).

Quoting from the first edition of this book I repeat the story told to me by Mrs. R.G. Ashby, of Ayr, to which I referred above. Mrs. Ashby wrote:-
wrote:-

"About the end of 1933 we obtained from Mr. A. Brown of Kilmarnock an outstanding Cobalt hen. She was exceptionally large with a fine head and excellent spots. She was bred from a normal Skyblue and a Mauve, and although the parents could have been obtained for a 'song' I thought they were too poor to trouble about.

"The main peculiarity was that the head, neck and nape were almost pure white with slight markings in places. Nearly all the flight feathers, primaries and secondaries, were edged with cobalt in the place of white. In fact it was almost a 'Cobalt-wing.'

POSSIBILITIES ANTICIPATED

"There appeared to be possibilities and it was decided to breed with her as a normal hen but at the same time experiment. She was mated to our very best Green cock, 2nd at the Palace, which was believed pure but he turned out to be split blue. This mating produced Blues, Greens, and a Dark Green. She was then mated to one of our best Blue cocks and she produced Blues and Cobalts.

"Mr. Andrew Wilson, of Glasgow, had a Blue from one mating and a

Cobalt from the other and he has bred from them paired. Now all the young from the pied Cobalt were normal in appearance. The Blue/pied × Cobalt/pied which Mr. Wilson had have produced normal birds. There is a little colour on the nape, but this appears to be the normal 'sheen.'

"The best Blue cock from the Green and Cobalt mating was then mated back to the pied mother this year. She had four in the first nest but one was trampled after a day. The other three turned out good birds: two pied Cobalt cocks and a pied Blue hen. All are marked similarly to the hen, except that the Blue has blue wing markings in the place of cobalt. She had a second nest of eggs but was badly egg-bound on the fifth egg. She was saved and the four eggs put under another hen. We were away on holiday for ten days and on our return found four young thrown out in the cage. Our maid had missed them and they were all dead. Each was a day or so old. We did not try again but we have now a good stock, viz.:-

"The old pied Cobalt hen, her two young pied Cobalt cocks and a pied Blue hen; the Blue/pied father, a Green/pied hen, Cobalt cocks and hens/pied, a Blue/pied cock and a Dark Green/pied hen, so we should have some fun with them this next year."

Mrs. Ashby said that "mottled" would probably be a better term to use than "pied" in describing these peculiar birds.

There was also an Opaline mutation in Australia during 1932 and one in Europe about the same time. There was a further British mutation bred by a Mr. Marriott of Wolverhampton from which a strain was formed.

This is no doubt the history of mutation which brought the British Opaline into existence. The terms "mottle" and "pied" were soon replaced by the more attractive name by which these birds are known to-day.

Our beautiful present day Opalines no doubt have their origin in these four separate mutations. Examples of all these mutations were available in this country during the development of the Opaline and undoubtedly they were all crossed in various pairings up and down the country.

In addition to what may be termed the ordinary Opalines some fine Opaline Cinnamons are exhibited. There are some very good Opaline Greys, and there are other Opaline variations.

Greys and Grey Greens. — At one time there existed two different breeding kinds of Greys and Grey Greens — the English Recessive and the Australian Dominant. The English Recessive birds were very dark in colour, even those masking Sky Blue and Light Green, but unfortunately the strain did not flourish and with the advent of the Dominant kind fell rapidly into the background. During the War period the Recessive English Grey mutation completely disappeared as it is now over forty years since the last specimens were seen.

The Australian Dominant kind caught the imagination of breeders and quickly became popular in birdrooms and on the show bench. There can be a Grey and Grey Green form of all the other varieties in three depths of colour — Light, Medium and Dark. At most exhibitions the Grey and Grey Green classes are now very well supported and others produce Best in Section birds.

In June of 1935 E.W. Brookes of Mitcham, Surrey, reported that he had bred real grey coloured birds from a pair of Cobalts. These English Greys as they were known were quite distinct in colour from any Mauves that could have been expected from a Cobalt to Cobalt mating. English Greys were of a dark dull grey tone varying in actual depth according to whether masking Sky Blue, Cobalt or Mauve. They were also bred in the Green series, the Grey Greens, and the character was of a Recessive nature.

It was the same year that Mrs. A. Harrison of Murrumbeena, Australia, reported that she had bred grey coloured Budgerigars from a Grey cock purchased from a bird dealer. The Australian Grey character was quickly found to be Dominant and their numbers rapidly increased with examples soon coming to Great Britain and Europe. The present day strains of birds carrying the Grey character are in the main descended from the birds first imported from Australia. A fuller history of the Greys and other mutant colours will be found fully explained in the 'World of Budgerigars'.

Yellow-faced. — All green coloured birds have yellow faces but those known as Yellow-faced belong to the blue coloured group, i.e., blue birds with yellow masks and yellow tinted wing butts and tails. This mutation exists in several different forms and include some with deep yellow masks known as Golden-faced. The two forms most frequently met with are known as Yellow-faced Blues Type I and Yellow-faced Blues Type II. The former having yellow on mask, wing butts and tail only whereas the other type has a general heavy overlay of yellow giving the body colour a sea green effect.

This strange phenomena was first reported to the Fancy by Mrs. G. Lait of Grimsby and Jack Long of Gorleston-on-Sea in 1935. However it was subsequently discovered that a strain of Yellow-faced birds had been breeding in Norfolk for a number of years before being reported by Jack Long. It is quite possible that both the Mrs. Lait and Jack Long's strains originated in the first place from the Norfolk mutation.

When the fourth edition of *The Cult of the Budgerigar* went to press the Yellow-faced varieties were miles behind the established colours in type. Since then a remarkable improvement has been witnessed. Although not numerous some magnificent birds with yellow faces are now being exhibited. The range of the variety has been extended, and we see Yellow Faced Cinnamons, Clearwings, and Opalines, and other combinations. For instance, the exhibit which was awarded the prizes for best Budgerigar at the National Exhibition of Cage Birds in January, 1959, was a Yellow Faced Opaline Cinnamon Skyblue cock.

BI-COLOURS OR HALF-SIDERS

Occasionally there appears unexpectedly a bird which is one colour on one side of its body and another colour on the other side of its body, there being a clear dividing line right down the centre of the head, breast, and back. These are known as bi-colours or half-siders. The first recorded appearances of one of these was at the Crystal Palace show in 1929, when Mr. C. Balser of Germany exhibited a bird evenly divided with blue on one side and green on the other.

There have also been seen birds carrying three distinct colours. These are tri-colours, a notable example of which was a hen exhibited by Mr. Niblo at the Crystal Palace in 1935 and which combined in its coloration blue, green, and yellow.

Since the recording of C. Balser's Half-sider in 1929 a considerable number of similarly marked birds have been bred and exhibited in a whole range of two distinct colours in Great Britain and throughout the World. Not only have perfect Half-siders been bred but others having different colours in varying amounts are known as colour Mosaics.

Several theories for the appearance of these very unusually coloured birds were put forward but it was not until Professor F.A.E. Crew and Rowena Lamy published a scientific paper on Autosomal colour Mosaics in Budgerigars that the position of these birds was clarified.

Professor Crew kindly sent me further information about bi-colours and tri-colours, which I quoted in *Cage Birds* of 15th March, 1935, as follows:-

"Examination of some twenty specimens exhibiting bi-colourism, together with a study of their pedigree and genetic make-up support the conclusion that this condition is not produced by any abnormal or unusual event connected with fertilisation, such as the existence of a binucleate egg, or the entrance of more than one sperm of different genetic content into the same egg.

"The accident which causes one side of some smaller portion of the body to show a different hereditary character from the other has its origin in a fault in the distribution of the chromosomes at the first, or some early division of the fertilised egg.

"From one cell carrying the full complement of chromosomes two new and complete cells normally arise. But occasionally it happens that in the process which results in the doubling and subsequent division of chromosomes a single chromosome may lag behind the others and fail to be included in either of the newly formed cells.

Clearflighted and Pieds

The breeding behaviour of the Flighted has now been solved and they reproduce somewhat on the lines first put forward by Mon. Raymaekers.

Birds can have either a single or double quantity of the Flighted character in their genetical make-up and, as would be expected, double quantity birds when paired to Normals all give single quantity Flight young. Single quantity birds when paired to Normals give 50% pure Normals and 50% Flighted. The markings carried by individual birds can vary from just a head spot in stages through to the perfectly marked specimens. As a general rule cock birds will carry the best pattern markings whereas hen birds are more inclined to have the head patch and a few clear flight feathers and this seems to apply equally to both single and double character birds.

A single character cock or hen paired to a Normal will produce 50% of each kind, the actual colour of the birds having no bearing on the Flighted character. Breeding experiments have shown that two Flighted mated together give a greater proportion of nicely marked birds amongst their young. There can be Flighted forms of all other varieties, both in the Green and Blue series, although it is the Normal kinds that show their colouring most clearly. With the more pallid kinds such as Yellows, Whites and Clearwings, the clear areas do not show up very well, although they are combinations of interest to colour breeders.

As it will be seen a little later, the Flighted character is used in the production of another combination that gives quite a unique colour result.

Recessive (Danish) Pieds

A few odd examples of Pied Budgerigars had been bred as far back as 1929 when Madame Le Callier of France exhibited two Yellow and Green birds at the Crystal Palace, London. Breeding strains of these and other Pied examples were not established and it was not until 1932 that a breeding strain was founded in Denmark — hence the term Danish Pieds.

The first example, a Green Pied, was seen at a Copenhagen Bird Show, and was bought for experimental purposes by K. Riis-Hansen and the late A. Reddersen who founded the strain. When these two gentlemen gave up the mutation it was taken over by Walter Langberg and later by C.af Eneljelm, then Curator of Helsinki Zoological Gardens, Finland.

It was not until 1948 that the first Danish Pieds came to this country when Herr Eneljelm sent two Green and Yellow Pied cocks and a Normal Green/Pied hen to C.H. Rogers, then of Abington, Cambridge. As these birds were very prolific breeders it was not long before the variety was well established in a range of different colours. Most of the present day strains of Recessive Pieds are descended from the Eneljelm birds.

For many years the Recessive Pieds were long, slender, round-headed birds like those first imported and were not very successful on the show benches. Owing to the perseverence of a few dedicated breeders the variety has been drastically improved and many strains do well at the shows, even amongst strong competition from the Dominant (Australian) Pieds.

Dark-eyed Clear Yellows and Clear Whites

The first information about these birds was contained in an article in 'Cage Birds' during 1947 under the heading of 'Black-eyed Lutinos'. Mon. Raymaekers — one of the well known Continental Colour breeders of that period had these birds appearing in his breeding aviaries containing Clear-flighted, Recessive Pieds and Normals, and thought they were a new mutation. They were first called Black-eyed Lutinos and Black-eyed Albinos as they were seemingly coloured like true Albinos and Lutinos except they had dark eyes and not red eyes.

It was quite some time before their breeding behaviour was sorted out from the very widely varying breeding results that were available and the final conclusion reached was that these Clear birds were not a mutant form but a combination of two already existing varieties.

When Recessive Pieds and Clear-flighted birds are mated together the two characters combine and in the second generation make a completely new form devoid of colour and all markings. There can be two genetical kinds of these Dark-eyed Clears, those having a single quantity of Clear-flight and those with a double, but both are exactly the same in their physical colouring. Their eyes are a deep plum colour without a light iris ring, the same as with the Recessive Pieds. In Chapter 12 details of the different pairings to produce Dark-eyed Clears will be found.

Dominant Australian Pieds

A few years after the Recessive Pied mutation appeared in Europe a further kind of Pied was developed in Australia. These first Australian Pieds were coloured like Normals but with all clear flights and tail, a clear head patch and a clear band across the chest from wing to wing. Because of this latter marking the variety became known as Australian Banded Pieds. For a time the great majority of these birds carried a good clearly distinct stomach band and were bred in numerous colours both in the Blue and Green series. The result of these pairings with other varieties was that the numbers of the Banded type became less and the broken coloured forms increased greatly. For a period the popularity of Dominant Pieds on the show benches was tremendous and many excellent birds were shown, but after a time they settled down to a steady flow of exhibits. In Chapter 12 will be found the breeding behaviour of this variety and suggestions on pairings for the production of these birds.

Slates

These birds are one of the five Sex-linked breeding kinds and are of British origins. Slates first appeared in the aviaries of T.S. Bowman of Carlisle round about the same time as Greys were being bred in Australia. They differ in colour from the Greys as they have dark blue tails, dull violet cheek patches and a slate blue body colour in the light form. The Mauve and Cobalt forms of the Slates are considerably darker, with the Mauves being the deepest coloured Budgerigars that can be bred, but are still some way from black. At the present time the Slate variety is quite rare, but a few specimens do appear at the largest shows each year.

Lacewing Yellows and Lacewing Whites

This variety was first noted by C.H. Rogers in 1948 from reports from a breeder who had discarded some of his red-eyed Yellow birds for having distinct cinnamon undulations and coloured tail feathers. Only one member of this family could be traced — a Light Green cock, and this bird paired to several Normal Green and Blue hens produced five red-eyed Yellow birds with cinnamon markings and coloured tails. From these five hens and some of their normally coloured brothers the Lacewing strain was formed.

Since that time many hundreds of Lacewing Yellows and Whites have been bred having Opaline, Dominant Pied and Recessive Pied markings as well as those with the usual undulations. During this last year or two suggestions have been advanced in the Fancy Press that Lacewings are actually a combination of the Lutino and Cinnamon characters. Although a considerable number of matings involving these two characters have been made, only an odd example or so of birds having the Lacewing – like appearance have been bred. This being so it may be that under certain circumstances it is possible to produce a similar type to the Lacewing. A great deal more experimental work will be needed before satisfactory conclusions are reached as to the relationship of these two differently evolved red-eyed kinds.

The Budgerigar Society has included Lacewings in their Colour Standards and formulated a scale of points which has undoubtedly encouraged breeders to include this variety in their studs. As far as I know Lacewings have not yet gained a Best in Show Award, but this is something that could happen in the near future with their increased popularity as show birds.

Spangles

News of this variety was revealed to British breeders in 1978 through an Article in *Cage and Aviary Birds* from an English fancier who had seen these birds whilst on a visit to Australia. It appears they were being bred in several aviaries in various parts of Australia so the mutation must have occurred a year or two before 1978. Spangles are a Dominant variety of rather a striking colour pattern which can be had in all varieties in both the Green and the Blue series.

Their colour is best explained by quoting from an article

by P. Gardener which was published in the magazine of The Budgerigar Society of Australia:

"**Spangle Cobalt.** Mask: white, throat spots: black with white centre, cheek patches: violet, body colour cobalt, wing markings with each feather edged with black, flight and tail feathers edged with black".

The above quotation is a specification for a good coloured example of the Cobalt form but individual birds of all colours can vary in their actual colouring. It is the single character spangles that show the characteristic feather markings most clearly as with the double character birds the pattern is more indistinct and even absent. Spangles are now being bred in Europe so it should not be very long before specimens will be appearing on our own show benches.

Crested

When this book and subsequent editions were first written Crested Budgerigars had been in existence but had not then been officially recognised by The Budgerigar Society. A Specialist Club, the Crested Budgerigar Club, was formed in 1962 for the development of the three kinds of Crested Budgerigars and through the efforts of the officers and members of the Club the numbers of Crested birds shown have greatly increased and have become a feature at all large shows. The Club has become an Associate Club of the B.S. who have included these birds in their Standards.

It was in 1920 or thereabouts that the first Crests were reported as being bred in Australia but nothing much was heard about them until the mid nineteen thirties and examples came to Europe and Great Britain during 1938.

Two other Crested mutations have been recorded — one in Europe and one from North America. The three mutations are all inter-related and reproduce in the same way which is rather more complicated than that of ordinary colours. A full history and breeding details of the Crested variety will be found in the Handbook of The Crested Budgerigar Club and copies can be bought from the Secretary. The Crested character as just quoted operates in a different manner to other characters but still follows Mendel's theory. There can be a Crested form of all varieties and colours with Full Circular, Half Circular and Tufted crests.

Other feather variations

Three other feather varieties have appeared amongst Budgerigar stocks — the Long-flighted, the Feather-legged and the Feather Dusters. The Long-flighted birds have large heads, very long, flatish bodies and extremely long flight and tail feathers. These features taken collectively spoil the fine outline of Budgerigars and The Budgerigar Society quickly barred them from the show benches. However it is through these birds that the bolder heads of present day exhibition stock are due to the careful use of Long-flighted characters in the past.

Feather legged birds have only appeared on odd occasions and have not been developed up to the present time. Their unusual feathering does not appeal to Budgerigar breeders like it has done to Poultry and Pigeon Fanciers.

The birds known to the Fancy as Feather Dusters have long, thin, weak feathers sticking out at all angles, they cannot fly and fortunately have quite short lives. It is thought by some breeders that they may be the result of a further mutation of the Long Flighted character due to excessive Buff matings. As they do not breed they do not constitute a danger to our lovely Budgerigars.

Pieds and Clear Flighted. — When the fourth edition of this book was printed the story of the Variagated (Pied) and the Flighted Budgerigar was confusing. People talked and wrote of Danish Pieds, Dutch Pieds, Harlequins, Penguins, Dominant Flighteds, Recessive Pieds, Finnish Pieds, etc.

The Budgerigar Society wisely clarified the position in so far as the classifying and exhibiting of these birds at the shows are concerned by dividing them in the Standard into three main categories, namely, Recessive Pieds, Dominant Pieds and Clear Flighted.

The genetics of these varieties are less confusing than they were five years ago, and because of this clarification some of the information which I gave in the fourth edition of my work would be redundant now, but I think the following should still be helpful to breeders:-

The Flighted Mutation, it is claimed, first appeared in Belgium within the last fifteen years. To describe these birds the terms "Clear Flights" or "Flighted" are now in general use, whereas at first they were described only as White and Yellow Flights. A Clear Flighted has white (or yellow) flights instead of the normal coloured flights, and with a white, yellow, or normal coloured tail. The ideal specimen would have all its primary flights yellow (in the green series) or white (in the case of the blue series), and with a white or yellow tail, and a white or yellow-coloured head patch.

I first heard of these from Mons. M.L. Raymaekers, of Brussels, honorary secretary of the Cercle Ornithologique de Belgique, who claims to have been the first to have bred them.

Mons. Raymakers, when writing to me regarding this mutant, said that the breeding behaviour of white and yellow flighted Budgerigars is not altogether in accordance with general Mendelian principles. He thinks their system of inheritance is similar to that of speckledness in Canaries, which Dr. Duncker described as "polymeric inheritance," in which three hereditary factors co-operate.

Apparently some parts of the body have a predisposition to be affected by these factors, viz. the flights, the tail, at the back of skull and the lower part of the neck. It is usual for the patch on the head to appear first, followed by the flights, the long tail feathers, and, lastly, the collar around the neck.

Rainbows

These birds were so named by their originators, the Keston Foreign Bird Farm, Ltd., who describe them thus:-

"The face and crown of the head are lemon, the moutachial markings being bright cobalt blue and the spots pale grey. The feathers of the back of the head are tipped with blue and yellow; the mantle feathers are blue tipped with green and the rump bright turquoise blue. The upper wing coverts are turquoise blue marked with dark grey and bordered with blue and the lower wing coverts are off-white merging into blue with a dark grey band and bordered again with the same blue, and the whole of these wing feathers are washed with yellow. The flights are dark grey on the inner web and blue and very pale grey, with a narrow white border on the outer web. The two central tail feathers are slate blue, the outer ones being pale yellow tipped with a blue grey and with a very narrow border of pale blue. The upper breast is pale green merging into bright turquoise blue on the lower breast and where the two colours merge is almost exactly the very beautiful blue green of the breast of a Hooded Parakeet. The vent is white.

"In the Cobalt variety of Rainbow, all the turquoise blue areas of the blue bird are a vivid cobalt shade and the rump being particularly beautiful, as it is deep cobalt above, merging into emerald green. Golden-faced Rainbows have the crown of the head, throat, and cheeks gold-yellow in place of lemon and the remaining shades of yellow on the body more intense."

The word "Rainbow" has not been adopted by the Budgerigar Society, who recognise this variety as the Yellow Faced Opaline Whitewing.

During the years that have passed some new colours have been hailed as potential popular favourites, and then they have gone into the limbo of forgotten things. An example is the Brownwing, a Budgerigar similar in markings to the Cinnamon, but not sex-linked.

Our experimental breeders are always working on new colour varieties, endeavouring to establish families from what are apparently new mutants, and in a few cases aiming to evolve new varieties from the old by crossing and selection.

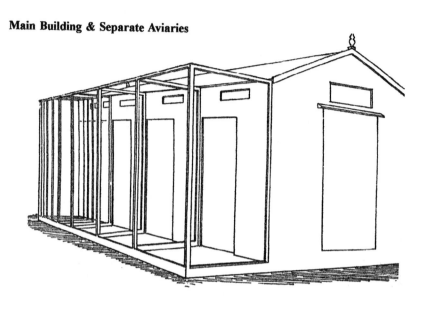

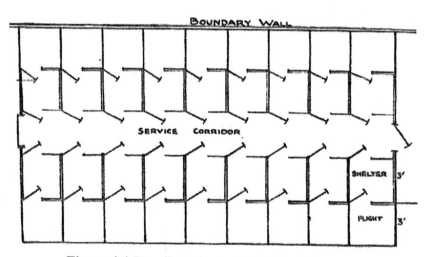

Figure 4-1 Breeding Block with Outline Plan
Designed by Dr M D S Armour who was probably
the most inflential breeder of exhibition budgerigars.
A number of references are made to him in the book.

CHAPTER 5

MARKINGS

THE COLOUR STANDARD

The Budgerigar Society's Colour Standard, compiled for the guidance of breeders, exhibitors, and judges, also gives particulars of the required markings in the respective varieties. My readers will find this Colour Standard quoted in full in Chapter 4.

From the Standard it will be learnt that adult Light Greens, Dark Greens, Olives, Blues, Cobalts, Mauves, Violets, Grey Greens, and Greys, and the corresponding Greywings, Cinnamons and Fallows of the same colours should be marked in the manner I will now describe.

First there is the mask, which covers the forehead and crown, and comes down the face in front of the eyes to a semi-circle below the beak. This semi-circle forms what is known as the bib, and which should be ornamented by four large round spots supported by a similar spot at the base of each of the two violet cheek patches. So there are in all six spots. The four circular spots in the centre of the bib should be set in line and equidistant. These spots are black in Normals, grey in Greywings, and cinnamon in Cinnamons. The bib and its decorative spots are often referred to by fanciers as the necklace.

There are waving or zebra markings on the cheeks, back of head, and neck. The wing coverts are laced, and the scapulars are scalloped — all black in Normals, grey in Greywings, and cinnamon in Cinnamons.

My readers will obtain a much clearer impression of the correct markings and their attractive undulation from the beautiful coloured and other pictures in this book than any words of mine can convey to them.

Perusal of the Standard will show that whilst all the Normal varieties named in the second paragraph of this chapter are marked in the way described, there are variations in ground colours to which attention must be given.

The mask and the ground colour of the wings of the Light Green must be clear buttercup yellow, which is again the ground for the Dark Green and the Olive.

Skyblues, Cobalts, Mauves, Violets and Greys must all have perfectly white masks and the ground colour of the wings must also be white.

The same requirements as to mask and wing ground colours apply to the Greywings, except that in the Greywing Green series yellow takes the place of the buttercup yellow in the Normal Green.

In the Cinnamon Green series the mask and ground colour of the wings has to be yellow. In Cinnamon Skyblues, Cobalts, Mauves, etc., clear white is required on the mask and wings. And this applies also to the Fallows.

The Hood

That part of the mask covering the face of the bird from the beak up to the crown of the head is sometimes spoken of as the hood; it is descriptive, but it is not an offical term. It should be wide, but it can't be wide unless the frontal of the skull is broad. Therefore this width of mask is not directly a matter of marking; it is a point of structure and width of feather.

The top outline of the hood should, in my opinion, go over the crown of the head exactly above the eye. If this line comes across in a position nearer to the beak, it gives a fore-shortened effect to the face. If it comes across nearer to the back of the head it makes the frontal of the head appear longer than it really is. Consequently, the position of the top outline of the mask can create a slight optical illusion, making a Budgerigar's head appear to be a little better or worse than it actually is.

This top outline to the mask should be as even as possible. In many specimens the line of demarcation between the mask and the striations on the head is a very ragged affair. This is a minor point, I agree, but it does have an effect on the general appearance of a bird. Dark markings known as flecking on the crown is a bad fault.

The Bib

The bib is more important than the hood, for the reason that because of its ornamentation it is more liable to be faulty.

The violet cheek patches present no problem to the breeder, and I have never known a Budgerigar to be criticised because of any failing in this characteristic marking.

Of all the component parts of the mask, it is the spots (constituting the necklace) which are the most important. They can fail in many different ways, viz.: They can be too small; too large; too many (multi-spots); unshapely; irregular in size, some being larger than others; set too high up towards the beak instead of being reasonably near to the base line of the mask; not equidistant, some being too close together, others too far apart; set too near to each other; one or more spots missing.

The spots should be reasonably big and round, but I would prefer the necklace to consist of spots a little smaller than is considered ideal if correctly set and uniform in size, than spots some large and others small, or spots irregularly placed.

Multiplicity of throat spots, mostly irregularly shaped, has become a serious problem with many otherwise excellent show specimens. This appears to be an hereditary failing which breeders could and should endeavour to eradicate from their strains by selective breeding programmes. Unfortunately they generally resort to any easy way out by pulling or clipping the undesirable surplus spots. This causes the masks of birds so treated to have a rough and unfinished look and, of course, does not lessen the problem in their offspring.

A vexed question discussed for many years was whether or not spots could be too large. Then the Budgerigar Society definitely decided that spots can be too large, and the Standard was revised accordingly. Spots too small are, of course, the more common fault.

It frequently occurs that the two centre spots are smaller than the others. Fanciers have withdrawn the feathers carrying these centre spots in the hope that when they grew again the spots would be larger. The idea was based on the assumption that spots increase in size with each moult up to a maximum point and that the pulling of the "spot" feathers would accelerate progress in the desired direction. But this theory did not work out in practice, and it has been proved that nothing can be done to rectify this fault of size inequality except, of course, producing the correct spots by skilful mating.

Another failing, less serious, is that of the four centre spots being too close together; they are bunched with quite a gap between the outside spots of the four and the spots at the base of the violet cheek patches. This is more likely to occur when the spots are too big.

Temporary Blemish

The case of the missing spot, or spots, differs from all the other failings which I have enumerated, inasmuch as this can be a temporary blemish, whereas the others are permanent. One feather of the mask moults just before a show, and with it away goes one of the bird's spots. Personally, if the remaining spots are good in every way, and the exhibit is attractive in all other respects, I do not too seriously punish it when making my awards. It can win, in fact, unless there is a specimen almost equally as good in all properties and with its spots intact.

The absence of more than one of the four centre spots is so disfiguring that a bird so unfortunate would have to "win by a mile" for its all-round excellence if it were to be placed by me above well-spotted competitors.

Good spots are so appealing to the eye, they are such a predominant characteristic of the marked varieties of Budgerigars, their excellence, or alternatively their deficiency, is so quickly apparent, that they have in the past undoubtedly received from some breeders and some judges more serious consideration when assessing the merits of birds than their true worth has warranted. There has been much controversy in the Press on this subject. It has been said that magnificently-spotted Budgerigars, otherwise of most inferior quality, have regularly defeated birds at the show of great all-round merit but inferior in spots.

But I believe there is now amongst knowledgeable breeders and judges a good understanding as to the correct value to place on spots when adjudging the merits of a Budgerigar, and that only those to whom the sight of a perfect necklace casts a spell which numbs their sense of proportion still think of a Budgerigar as a creature of spots and spots only! On the other hand, the value of spots as a show property must not be underestimated.

The base line of the bib should be cleanly cut, and an unbroken sweep of this line from cheek patch to cheek patch is preferable to there being a slight break, in the shape of a V, in the centre of the line, giving a scalloped effect. This point, however, is definitely a minor one, and providing the outline to the bib is gracefully curved, no serious criticism is called for.

The whole mask, which is the hood and bib combined, should be free from striations.

Before passing along to the wing markings I will refer to a slight failing in Budgerigars which appears to be difficult to eradicate, viz., an extension of the striations of the neck on to that part of the body colour which is between the wing butts and the striations covering the cheeks. If this blemish becomes too prominent it is unsightly. A little of it is not taken seriously by our judges.

The Standard says that the markings of the wings should be well defined; in other words, there should be a sharp contrast between the ground colour and the dark zebra markings.

Structure of the Markings

I have before me as I write a well-marked adult Cobalt Budgerigar cock. I examine one of the small feathers situated in the centre of the side of the wing. There is an outer band of clear white, then a black band, followed by another band of white, and then a grey band which extends to the point where the quill of the feather emerges from the skin.

It is the outer band of white and adjoining band of black which control the appearance of the markings as we examine a bird as it stands in its cage before us. I notice that in the feather which I am inspecting these two bands are similar in width. Had the black band been much wider than the white band, then the black markings would have been too heavy, and we should have had a specimen such as is sometimes described as "too heavily marked on wings."

The proportionate width of these white bands and black bands has undoubtedly a bearing on the brightness or dullness of the wing markings. But there is another factor, and that is the purity or otherwise of the white bands on the feathers which, collectively, constitute the white ground colour. Exactly the same remarks apply, of course, to the yellow band on the feathers in the case of the Green colour varieties. If these lighter parts are dull then the bird concerned will be what is so often termed in show reports as being "smudgy in markings."

Must be Jet Black

In the Normal marked varieties all the black markings which I have described should be really black, jet black, in adult birds, not brown. Otherwise, however pure in white or however rich in yellow the ground colour may be, there cannot be achieved that vivid contrast between the light ground colour and the black markings which is one of the most appealing features of the Normal varieties — not observable to a similar degree in any other Budgerigars.

In Greywings, as the name implies, all these dark markings must be grey, not black. A simple definition is that they should be in depth midway between zero and black.

Although I think it is now almost universally agreed that "half black" is the ideal depth of colour of the markings in a Greywing, the variations from this in birds in the aviaries and even in birds exhibited are numerous. As a matter of fact, the fixing of depth of colour in markings in Greywings presents a problem difficult to elucidate. I write about it at length in Chapter 12.

But even though this difficulty is recognised, that is no excuse for Greywings very lightly marked on the wings or Greywings very dark in markings being placed high up in their classes. I admit that it is rare to see a prize awarded to a bird whose markings are so ghost-like that at a first glance it is mistaken for a white, but it is not such a rare occurrence to see red tickets on the cages of Greywings so dark in markings (accompanied by depth in body colour) that they are but little different from Normals in appearance.

The fact that the correct depth of markings is not so easy to produce in Greywings as in the Normal colours, should make it all the more worthy of being honoured when it is there — providing always, of course, that the bird is sufficiently good in type.

The colour of the markings in Cinnamons varies much in individual birds. Cinnamon brown is called for by the Standard which recognises that this is usually deeper in cocks than in hens.

It is not desired that Light Yellows, Dark Yellows, Olive Yellows, Yellow-wing Greens, Whitewings, Whites of light suffusion, Lutinos and Albinos should be marked in any way.

All that I have written about markings in the Normal marked varieties is also applicable to the Yellow Faces, except that, as the name implies, they must have a yellow mask instead of the ordinary white one, and yellow marked tail feathers are permissible. Fallows are marked similarly to Normals, the markings being dark brown.

Opaline Markings

It is when we come to the Opalines that there is quite a different story to tell. In these handsome birds the striations or wavy markings extending from the crown of the head to the base of the neck are much thinner than in the Normal varieties, giving a somewhat grizzled appearance. To be ideal the saddle should be clear of markings. The ground colour on the wings, instead of being white as in Normal Skyblues, or yellow as in Normal Greens, should be the same as the body colour of the bird. A rather lighter shade is accepted. The black markings on the wings should be as in the Normals. The distribution of black and ground colour on the wings should be equal in quantity. The spots should be as in the Normals.

A clear saddle is often accompanied by a deviation from the normal in the wing markings, which are in these cases rather light and patchy. The smaller quantity of pigment which causes the saddle to be light has a similar effect on the wings. It is a natural corollary, for which a judge has to make a sensible allowance. But he should not go so far as to give an Opaline first because it has perfect normal wing markings, or another first because it has a perfectly clear saddle, and an almost clear wing. It is the happy medium which is required. I have seen judges leave out of the cards all the birds (including some of better type than the prize winners) because they had not completely clear saddles, and others treat with similar ruthlessness all those birds which deviated somewhat from the normal in their wing markings. I do not call this good judging.

After their first moult young Budgerigars are garbed in adult plumage and are marked as I have described markings in this chapter. Prior to the change from their infant feathering, their foreheads are barred with thin waving lines. On the throat in the space which will ultimately be the necklace there are no defined spots, but an obvious presence of dark pigment observable in the form of flecks rather than any regular formation. I have observed that as a general rule the more dark feathering there is apparent here in the chick prior to the first moult, the larger are the spots when it is in adult plumage.

In unmoulted babies there is not that sharp contrast in the wing markings which we see in the adult. The ground colour of yellow or white (according to the colour variety) is comparatively dull, and the black, grey, or cinnamon markings have not that intensity or clarity which they will develop when the adult stage is reached. These remarks are, of course, not applicable to the unmarked varieties.

In Chapter 4 there was a description given of the markings of the Clear

Flight. Ideal pattern set for the markings of the Pieds has been devised, and can be found in the Budgerigar Society's colour standards in Chapter 4.

Figure 5-1 Training Young Birds

71

Figure 5-2   An Outside Flight

CHAPTER 6

AVIARIES AND APPLIANCES

DESIGNING AVIARIES

When commencing to write this chapter I am faced with a problem, common to any author who writes on the housing of livestock and who has to appreciate the fact that his readers consist of people varying greatly as regards financial circumstances, and also differently placed in so far as space on which to erect buildings is concerned. Consequently, I have had to give much thought to the best means of making what I write of equal value to the rich man and the poor man, to he who has a large garden or field, to he who only possesses a small yard, to he who intends to keep very many Budgerigars, and to he whose idea is to have one, or at the most two, comparatively small buildings to serve as quarters for his birds.

Budgerigars will thrive and breed most satisfactorily in almost any kind of aviary providing certain essentials are not overlooked, viz., by means of a suitable shelter, freedom from damp and draughts; protection from the direct rays of the sun during the hot days of summer; avoidance of a structure which becomes sometimes insufferably hot and sometimes very cold, for instance a house almost entirely covered with glass, or with corrugated iron, or one with the wrong aspect, that is to say, facing east or north.

So the young fancier can be assured that his inability to spend a lot of money on aviaries or his not possessing a large amount of land on which to erect them, need not deter him from commencing in the hobby.

Most of the aviaries owned by those breeders and exhibitors who have taken up the breeding of exhibition Budgerigars very seriously are more useful than ornamental, but there is no reason why those who are by nature artistic should not combine elegance with serviceability by means of rustic woodwork, fancy roofing, climbing plants, attractive painting and other adornments. A typical aviary in which the beautiful and efficacious have been skilfully combined is illustrated.

I have decided to approach the problem outlined in the first paragraph of

73

this chapter in the first paragraph by describing the new and rather elaborate aviary which we have had erected where we now reside.

The outer walls are constructed of 1 in. clear quality Western red cedar weather boards, secured to 3 in. by 2 in. framework with galvanised nails, and bolted at all section joinings and corners.

Clear cedar wood was selected because it is rot and insect proof, very durable, free from knots, and of an attractive colour; hence it has not to be painted. Soon after the aviary was erected it was treated with linseed oil and turpentine, and once annually linseed oil alone will be applied.

It has a mono-pitch roof, which is covered with green mineral felt, stud nailed to ¾ in. tongued and grooved boarding, supported by 4 in. by 2 in. rafters, with a span width of 10 ft. Rain water is disposed of by means of asbestos cement rainwater gutters and down pipes connected to the main drainage system.

The whole of the interior is lined with ⅛ in. hardboard for insulation purposes, and sub-divided internally with stud partitions covered both sides with hardboard to form three main sections.

The frames in the flights are covered with angled tin to prevent the destruction of the woodwork by gnawing. These contain eight flights on the outer sides and 120 training or breeding cages on the inner sides. These cages are fastened to the walls.

By the use of partitions the show preparation room, office, food store and appliance store were sited at the ends of the respective wings.

The flooring throughout is 1 in. tongued and grooved boards on 4 in. × 2 in. joists at 18 in. centres, and the whole mounted on timber sleepers, purchased secondhand.

Ventilation is provided by large and small windows to the flights and other rooms, above which there are smaller windows that can be opened when it is not desired to open the large windows because of weather conditions. All these windows are backed with removable wire-netted frames, so that the birds cannot fly out when the windows are opened. There are also baffled louvre ventilators at the eaves, which provide ventilation when all the windows are closed.

In the construction of the interior flights ½ in. mesh wire netting was fitted into suitable timber frames. In each flight there is a table on which food and grit vessels are placed. There are long round hardwood perches, 3/8 in. diameter, and what I term "V" formation perches (see illustration facing page 89).

There are three main entrances to the aviary, one to each wing. The doors are of single type, with the top sections glazed.

The electric lighting system includes in each wing one half-watt coloured lamp which burns all night to avoid night frights. The colour of the lamp is blue. Thermostatically controlled tubular heaters are fitted. Pyrotenax

Figure 6.1 Exterior View of the Watmough Aviary.

Figure 6-2   Interior View of the Author's Aviary

copper cable is used throughout the electric installation.

In the show preparation room there are an earthenware sink, an electric geyser, etc.

All the interior walls are decorated light blue. The cage walls and the wire fronts have been treated with white cellulose.

The training and breeding cages are built in tiers of three. The bottom tier of cages is mounted on legs and bearers 14 in. above floor level. This leaves a space suitable for storage, which is covered with wood, with suitable doors.

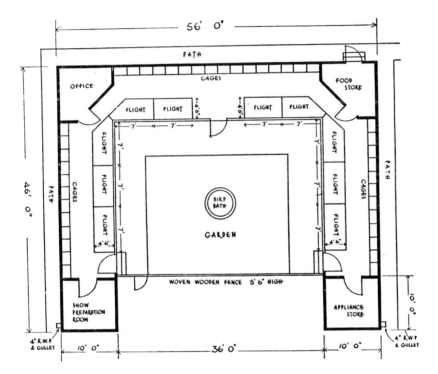

Figure 6-3   A Plan of the Author's Aviary

At intervals along the base of the top tier of cages brackets are fixed to take movable wooden platforms, on which can be placed, when required, rows of show cages when birds are being compared. These platforms are each 6 ft. 6 in. long and 8 in. wide. Each cage is 27 in. long by 18 in. high and 16 in. deep, but as there is a sliding wood division between each cage we can throw two, three, four, five, six or more cages into one to give the birds greater freedom of movement, when they are being used as training cages, or for any other purpose instead of breeding.

Each cage bottom is fitted with a 1¼ in. deep removable metal tray. This is pulled out for cleaning by means of a 1½ in. deep wooden flap, which is hinged to the 1½ in. deep bottom rail. This flap has a pull knob.

The wire front of each cage is 24½ in. by 14½ in. It fits into ½ in. by ½ in. top and bottom wooden carriers. The door in the wire front is 9 in. by 9 in., which is sufficiently large to enable a nest box to be lifted out without tilting it.

The perches in the cages are 3/8 in. hardwood, and run from front to back. In each cage there are food and grit vessels, and a modern plastic drinker is attached outside the cage front.

The outside quadrangle formed by the outer walls of the three wings of the aviary has been tastefully laid out as a garden by my wife. Across its front there is a 7 ft. high wooden woven fence. Readers will find all the major dimensions of the establishment on the accompanying plan.

This aviary at Lintonholme is a dream materialised. It constitutes my ideas of a perfect Budgerigar establishment, based on my long experience and the faults in detail and principle which I had discovered in our old places at Idle.

Some fancier visitors to Lintonholme express surprise that there are no open flights, and I have to give them the following explanation.

Close observation has convinced me that although fresh air, correct ventilation, and plenty of sunlight are essential to well-being, complete exposure to hail, cold, rain, snow, and fog can be injurious; and I have long since ceased to consider it to be wise to allow the birds to remain in flights all night. Please do not imagine that I am advocating the coddling of Budgerigars — far from it — but, on the other hand, there is no sense in inflicting on Budgerigars conditions which the fittest and healthiest human beings would not tolerate.

I decided, therefore, that our new aviary should completely meet the following needs:-

1. Combine the advantages of the open-air flight with those of the covered flight.
2. Enable the owner to observe, feed, and tend the birds himself under cover and in comfort.
3. Be easy to keep in a clean and hygienic condition.
4. Be perfect as regards ventilation, light and durability.

In my opinion our new aviary fully meets all these requirements. Its erection has been a very costly enterprise, because everything therein is of the best, as I intended it should be. I do not say to my fellow fanciers, "Go thou and build likewise", but I do advise them to embody in any aviary they may build or any buildings they may convert into an aviary, the basic principles I have described. You can do this whether your new aviary be large or small.

Figure 6-4 The Author's Aviary. With surrounding flower beds the aviary and garden make a most attractive picture

Figure 6-5 A Rustic Budgerigar Aviary that is both picturesque and practical

Figure 6-6 Exterior view of a Useful Bird Room

Left: Interior with show cages above the breeding compartments

Below: Set of "V" perches for hanging on the wall framing a perchless cardboard nest box.

If you carefully study the plan and photographs you will appreciate that the construction is such that it can be copied in a building of any size, large or small.

Taking our aviary as your standard, you can build 20 ft. of it, or any other length to suit your purpose. It is because of this facility that I have made the description and the photos of our aviary the bedrock of this chapter.

Some fanciers have an aviary but not a separate birdroom, such as we had at our old house, and which for many years served us so well. We do not need one now because all the special birdroom requirements are met by the aviary itself. I have reproduced pictures of this room (facing page 89).

It is 22 ft. long by 6 ft. 6 in. wide by 9 ft. high at the front and 6 ft. 6 in. high at the back, the roof being a lean-to. The structure is made of 1 in. boarding, the roof being covered with good quality felt.

One of its most valuable features is the abundance of light which is provided. At each end there is a window 3 ft. by 2 ft. In the front of the room there are very large windows, four in number, and each 4 ft. 6 in. by 3 ft. They open inwards, being fastened back securely to hooks in the inside of the roof. To avoid the risk of birds escaping when the windows are open, attached to each frame on the outside there is a half-inch mesh wire netted shutter. The entrance door is 2 ft. 6 in. by 7 ft. It is in the centre of the room.

To the back wall there are attached three tiers of breeding cages, the average size of each being 3 ft. long by 1½ ft. from front to back and 1½ ft. high. In each row the cages are divided one from the other by sliding wooden divisions. These enable the cages to be doubled or trebled in size at will; in fact, the birds can be given the full run of 21 ft. if so desired. The cage fronts are similar to those described earlier in this chapter. The perches in these cages are as those described above.

Provision for Show Cages

The roof of the top row of cages being flat and 1 ft. 3 in. away from the roof of the room itself, there is provided a long and suitable space for a line of show cages. There are also movable platforms attached by a suitable system of hooks to the front of the training cages. Each platform is 6 ft. 6 in. long and 8 in. wide.

Below the bottom row of training cages there is a space 1 ft. high. Behind this in the back of the building itself there are louvre ventilators through which pure air passes under the cages and into the room. A strip of ½-in. mesh wire netting 3 inches deep runs the full length of the room above the large front windows. This enables vitiated air to leave the room, though when the windows are open, which is very frequently, particularly in summer, there is an abundance of fresh air — much more, of course, than can be provided by the system of ventilation described, good as that system is.

Three 100 watt electric lamps are provided and there is a tubular electric heater, thermostatically controlled.

The outside woodwork is creosoted. The inside walls are painted oak colour, except the cages, which are treated with white cellulose inside and black varnish paint outside.

Primarily this bird room was used by us for birds when they were being prepared for exhibition, and for young stock for a period after they had left their parents. I can thoroughly recommend the principles which it embodies to anyone who is requiring a place of this kind.

I trust I have conveyed to my readers all the essential requirements of the different types of Budgerigar houses and which they can without difficulty apply to their own particular circumstances, the space at their disposal and the amount of money which they desire to spend.

Sectional Structures

A number of well-known cage bird appliance makers manufacture most suitable Budgerigar aviaries and bird rooms. These are usually delivered in sections which can easily be erected in accordance with the instructions supplied.

And writing of these sectional buildings prompts me to advise anyone who has an aviary constructed to have it made in sections, so that in the event of removal it can be transferred to a new site without any particular difficulty.

Importance of Aspect

At the commencement of this chapter I said that Budgerigars will thrive and breed most satisfactorily in almost any kind of aviary providing certain essentials are not overlooked and I gave examples of these essentials. I will now be more explicit.

An important matter is that of aspect. If at all possible it is always better for aviaries to face south or thereabouts. The worst aspects are north and east, the former being the worst of all, because of the little sunlight which comes to us from that direction, and because it is usually the coldest.

Good Ventilation Essential

In the erection of Budgerigar aviaries careful attention should be given to ventilation. If at night the birds are fastened in badly ventilated houses, even though during the day they have access to open flights, illness may be caused.

Ventilation means the removal of air which has become impure by respiration, and its replacement by fresh, pure air. Air is a mixture of gases, and like all gases it expands as it becomes warmer, and as it expands it becomes lighter and rises. Nature abhors a vacuum, and consequently if by means of proper ventilation the used air is able to leave the room, its place will be taken by fresh air, providing, of course, there is an entrance for it.

This simple scientific fact makes it clear that in order to arrange for the speedy removal from the aviary of air which has become warm and impure, by its passage through the Budgerigar's lungs, a ventilator of sufficient capacity should be fixed *as high as possible,* and inlets for fresh air as low as possible. But they should be so placed that they do not cause draughts. Some modern ventilators work on a principle of balanced louvres, which obviate draughts.

There are many well-known types of ventilators, and it is unnecessary for me to enter into a detailed description of them. If you purchase your houses from manufacturers who specialise in aviary construction it is unlikely that their ventilation will be incorrect. If you engage a local joiner to build your Budgerigar accommodation, he will be able to advise you.

A room with a span roof is the easiest type of erection to ventilate. A louvre ventilator can run nearly the full length of the ridge. Another plan is to let both long sides of the shed finish about two inches short of the roof, leaving a space through which the fresh air can enter freely. This space must be covered with strong perforated zinc; otherwise, of course, the birds would escape through the aperture. As an alternative, box ventilators of any recognised pattern may be fitted, or a row of holes, covered with perforated zinc, can serve the purpose. In the case of a lean-to roof, ventilators of one of these kinds should be fixed at the highest point and also at the eaves or, better still, much lower, for the reason previously indicated. Ventilators of the Colt type can be strongly recommended. They are excellent.

The well-known louvre principle to which I have referred above, consists of a pent house raised above the ridge of the shed and which permits of a current of air passing without draught between it and the roof.

Perhaps sub-consciously when I write about housing I have always the cold bleak north in my mind. More liberties as regards weather can perhaps be taken far south where normally climatic conditions are superior to those experienced by us who reside in the northern counties of England and Scotland. But, even so, I would not use less than 1 in. boarding anywhere. For instance, ½ in. wood in a hot climate is likely to warp.

The majority of Budgerigar fanciers erect wooden buildings for one or more of a variety of reasons, particularly expense and removability where the owner does not own the property on which the aviaries are erected or does not necessarily intend to remain indefinitely in the same residence. But happy is he who can make his Budgerigar houses of brick, or who has perfectly suitable brick buildings which he can convert into aviaries.

Bricks are superior to wood because they maintain a more equable temperature throughout the year, viz., warmer in winter and cooler in summer, warmer at nights, cooler in the daytime; and then, of course, they are much more durable.

Nest Boxes

After experimenting with various types of nest boxes I have come to the conclusion that providing certain essential requirements are not overlooked the actual pattern of the nest boxes is not by any means one of the most important factors in successful breeding, and almost any of the popular types of Budgerigar nest boxes which are made by cage bird appliance manufacturers will satisfactorily serve the purpose.

. I have observed successful rearing in boxes of the most simple kind and unsuccessful rearing in elaborate contrivances, though this does not alter the fact that a well-made and sensibly designed nest box must be an advantage both to the birds and their owners. What then are those essentials to which I have referred?

The box must be neither too large nor too small. The entrance hole should be at such a distance from the base of the box and so situated that the chicks cannot easily get out of it before they are 30 days old, which is the time when normally they come out into the aviary. The entrance hole must also not be too large. I find that a hole 3/8 in. or 1½ in. in diameter is quite satisfactory.

Figs. 1 and 1A depict a box which is typical of what is known as the "desk" pattern. Suitable dimensions for a box of this type are approximately 6 in. long by 7 in. wide by 5½ in. high at the back and 2½ in. high at the front, with a base about 1 in. thick.

The front half of the roof of the box is hinged to facilitate inspection. The bottom is concave, as should be all nest box bottoms, so that the eggs roll towards the centre, and so that the hen can easily keep them under her when sitting without the risk of one or more being pushed to the sides of the box. The diameter of the concave is about 5½ in.

The system of ventilation consists of a number of holes on either side, each hole being about ⅛ in. in diameter.

Fig. 2 is an example of the upright type of box. The width of the box illustrated is 7 in. and the height 8 in. The hinged inspection lid is at the top. These upright boxes are made in several designs. Some are rectangular, some hexagonal.

In addition to these simple forms there have been designed nest boxes possessing what are claimed to be improvements. For instance we see in Fig. 3 a nest box which the designer, who was a successful and practical fancier, considered to be more satisfactory than all the other kinds of nest boxes used at any time in his own aviaries. This box is made of plywood of the thickness of 3/8 in. It is oblong in shape with a sloping top, its dimensions being 8 in. long by 5 in. wide by 7 in. high at the back and 5¾ in. high in front. It has a loose base, which is made either of oak or deal as preferred. Nest boxes, by the way, are usually made in white or red deal. The concave is 3¾ in. in diameter. It is at one end of the bottom itself, leaving a flat portion on the base 3 in. by 4 in. The back of the base is cut slantwise, providing a space into which dirt falls when the base is pulled out instead of resting on the top.

The front of the box downwards for 3¼ in. consists of a door which lifts upwards. The remainder of the front forms the protecting ledge which is actually fastened to the removable base. The entrance hole, which has a diameter of $1^3/_8$ in. is at one end, and underneath, as will be seen from the illustration, there is a perch. The ventilation system consists of two holes on the opposite end to the entrance hole, each hole being ¼ in. in diameter.

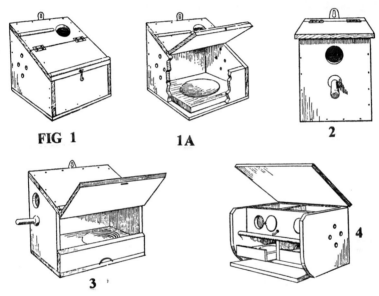

Figure 6-7   Some typical nest boxes used for Budgerigars

Common Principles

I have selected this particular box as my Fig. 3 because it embodies principles which are now applied to many of the advocated nest boxes. We have here, for instance, the removable base, the chief advantage of which system is that it greatly facilitates cleaning out. As soon as an owner finds a box sufficiently dirty to demand cleaning (too dirty or wet for the birds to be expected to clean it themselves), all he has to do is to slip out the dirty basin and put in a clean one, although, of course, similar ease of cleaning can be secured by exchanging a dirty nest box for a fresh one.

At one time I disliked the idea of having an inspection door in the front of a nest box. I thought that the sudden opening of this door would frighten the hen and flush her off, with possible damage to the eggs. But those who use boxes with these doors attached tell me that in actual practice the danger to which I refer is non-existent, and it must be agreed that the method saves considerable time when making a tour of the boxes during the breeding season, because the owner need not take the nest boxes from their hooks in order to look inside.

Debatable Point

As to whether the concave should almost occupy the whole of the base or whether there should be a flat portion as in the box illustrated in Fig. 3 has always been a debatable point with me. I will put the pros and cons. The advantage of the flat portion — which by the way should be the nearer to the entrance hole — gives the hen the facility of coming down on to it instead of on to the eggs themselves with the possibility of damage to them. She drops on the flat and then walks gently on to her eggs.

The possible disadvantage is that young chicks may wander on to the flat part away from the hen and thus be deprived of the warmth provided by the hen's body and also the warmth of their brothers and sisters which can be so advantageous to them, particularly in the cold days and nights of the early part of the breeding season. Young Budgerigars are inclined to move into the corners of a box at a very early age if they have the opportunity of doing so, and it has always appeared to me to be an advantage if, because of the shape of the box and the size of the basin, they were so confined that they could not get away from the hen.

Still, here again experience is superior to theory, and I have never received any complaints from those who have used boxes with basins similar to those about which I am writing.

Again in theory it would seem that where one has the concave practically filling the whole of the basin there is a danger of a hen breaking eggs as she comes straight down on to them; but once more I doubt if many, or any, eggs are broken in this way.

Just as the wild Budgerigars in Australia will go straight on to their eggs, so are hens kept in aviaries able to do so without danger of breakages. This is but one more example of Nature's wisdom. The hens instinctively know how to descend on to the nest without doing any damage.

I once experimented by putting a little landing board beneath the hole inside the box, theoretically for the hen to rest on before going on to the eggs, but I did not find it to be any advantage.

Apropos this risk of breakages, a friend of mine who had visited a large Budgerigar establishment in France once told me that the nest boxes employed there were 12 in. deep and only about 4 in. wide, with the hole at the top. Yet eggs were rarely if ever broken, and when the chicks were thirty days old they ascended what was virtually a tube and came out into the aviary in the normal way.

Fig. 4 illustrates a double nest box of a pattern which can also be purchased in the single form if desired. Here again we have the removable basin with protecting ledge and an inspection door.

With this double box, as soon as the hen has laid in one of the two compartments the hole of the other compartment is closed by means of a swing shutter. A 1½ in. hole is provided in the centre partition through which the hen can obtain access to both nests. Those who use these double boxes tell me that the hen will often lay the eggs of the second nest in the enclosed half of the double box. Obviously if the hen does behave in this way, the advantage is that there will not be newly laid eggs and chicks of the first round in the same nest. This is certainly desirable, because a hen which is sitting on eggs in the same box as chicks which have not yet gone out into the aviary is often disturbed and sometimes eggs are damaged because of this overlapping between the first round and the second round. But will she always behave in this manner? I doubt it.

I do not consider that any nest boxes should exceed in floor dimensions those which I have given in describing the illustrations accompanying this chapter.

I consider that ventilation is important, although in the patterns I have described the arrangements for the egress of used air and the ingress of fresh air are ample. The entrance hole itself is, of course, the major means of ventilating the boxes.

Seed Hoppers

One method of arranging for seed to be always available to Budgerigars is the provision in each aviary of a seed hopper. These usually consist of a glass-fronted container, a chute down which the seed slides to a position opposite a row of feeding holes, a perch on which the birds stand when they are eating, and a deep tray in which the discarded husks collect.

Sufficient seed can be placed in the upper container to provide food for a considerable period; thus it is unnecessary to replenish daily, which saves the owner much time on his morning tour of the establishment.

As the seed is eaten that which is in the container slides down to the front of the feeding holes, and the birds always have the facility to satisfy their appetites so long, of course, as the hopper is not allowed to become empty. As the husks fall into a tray below, there is no necessity to blow these off, which arises when the food is placed in pots or on trays. Numerous patterns of these metal automatic seed hoppers are on the market in normal times and they are made in various sizes.

Hoppers are not suitable for soaked seed. In fact, many fanciers regularly feed their birds in earthenware or glass food vessels, which are, of course, also suitable for grit and water. These can be purchased in various sizes from the appliance manufacturers, who advertise in *Cage and Aviary Birds*.

In every Budgerigar breeding establishment such appliances as are below enumerated are required:- Brushes, scrapers, buckets, water jugs, suitable tools for doing necessary repairs, and other appliances referred to in this book, e.g, a hospital cage, spraying cages, a spray, etc. — all obtainable from the appliance makers.

Figure 6-8   One Type of Nest Box

CHAPTER 7

FIRST PURCHASES

MAKING A CHOICE

The novice who is commencing in the Budgerigar Fancy in a small way with (say) not more than four pairs of birds, will probably read Chapters 13 and 14 in this book with mixed feelings. He or she may say: "All this advice about selection, in-breeding, the founding of a strain, how to introduce out-crosses, etc., is all very well for the owner of a large stud, and it may be all right for me in a few years when I have a much more extensive establishment and more birds to breed from. But here I am at the beginning of my career and I have to buy some birds with which to lay the foundations of what I hope will eventually develop into a successful exhibition team. How do *I* proceed?"

I appreciate the point of view of young fanciers who cannot commence with many pairs, and I realise that the majority of new Budgerigar keepers are men and women who wish to begin in a small way, and that is why I have especially devoted this short chapter to them.

Although in the first breeding season they must perforce use only stock bred by other owners, from whom they have made their purchases, in the second and subsequent seasons those principles which I have described in the chapters headed "How to Breed Winners" and "In-breeding" can be applied whether an owner possesses few or many pairs. But the initial breeding stock has obviously got an important bearing upon future results, and if the beginner starts with poor material it is not likely that he will breed youngsters in the first year sufficiently good to serve his purpose in founding what he hopes will eventually be a successful show team, nor suitable for him to make use of them in accordance with the established principles which I shall describe in the other chapters referred to above.

Therefore, I want to emphasise the importance of a maxim which has become almost hackneyed, viz., **quality before quantity.** In other words, if your initial expenditure must be limited, spend your money on comparatively few good well-bred birds in preference to twice the number of inferior specimens. So many young Budgerigar fanciers make the mistake of filling their aviaries with faulty birds merely because they want to have a display of colour for their friends to see. It would be much more profitable to them to expend the same amount on only three, four or five pairs which, whilst not necessarily good enough to be exhibited, are satisfactory breeding stock possessing more good properties than bad ones — well-bred and obviously likely to produce offspring better than themselves and capable of forming the basis of a collection which will be a credit to their owner and eventually bring honour to them.

Of course, this advice does not apply at all in the case of those people who do not desire ever to become exhibitors, but who merely want to own aviaries full of Budgies as an adornment to their gardens.

IMPORTANCE OF GOOD INITIAL STOCK

It is wise not to be too cheese-paring when making the first purchases. A few pounds extra spent at the beginning can come back fourfold ultimately, providing always, of course, that one obtains value for money; and this is not difficult to ensure in a Fancy containing so many good breeders, so many good birds and so many genuine devotees.

It is impossible for me or anyone else to tell novices how much they ought to spend on Budgerigars of particular colours, as everything depends upon the quality of the birds offered and the quality of the stock which has produced them. I have sufficient faith in my fellow fanciers to say that in the great majority of cases the beginner will be given a square deal, will receive sound advice from the seller as to how to mate the birds bought in the first season, and will not be charged unfair prices.

Just as in the next chapter I shall say to those who have birds for sale that they should be willing to send birds on approval under the usual conditions, so I think it is only right that buyers should usually desire to see that which they are asked to buy before finally making a decision. Having got the birds before them and having formulated ideas, as they ought to have done, as to what are the essential requirements in a good Budgerigar, they can then buy or not buy as they may think fit.

Alternatively, if they have a friend who has more knowledge than they have, they can let him see the birds before deciding. But if the potential purchaser feels that he is as yet himself incapable of selecting birds, and if he has no one else to whom he can refer, then having specimens sent on approval will not serve any useful purpose, and it is better in such a case to place one's trust entirely in the breeder from whom one intends to buy and leave it to him or her to select the birds in accordance with the amount to be expended and the number of pairs which is required. Such trust as this will rarely be abused, although, of course, it is advisable for a purchaser to use normal business sense when selecting the advertiser to whom he is to write. In ninety-nine cases out of a hundred, when the absolute novice, who admits his ignorance, tells an older fancier that he leaves himself entirely in his hands, he who did not strive to give complete satisfaction would indeed be a knave. True, we hear of cases in which advantage is taken of beginners, but I am sure that such conduct is not common, and, after all, no business or hobby can ever be entirely free from those whose consciences are elastic, to put it mildly. But in the Budgerigar Fancy these are comparatively few, and most of their names are known.

The novice who can only commence with, say, four pairs will be well advised to specialise in a particular colour or group of colours. As to which colours he shall commence with is entirely a matter of personal taste. It is a good plan in the first place to go to a show, see all the different colour varieties on exhibition, decide which attract the most and then follow the dictates of one's fancy.

If your particular favourites are Light Greens or Lutinos, and your collection in the first year must be confined to four pairs, then I should advise you to have all your birds of the one variety. If your fancy leans towards Mauves, Cobalts, Violets, and Blues, you can commence with a small stud containing most of these colours, because they can often be inter-mated with considerable advantage, as advised in Chapter 12. I name the above colours, of course, only by way of example.

BEST TO SPECIALISE

My point is that the man or woman who is only buying a few birds to begin with should definitely specialise. The probability is that later the young fancier will become so enthusiastic over the Budgerigar that he will decide to extend his scope and accommodation, and then it will soon be enough for him to take up additional colour varieties.

Of course, if the beginner is able to purchase, say, twenty pairs at the start, there is no reason for him to specialise in the manner I have described, though even such as he should not keep *all* the colour varieties.

There are patent reasons why the specialisation which I advocate is so necessary. To take an extreme case, if the four pairs purchased were composed of, say, one pair of Light Greens, one pair of Greys, one pair of Lutinos, and one pair of Clearwings, it would not really be desirable with an establishment of this size to mate any of the youngsters from one pair with the youngsters of any other pair in the second breeding season, because the colour crosses are unlikely to be suitable. Consequently, quite a number of new purchases would have to be made, whereas if the policy of the owner were to specialise, the young stock of the first year would themselves provide him with a series of matings, in addition, of course, to his being able to use again the birds bought at the outset.

Another cogent reason why it is unwise to depend solely on one pair of one colour to found a family of that colour is that they may fail to be successful stock birds. Due to the fault of the cock or the hen, or both, they may not "nick" — as fanciers say — whereas if one has four pairs of the same colour or group, the chances are that one at least will be successful, and then it is they and their progeny which will lay the foundations of success. It is not always by any means easy to breed winners even with a number of pairs, so how greatly is the breeder handicapped when all his hopes have to be centred in only one pair.

Novices often ask me what essential qualities they should look for in the birds which they buy for breeding purposes. My answer is that they must study the Budgerigar's exhibition requirements and the most common faults, and secure in their purchases as many of the former and as few of the latter as possible, always bearing in mind that the better the bird the more expensive it must be; that there is no such thing as a perfect Budgerigar; that the most successful show birds — even if the owners will sell them — will be comparatively expensive; that it is possible to breed good youngsters from birds that are themselves not of sufficient merit to win prizes but which are well bred and of that general type which one associates with show Budgerigars as distinct from under-sized, slim, small-headed specimens, such as are kept as pets.

You must expect minor faults, but wasters are dear at any price if the object is to breed from them.

All this, I am afraid, is abstract advice, yet how can I be definite without the birds which someone is thinking of buying actually in cages before me? The novice can adopt no better procedure than to formulate his own ideas as to what he should and should not have in a Budgerigar which he buys by visiting shows and studying the winning exhibits, reading assiduously all that he can about the exhibition properties, and interrogating older fanciers whenever the opportunity presents itself. We all learn by experience in Budgerigar culture, as we do in every other walk of life.

CHAPTER 8

GENERAL MANAGEMENT

CONSTANT ATTENTION ESSENTIAL

In this chapter I shall describe all those things which the Budgerigar fancier has to do in connection with the management of his or her birds and to which separate chapters have not been devoted.

If I were asked to name one word which epitomises the secret of success in livestock culture, that word would be *attention*. Constant and careful attention to all those items, many of them *apparently* unimportant, plays a big part in the achievement of success in our hobby.

Having decided on a good system of management, it is essential that the breeder should ensure its being carried out, without any slackness or omissions. It is the meticulously careful, painstaking fanciers who rank supreme in the prize lists. They are thorough in all that they do, and thoroughness in anything always brings its own reward.

Budgerigars are easy to manage compared with many birds and animals. They do not make excessively exacting demands on a man's or woman's time, and yet they will suffer from neglect as will any living thing. If my reader formulates a good simple daily programme, and keeps to it religiously, never putting off till to-morrow what can be done to-day, never through laziness or indifference saying "I will not bother," he or she will discover that looking after a Budgerigar establishment is not a very difficult matter and a constant source of pleasant recreation. It is the careless, inattentive breeder who obtains the least fun out of the game, because he gets so far behind with his work that he becomes overwhelmed and what should be a pleasurable recreation becomes something of a burden.

Those who are able to employ a good spare or full time man or youth to clean out the aviaries and do other work connected with the birds can keep efficiently a larger number of Budgerigars than breeders who have to rely entirely on their own pair of hands. Those who are in the latter class should avoid keeping a bigger head of stock than they can satisfactorily manage. In other words, they should not give themselves so much to do that it frequently becomes difficult for them to keep up with the daily routine.

I have always found it best to draft a programme and adhere to it strictly except, of course, when business or other circumstances unexpectedly interfere. And, having formulated your programme, do not vary it, except in accordance with the particular demands of the different seasons of the fancier's year and unless you become absolutely convinced that certain variations are really desirable.

I am afraid some novices are inclined to adopt almost every new idea about which they read or which is suggested to them, without first giving sufficient thought to the proposal. Thus they are constantly changing their methods of feeding, management, etc., not always with benefit to their birds or satisfaction to themselves. Keep your mind receptive to practical advice, of course, but do not be for ever changing your system without any patent need, and do not develop into a faddist.

REGULAR CLEANING

Cleanliness of the aviaries and all appliances is of tremendous importance. The aviaries should be cleaned out at least once weekly. Never in any circumstances should this cleaning be deferred beyond a week. Dirt is the most common cause of disease. It harbours deadly bacteria, and I am sure that many deaths amongst Budgerigars are attributable to a lack of cleanliness in their homes.

For cleaning out, a scraper, a fairly stiff long-handled brush, a hand brush, a bucket and a shovel, all the appliances required.

The scraper should be used for loosening all excreta. I prefer a scraper with a triangular shaped head, because by means of one of these you can more easily remove dirt from the corners.

The dirt which is collected should not be stored anywhere near the aviaries; in fact, the best thing to do is to burn it.

All drinking pots, grit vessels and other receptacles should be cleansed in hot water, in which it is quite a good plan to dissolve ordinary washing soda, say one-tablespoonful to a gallon of water. Soda is a good disinfectant though there are advertised disinfectants which are even more efficacious.

Once per fortnight, at least, after the usual cleaning by scraping and brushing, it is an excellent thing to mop out the aviaries well with hot water and disinfect them.

Treatment of open flight floors at the weekly cleaning will, of course, depend on their covering. If they are concrete they must be well swept and swilled. If they are covered with any other material they should be kept trim and neat by being treated weekly in the most suitable manner. The best method to adopt will readily suggest itself to the owner.

At one time, whilst I never had nest boxes cleaned out when they contained eggs, I was an advocate of cleaning them fairly regularly during the period when they were occupied by chicks. Experience has taught me that, providing the excreta remains dry and powdery, no harm is done to the youngsters by its remaining.

As soon as the chicks leave the box the parents almost invariably clean out the nest themselves preparatory to the next laying. Anyone who has observed them doing this work will agree that they thoroughly enjoy it and that it is obviously instinctive with them and a perfectly natural process.

In the case of what we term a wet or dirty nest, in which the excreta is never dry, fairly regular cleaning out of the nest box is essential. The simplest way is to slip a clean base into the box, cleaning the dirty one later. A surplus of these bases should always be kept at hand. Of course, this can only be done when nest boxes with detachable bases are in use, and they are the kind that should always be employed.

ANNUAL "BIG CLEAN"

In addition to the weekly cleaning, and at least once annually, there should be a special cleaning down. If this can be done, both in the early spring and in the autumn, so much the better, but if the fancier feels that once per annum is all he can carry out, then I think it is better to do it in the early autumn when all the birds have finished breeding. Then everything will be spick and span for the exhibition and selling season and the aviaries in a fit state to withstand the ravages of the winter.

It is a good plan to commence the annual "big clean" in July or August. Woodwork and netting which may have become deficient should be repaired. Roofing felt should be renewed where necessary or perhaps recoated with one of the excellent tar products sold for the purpose. The outsides of the houses should be given a fresh coat of creosote every second or third year, as required — less frequently if they are painted.

After the inside walls have been thoroughly brushed with a hard brush, they are all distempered afresh. After creosoting, painting, or distempering, care is taken to keep all the birds away from the newly treated surfaces until the medium used is thoroughly dry. I do not advise creosote for internal walls, and on no account for the insides of nest boxes. In the case of cedar wood treatment once annually with linseed oil is all that is necessary, as I pointed out in Chapter 6.

Wood boxes should be cleaned, soaked in boiling water, disinfected, and stored away in a dry shed or cupboard for the winter, though those who use cardboard nest boxes should burn them at the end of each breeding season (see Chapter 6). After thorough cleansing and disinfection the wood bases should be stacked away.

All show and training cages should be re-enamelled or cellulosed, and similarly, all other appliances renovated or renewed. As much care should be taken with all this work as is exercised by the ladies when they are conducting spring cleaning in the home. Nothing should be left undone that it is obvious should be done.

The feeding of Budgerigars can be an easy matter compared with the feeding of many other birds and animals, because by the employment of hoppers it becomes unnecessary to give a fresh supply of food daily. The hoppers, which are described in Chapter 6, need only be filled with seed periodically, but the owner must never allow the containers to become empty. As I emphasise elsewhere, Budgerigars must always have food available to them, and, therefore, never in any circumstances, must the renewing of the seed in the food vessels be overlooked or there may possibly be fatal effects.

Whilst it is quite all right to give dry seed to the birds by means of hoppers in the manner described above these appliances are not suitable for seed which is damp because of its being treated in the way which I describe in Chapter 9. Seed so prepared should be fed in earthenware or plastic pots.

CLEAN DRINKING WATER

Every day fresh water must be put into the drinking vessels if open earthenware or plastic pots are used. In our new aviaries at Lintonholme in both the aviaries and the cages modern plastic drinkers are fitted. These protect the water from dust, etc., and we do not find it necessary to change the water more often than every other day, at most. Although Budgerigars are such light drinkers (they drink more when they are rearing chicks), the water must be there for them when they do want to drink; and it must be clean water placed in a position where it is shaded from the sun. The fancier who is so fortunate as to have a running-water system installed in his establishment is saved the duty of giving water daily, but he must see that the trough through which the water flows is always quite clean. Not many breeders are so blessed.

A watchful eye must be kept on the grit pots to see that they have not become empty. Any greenfood left uneaten must be removed, as stale greens can be harmful.

The carrying out of the simple routine tasks above referred to need not occupy a lot of time, and it is wise to make the first tour of the aviaries in the early morning. Sometimes one may detect a bird which is ailing. Immediate attention may mean the saving of its life, whereas if it is left until later in the day it might die.

I must leave the actual planning of the daily programme to my readers themselves because people's circumstances differ, and they must organise the work of managing their birds according to what best suits their convenience. But I do say again to them — formulate a programme and stick to it as closely as is humanly possible. Arrangements can usually be made so that the larger tasks are left to the week-end.

The installation of artificial light in the bird room is almost essential to the business man who is usually not able to see his Budgerigars on weekdays from his early-morning tour until he returns home in the evening, when he has, for instance, to do all those things necessary to the preparation of his exhibits for the shows described fully in Chapter 17 and which he could not do on the dark evenings of winter if artifical light were not provided.

SEPARATE THE SEXES

When the breeding season is over it is advisable to separate the sexes, and if the accommodation permits, it is wise to keep the cocks out of sight and sound of the hens, though this is not absolutely essential and certainly not always practicable. Once this can be done he birds are inclined to show a greater keenness to breed when they are mated in the spring. If the cocks and hens are kept together in the autumn and winter they form alliances, and when the owner mates them as he desires at the commencement of the breeding season they often for a period, display a lack of affection towards partners which are not of their own natural selection.

Where several pairs are kept in one aviary, this can be a great nuisance, because the cock may go over to a hen which it so happens has been his loved one during the non-breeding season. In any circumstances there is always a possibility of Budgerigars changing their mates contrary to the desires of the owner when a number of pairs are in the same aviary, but the risk is increased when the sexes have not been separated. This particular risk does not, of course, arise when only one pair is kept in one place, which is the ideal method, as I shall explain more fully later.

As soon as the young birds have passed through their first moult their ceres will indicate their sexes. Those of the cocks will be blue, except those of the red-eyed and Recessive Pied varieties where they will be purplish flesh coloured and those of the hens, brown.

Budgerigars do not moult at regular times, as do poultry and other birds. After their first moult as babies, which commences when they are ten to twelve weeks old, their coat-changing process is somewhat erratic. Sometimes they cast only a few feathers now and again. At other times they moult freely and speedily, which is what I like them to do, because then you can rely upon their assuming a new coat and being much brighter and more attractive in appearance when they are exhibited. They usually have an approximately full moult about October. Judging from observation of our own birds in the aviary at Lintonholme this process apparently coincides with the normal autumn fall in temperature.

Owing to this irregularity of the moult, it is not possible to assert how long a Budgerigar takes to complete the process. As some guide I can say that it takes six or eight weeks for a bird to grow a completely new tail, and if it drops a spot it is about three weeks before it reappears.

When a bird is casting a lot of feathers, and when it can be said to be having a full moult, a watchful eye should be kept upon it, and greater care than usual should be exercised in protecting it from chills.

A more or less full moult taxes a Budgerigar's system. A certain amount of the nutrition which it secures from its food has to go to the "feeding" of the new feathers, and its physical condition falls below the normal. Most of my readers will have noticed how moulting is often accompanied by loss of flesh. Cod liver oil (or synthetic vitamins) is never of greater service than when a Budgerigar is changing its plumage.

Changes of temperature will sometimes set birds off moulting, and this at any time of the year. That is why exhibition specimens so often commence to cast feathers when they return from a show. They have experienced varying degrees of heat and cold whilst travelling and whilst benched in the exhibition hall or tent. Note also how quickly Budgerigars will begin to moult when they are transferred from the bird room — with its more or less equable temperature — to an outside aviary.

PROTECTION FROM CHILL AND FOG

Although Budgies are so hardy, and although an abundance of fresh air is invaluable to them if draughts are avoided, reasonable care should at all times be exercised to protect them from chills. For instance, whilst birds that are kept in open-air aviaries enjoy and may be refreshed by a shower of rain, the house doors should be closed and the birds put under cover on wet afternoons sufficiently early for them to become completely dry ere they retired for the night. It is always dangerous for domestic animals and birds to go to bed with wet coats.

Then always see to it that the stock is kept inside when fog prevails. Fanciers must use common sense in deciding when it is unwise for their Budgerigars to be allowed access to open flights, but there is no need for them to err in the direction of coddling. These remarkable little Parakeets are vigorous, but they are, after all, only flesh and blood, and they must have reasonable protection. But you will have read much more already about the question of exposure to the elements in Chapter 7.

In Chapter 7 the importance of correct ventilation is stressed. Never is lack of ventilation more harmful than when the house doors are closed at night. Unless provision has been made for the egress of used air and the ingress of fresh air, before morning there will be a serious lack of oxygen and the birds will be breathing air charged with carbon dioxide — a state of things calculated to cause ill-health amongst them. And the danger will be much increased if there are too many Budgerigars in one aviary. Overcrowding must be avoided in any case, but overcrowding plus bad ventilation is ruinous.

BATHING AND SPRAYING

Voluntary bathing cannot be other than good for Budgerigars but, unfortunately, if you place an earthenware or zinc bath in the flights and fill it with water, they will not make use of it as do pigeons and other birds. Some individuals will bathe, but not the majority. If a considerable quantity of long grass is put into the bath the Budgerigars will roll and play about in it, getting quite wet, though actually in our aviaries in Lintonholme we do not make this provision. One friend of mine sprays his birds with a large garden spray as they stand on their perches. But in spite of what I have just said, bathing is not an *essential* part of Budgerigar management.

As winter approaches you will have decided which birds you are desirous of advertising for sale. It is advisable, if possible, to keep these to themselves in aviaries separate from the stock which you are retaining for your own purposes. Then when prospective customers visit you with the object of buying birds, you can show them all that you have for disposal in one collection, which facilitates their selection. Similarly, when you receive inquiries, having the "sellers" all together saves you much time in choosing birds to satisfy the requirements of potential customers.

When advertising Budgerigars it is most desirable to describe them accurately, not making over-statements about their merits. Apart from the ethics of the matter it is bad business to mislead buyers. A disappointed customer will never again buy from the same seller and neither will his friends.

Selling Surplus Birds

In the same spirit, always show your own confidence in those specimens which you offer by being willing to send them on approval either against cash or under *Cage and Aviary Birds'* admirable Approval System, or, of course, without such protection in those cases where the prospective customer is personally known to you. When forwarding on approval a condition should be made that if the birds are not returned within four days it will be understood that they are sold. One bird or two birds can quite safely be dispatched by rail in a box. Seed must be put on the bottom, and it is wise not to be sparing of it, perchance there is abnormal delay on the line. Make sure that the box is sufficiently well ventilated without its being draughty. We use boxes made of strong cardboard, plywood or a mixture of both.

Danger of Vermin

In spite of the measures that may be adopted to keep mice out of the buildings (described in Chapter 7) these rodents are adept at getting into aviaries, corn stores, etc. They can be a great annoyance, and even an expense, because they will eat as much seed as the Budgerigars themselves if they are able to reach it. Another advantage of seed hoppers, as compared with pots or trays, is that they can be fixed at a height and in such a position that mice cannot reach them. All food should be so stored that it is inaccessible to mice. Mice, like rats, are carriers of disease, and seed fouled by them can be dangerous. If mice become numerous they destroy woodwork, etc.

Unfortunately, it is not possible to trap these vermin in the aviaries because of the danger of trapping the birds instead of the mice! Traps can be set in the bird room, cupboards, etc., and the colony of mice reduced by this method, but the best way to destroy them quickly in considerable numbers is by the use of one of the modern methods used by Ministry of Agriculture pest officers. In fact, by arrangement they will do the job for you if you have a big number of mice. A good cat will assist, but, of course, it must be kept away from the birds.

Rats are the most dangerous vermin, because they will kill the birds if they get the chance. They can be destroyed by the same means as those employed to kill mice. Ferreting is effective if the rats' runs are suitable. If there are many rats and the usual methods fail, the services of a professional rat-catcher or a pest officer should be utilised.

In the case of open-air aviaries, precautions should also be taken to prevent cats from running over the top of open flights. Budgerigars are so alert and swift that it is a rare occurrence for a cat to injure a bird through the wire netting, but its appearance alone can be alarming to them and cause them to fly about the aviary dangerously. One's own cat can be trained not to go on to the netted roofs by hitting it (not cruelly) when it offends in the manner described.

The birds must not be allowed to remain in open flights all night, even during the heat of summer. Apart from the fact that great changes can occur in the weather during the night-time, after dark they may become seized with panic and dash about recklessly in a state of wild alarm, heedless of the danger of injuring themselves. This is known as a night fright. The sudden flash of light, reflected in the aviary, is a common cause.

One of the first and most elementary things a novice has to learn is how to catch a Budgerigar when it is flying about in the aviary. The correct method is to use a net. The one which we employ is 14 in. in diameter. The frame is made of wood and the net of linen. The handle is about 8 in. long. It is not advisable to have a long handle as it gets in the way when the net is being used, although if the aviary is unusually high a longer handle is a necessity.

If care is used a Budgerigar can be caught without any risk of accident as it is flying, or when it is clinging to the netting. Care must be exercised to avoid hitting it with the wooden frame.

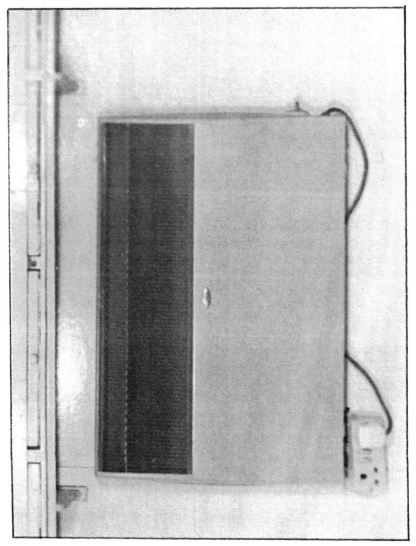

Figure 8-1 A Type of Electric Heater which is most suitable for Budgerigar Bird Rooms

Figure 8-2   Feeding Pots and Foods

CHAPTER 9

FOOD AND FEEDING

THE STAPLE DIET

The staple diet of Budgerigars consists of canary seed and millet. The former is the seed of the grass *Phalaris canariensis,* a hardy annual bearing beautiful flower spikes in summer followed by a fruit which contains the seed that we give to our birds. There are a number of grades, qualities, and varieties, the best known being Australian, Morocco, Turkish, Mazagan and Spanish. The order in which I have written them corresponds with the variation in size, commencing with the small Australian canary seed and ending with the largest of all, the Spanish, which itself varies from a Bold to a Mammoth Grade. Canary seed is still being grown in England, but not by any means in the quantity in which it was being produced during the war, when canary and millet seed could not be imported. The ability to grow this seed satisfactorily in England was a war-time discovery.

Millet seed is a cereal grown, so far as its use as a bird feeding seed is concerned, in Europe, Australia and Turkey. It is especially suitable for cultivation in those lands where there is a low average rainfall and the soil is too poor and sandy for wheat or even maize. It is a small grain, the seed of the grass *Panicum miliaceum,* which grows up to 12 ft. high and produces its seed in a tuft at the summit of its stem.

The best known millets used by bird keepers and which are purchasable in this country are the following:-

White millet — Italian, Smyrna and Australian. Yellow Millet — Bombay and Persian are not much in demand at present, the Indian type (Small Panicum) being more popular. Spray millet in bunches is French (Millet-en-grappes) and Italian. Attempts to grow millet in Britain have not proved so successful as the production of canary seed. A large percentage of the millet at present used by Budgerigar fanciers comes from Australia.

With canary seed and millet, as with other seeds to which I shall refer later, it must be borne in mind that seeds can vary considerably in quality even though they are of the same variety. This variation can be due to one or

103

more of several causes, including *(a)* quality of seed sown; *(b)* weather conditions during growing period; *(c)* harvesting when mature and unspoilt by adverse weather; *(d)* drying and preparing; *(e)* grading; *(f)* cleaning and screening.

GROATS v. OATS

Some fanciers use oats or groats as an addition to the feeding mixture all the year round or at certain times. Some use pinhead oatmeal and others wheat. To our seed mixture we add a small quantity of groats and good sound Canadian wheat. Wheat of inferior quality should never be fed to Budgerigars.

The oat is a grain with which everyone is familiar and it is quite unnecessary for me to describe this product of British soil. The groat is the oat from which the husk has been removed. Pinhead oatmeal is kibbled or cut groats. The only advantages that the groat has over the oat is — (1) only oats of very good quality are de-husked to become groats; and (2) they are an excellent medium for the giving of cod liver oil, because as they are without husk, the oil easily percolates into the grain, hence there is less wastage, and the owner is certain that the birds are getting the quantity of cod liver oil he wants them to have. Otherwise the groat has no advantage over the oat — certainly not oats of the best quality. In my experience an *excess* of oats or groats is calculated to make the birds rather loose in feather and they are inclined to be fattening.

Oats, groats, and wheat should never be more than a comparatively small part of the food mixture.

Recently we have added a small quantity of linseed to our seed mixture. It is a recognised fact that it is one of the best of all bird and animal conditioners. It can provide that little bit extra which puts the finishing touch to a conditioning regime. It was my father who first taught me its virtues when I was a youth and we kept horses. "It's linseed that puts the sheen on their coats", he said to me. Linseed mashes for horses, linseed cake for cattle are recognised as being indispensable.

Linseed is never more useful than when animals are casting their coats, and so in the case of Budgerigars it should be of particular value during the moult.

Unfortunately, Budgerigars do not usually take to eating linseed with any degree of enthusiasm, though if they once try it, they continue to eat it; and if they are brought up with it from birth there is no difficulty.

Probably the reason for its ability to put a sheen on the coats of horses and the plumage of birds is its very high fat and silicon content. It is rich in protein, which is of particularly good quality. It certainly "feeds" feather. It provides essential vitamins, and it contains some desirable trace elements.

Because of its high fat and alkaloid content it should be used in moderation.

It is a mistake to exercise false economy when purchasing seed, and I warn my readers against the dangerous practice of obtaining inferior qualities merely because they are cheaper. Generally speaking, the most expensive grades are the best.

Only by experience can fanciers learn to appreciate good quality seed by appearance, cleanliness, plumpness, sound kernels (which is very important), and sweet taste, and, therefore, they should always purchase their supplies from reputable firms who have a thorough understanding of the Budgerigar's needs.

On this page an analysis is given of the seeds used in the feeding of Budgerigars, and of other grains for comparison purposes. These figures given can be accepted as being approximately correct, although analyses are subject to some variation in accordance with the actual quality of the seeds.

	Proteids (Albuminoids)	Fats or Oils	Carbohydrates	Salts and Minerals
Canary Seed	13.5	4.9	51.6	2.1
Rape Seed	19.4	40.5	10.2	3.9
Hemp Seed	10.0	21.0	45.0	2.0
Maw Seed	17.5	40.3	12.2	5.8
Niger Seed	17.5	32.7	15.3	7.0
Millet Seed	11.3	4.0	60.0	3.0
Sunflower Seed	16.0	21.5	21.4	2.6
Linseed	25.0	40.0	18.0	5.7
Peas	22.0	2.0	53.0	2.4
Beans	24.0	1.4	44.0	3.6
Tares	25.0	1.5	46.0	3.0
Lentils	29.0	1.5	44.0	2.3
Wheat	11.0	2.0	70.0	1.7
Barley	10.0	2.4	70.0	2.0
Oats	12.0	6.0	62.0	3.0
Maize	10.0	7.0	65.0	1.7
Rice	5.0	0.5	83.0	0.5
Green Vegetables	2.0	0.5	4.0	0.7

Carbohydrates provide heat, force and vital energy by their oxidation or burning up within the body.

Proteids (albuminoids) form tissue and build up and repair wastage of body substance.

Fats provide heat and energy.

The mineral substances are bone providing, and they also supply chemical salts to the glands, the blood, and the digestive fluids of the body. Then there are the vitamins, but these I will deal with separately later.

The perfectly balanced ration for a Budgerigar would consist of just the correct proportion of proteids, carbohydrates, fats, minerals, and salts to fulfil the bodily requirements of the bird. Experience has taught us, particularly during the war, that analyses are not by any means a certain guide. For example, the differences in the percentages between oats and canary seed are not, prima facie, sufficient to indicate any great difference in nutritional value. Yet oats, useful as some consider.them to be as an auxiliary food, are incomparable with canary seed in so far as Budgerigar feeding is concerned. This may be due to variation in the qualities, as apart from the quantities, of the constituents of the two grains. For instance, the protein in canary seed might be superior to the protein in oats. Be that as it may, our birds certainly do much better when canary seed and millet seed are the staple diet.

Up to comparatively recently there had not been carried out with Budgerigar feeding extensive experiments such as there have been in connection with poultry culture, and to a great extent we have had to rely on "trial and error", and feed our birds on those seeds, etc., and in those proportions which have given to others and ourselves satisfactory results, and on the Budgerigar's natural instinct to eat from the food we place before it just sufficient of each kind to satisfy its system's demands. Under the sponsorship of the National Council of Aviculture there is now proceeding at the University of Reading research into French Moult. A very important part of this work is the study of nutrition in Budgerigars. At Reading the authority on nutrition is Prof. T.G. Taylor, who has a special interest in Budgerigars. Therefore, it is pleasing to me to be able to say that there is now a more scientific approach to the feeding of our birds than ever before.

FUNCTION OF FOOD

The purpose of food is to develop growth in the young, and in birds of all ages maintain and repair body substance and produce heat and energy; and the perfect diet must necessarily be so constituted that it meets all these requirements. It should be so flexible that it can be changed suitably in accordance with the particular seasons of the year, the facility or lack of facility for exercise, the condition of the Budgerigars at stated times — for instance, whether they are too fat or too thin, or moulting — and it should particularly be adjusted within reasonable limits when the parent birds are feeding youngsters.

In actual practice with this species we are somewhat limited as to the food which they will eat, there being many additions which we could make to their dietary if they would co-operate with us by consuming them. But I have found in my experience that Budgerigars are somewhat particular as to what they will eat and what they will not eat. I always argue, however, that birds and animals will naturally usually select those things, if available, which are good for them and that we need not worry unduly because of our inability to induce them to experiment with foods which we rightly or wrongly think would be to their benefit; and it is gratifying to realise that a comparatively simple diet is sufficient to keep Budgerigars in good health and condition.

I have already said that in normal times their staple food consists of canary seed and millet, and I have as yet been unable to improve upon them as the main components of the dietary. We have varied our mixture in our own aviaries at infrequent intervals, always with the idea, of course, of improving it.

Millet sprays are rather expensive. Apart from this it is quite a good practice – though not essential – to hang them up in the cages or aviaries, say once per week. They are particularly beneficial to the youngsters in the nursery. The seed of French millet spray is of high quality; in addition, the birds particularly enjoy picking it, an activity which I am sure acts as a tonic.

VITAMINS

Before I pass along to the subject of green foods, roots, and possible suitable additions to the dietary during the breeding season, I think it will be helpful to my readers, if I say here something about the important question of vitamins, the study of which is a science and has undoubtedly proved to be of tremendous importance in the feeding of human beings, animals, and birds. These vitamins are elements in food which have a very important bearing upon health and which should be provided in ample quantity not only with a view to maintaining physical condition but also as a preventative of disease. The vitamins consist of the following:-

VITAMIN A (Fat Soluble) — assists growth and increases stamina and the resistance to disease.

VITAMIN B (Water Soluble) — its presence strengthens the nervous system and is therefore conducive to good health generally. Its deficiency is a common cause of neuritis and various nerve disorders.

VITAMIN C (Anti-Scorbutic) — its deficiency causes skin diseases.

VITAMIN D (Anti-Rachitic) — assists in the formation of bone and its absence causes rickets.

VITAMIN E — prevents sterility and increases fertility.

These vitamins in varying quantities are in all the foods which we give to Budgerigars.

The most important vitamins to the Budgerigar keeper are Vitamins A and D, which are contained in cod liver oil. Because of the probability that the ordinary foods do not provide a sufficiency of Vitamins A and D, many of us are of the opinion that cod liver oil of the best quality is a most valuable auxiliary food (I look upon it as a food and not as a medicine).

107

HOW TO GIVE COD LIVER OIL

The recognised method of giving cod liver oil is to include one teaspoonful of oil with each pint of seed. It should be well mixed into the seed with the hands until he who is doing the mixing is satisfied that it is fully distributed. The job should be done thoroughly in order to prevent some parts of the mixture carrying more of the oil on the husks than other parts.

At Lintonholme we use cod liver oil all the year round except when the birds are breeding and even then if sunshine is as notable by its absence as it is here in some summers. It is particularly beneficial during the winter when there is at times an almost complete absence of sunshine and when the actinic value of the sun's rays is low. During the summer when the sun is shining daily and when good health can be maintained more easily than at other periods of the year, vitamin deficiency is not so likely to occur and cod liver oil is therefore not then so necessary as on other occasions.

I do believe that a course of cod liver oil prior to birds commencing to breed not only strengthens them for the task which is before them but also puts them into such a state of health that egg binding is not likely to occur.

I have stated above that cod liver oil should be given in the proportion of one teaspoonful to one pint of seed. The usual method is simply to put the oil in the ordinary canary seed-millet mixture and distribute it by hand, mixing so thoroughly that every bit of seed becomes coated with the oil.

AN ALTERNATIVE METHOD

An alternative way of administering cod liver oil is to mix it with a de-husked grain. (Groats, as I have already said, are particularly suitable for the purpose.) The advantage of this system is that the whole of the oil is absorbed, whereas without doubt when cod liver oil is mixed into canary seed or millet some oil is lost when the birds de-husk the seed. It is essential that only cod liver oil of the very best quality and highest vitamin content should be used.

Halibut liver oil is many more times richer in Vitamins A and D than is cod liver oil and, therefore, of course, a much smaller quantity will give equal results. But it is not so good for our purpose as cod liver oil because one cannot distribute very small quantities of halibut liver oil over a pint or more of seed.

All the above remarks about cod liver oil are a reprint of what I wrote about it in the fourth edition of *The Cult of the Budgerigar,* and it remains good advice.

Since then I have given much thought to the question of providing our birds with the essential Vitamins A and D by means of one of the excellent synthetic vitamin solutions, which, incidentally, I have found most beneficial to myself and responsible for some of that excess of energy which my friends tell me I possess, and which is inconsistent with my age. Note that these synthetic Vitamins are not medicines, and they are not dopes.

Some fanciers have told me that when they have given cod liver oil to their birds during the breeding season, the chicks have sometimes been bilious. This has not been my experience, and I do not think it should occur unless too much oil is mixed with the seed.

I have consulted Prof. Taylor about this question of cod liver oil *versus* synthetic vitamins, and this is what he says:-

"I consider that cod liver oil, when added to the seed fed to Budgerigars at the normal rate of one teaspoonful to one pound, is entirely beneficial. It may, however, prove harmful if a poor quality oil is used, or if a good quality oil is fed, but allowed to become rancid. The only reason for feeding cod liver oil is for its content of Vitamins A and D, and the oily part is just a carrier for the vitamins. No benefit is likely to result from the non-vitamin portion. If A and D are given in some other way, this is just as good as the traditional method."

Abidec is the synthetic vitamin mixture which I take almost daily, though other very good ones are obtainable. I use it in capsules; for the birds I buy it in liquid form. As Abidec (and other similar products) contains Vitamins B, E and C in addition to A and D, it is superior to cod liver oil to that important extent.

A synthetic vitamin solution cannot satisfactorily be given to the birds by adding it to the dry seed. Therefore, the most simple way is to put it in the drinking water.

When fresh water is given daily, there can be a wastage of the vitamins added to it. In aviaries in which the plastic drinking fountains are provided, to which I referred in Chapter 8, the vitamin solution can be put into the water once weekly, and the water left unchanged for three days, unless, of course, it has been consumed. Although excessive provision of synthetic vitamins is undesirable, the fact is that there is little danger of the birds taking vitamins in excess; their bodies will only absorb as much as they require.

One weakness — perhaps not serious — in the system of administering vitamins through the drinking water is the variable desire of Budgerigars to drink, and from this point of view mixing the vitamins in the water used for soaking may be a more efficacious system in those aviaries where soaked seed feeding is carried on.

There are on the market emulsions, etc., containing cod liver oil, which can be given instead of the raw oil, and mixed with the seed in accordance with the directions.

Green foods and roots are beneficial to Budgerigars, though not so *essential* as at one time we all thought. They should if possible be provided daily during the breeding season and *at least* three times per week when the birds are not engaged with parental duties.

The richer the soil on which the greens are grown the more nutritious they will be.

As autumn approaches the early wild plants, particularly following a season of extreme heat and dryness, lose their feeding value, and it is then advisable to discontinue using them and commence to give cultivated greens or roots.

When seeding grasses are available they are a valuable addition to the Budgerigar's dietary — in fact, they are considered by many to be the best of all green foods — particularly for adults rearing chicks, and youngsters after they leave the nest. They possess desirable properties additional to those contained in dry seeds. The birds eat them with great relish.

As agriculture has become more scientific so has the use of fertilisers (as distinct from the old-fashioned horse and cow manure) and insect and other pest destroyers have become the regular practice. Hence the need for care when gathering wild greens. They should not be gathered at the road side or in fields which can possibly have been fouled.

Common chickweed is well known to everyone who owns a garden. In addition to possessing the other properties for which greens are valuable it is said to be rich in Vitamin E, and for this reason it is claimed that it increases fecundity. It grows profusely as a weed, and there is usually little difficulty in gathering ample quantities of it.

The common dandelion is an admirable tonic, but I do not think it is a green which should be given too frequently.

Groundsel, like chickweed, is easy to find and is given to Budgerigars by some fanciers. Others, however, speak disparagingly of it and consider that it is inclined to cause diarrhoea. As there are plenty of other greens to be had for the gathering, perhaps it is safer not to use groundsel.

The birds like plantain, and it is a good food. It is inclined to be slightly astringent in its action.

SHEPHERD's PURSE A TONIC

Long-leaf plantain is also a useful green, as is common shepherd's purse. This plant is both a tonic and an astringent. On the first signs of scours in a rabbit many practical breeders of these animals give to the sufferer a feed of shepherd's purse, and a complete cure is often soon effected. Budgerigars thoroughly enjoy picking the seeds from this plant.

Of course I could go on and on describing wild greens which can be given to Budgerigars — there are so many of them — but I think I have named sufficient to give my readers ample choice, in addition to which they might consider, if they wish, those other weeds favoured by rabbit breeders, who have studied the green food question seriously, viz. common burnet, hogweed, clover, coltsfoot, cleavers (also known as cly, sweetheart and goose grass, and which is beloved of geese and turkeys), common nipple-wort, and sow thistle.

But, after all, it is advisable for the fancier who is not a botanist to confine his attentions to those plants with the appearance and value of which he is familiar, because there are some wild greens which are definitely dangerous to birds and animals, well-known examples of which are arum (cuckoo-pint), anemone (windflower), autumn crocus, belladonna (nightshade), white bryony, celandine, figwort, fool's parsley, hemlock, etc.

When suitable wild green food is unobtainable the Budgerigar breeder must turn to cultivated greens and roots. A fresh lettuce is a useful food, but particular care should be taken not to put more into the aviary than will be quickly eaten. Once lettuce leaves begin to turn yellow in my view they can simultaneously commence to be unsuitable as food.

There is nothing superior to perpetual spinach as a cultivated green. Chicory is another good green food.

Some breeders give their birds those green vegetables which they eat themselves — cabbage, brussel sprouts, kale, watercress, celery, etc.

In the winter many fanciers substitute the wild greens of summer by putting in the aviaries apples, beetroot, swedes, or carrots. Of these I prefer carrots, which I think combine all the essential requirements.

Young carrots, cut into four by slicing down the middle, are readily eaten by Budgerigars when once they have got used to them, and their composition is such that they balance green food deficiency when wild plants are unobtainable, and they are rich in vitamins. We use a lot of carrots in the aviaries at Lintonholme.

Differences of opinion exist with regard to the value of green foods and roots as an auxiliary diet. Although it is unwise to give these products too profusely, I think the majority of keepers consider that *reasonable* supplies of them are beneficial to the health of their birds. There are some fanciers who only supply these foods occasionally, and there are a small minority who do not utilise them at all.

My own view is that the *lavish* use of greens is undesirable. They are not by any means so important as the staple diet of canary seed and millet. A little at a time given more regularly is, in my opinion, preferable to giving greens or roots infrequently, and then in large quantities, with the result that the birds literally gorge themselves, which can be particularly dangerous if they are feeding chicks.

Green foods or roots given in a sensible way do serve a valuable purpose, because they contain a relatively high percentage of desirable vegetable salts and vitamins and they have a cooling effect on the system. They also counteract obesity.

111

DRIED GRASS OFFERED

I have said above that I do not consider greens to be so essential as at one time we all thought they were. During the war when my aviary attendant was away on service and I was every day crowding two hours into one, I often found I could not give greens for quite lengthy periods, and yet the fact remains that although the stock were being mainly fed on a substitute diet they did not apparently suffer. I do not say that they would not have been better if they had been getting greens frequently, but there were certainly no apparent ill-effects. Nevertheless, I became rather worried about the absence of green foods and I found a very good substitute in dried grass. I mixed the dried grass into the soaked seed, to which it adhered, and in that way the birds got a proportion of it. Some, of course, was cast away with the husks. I do not particularly recommend dried grass, though it was useful in the abnormal days to which I have referred.

The provision of tree branches in the aviaries, breeding and training cages for the birds to chew the bark and much of the wood is a commendable practice. The enthusiasm with which they attack the newly introduced branches is convincing evidence that they provide something which Budgerigars require, and which they get in their wild state.

Mr. E.W. Buttner, a learned South African student of nutrition in Budgerigars, has told us how in the bush in Australia the birds gnaw the eucalyptus trees and of his satisfactory experiments with feeding ground eucalyptus wood to his own Budgerigars. We find at Lintonholme that our birds enjoy the bark and wood from any tree, but I wish we had eucalyptus trees available.

Care must be taken to avoid taking branches from poisonous trees, of which there need be little risk in view of the following letter from the Forestry Commission in reply to an enquiry which I addressed to that body:-

"Only the yew (*Taxus baccata* L.) and the laburnum (*Laburnum anagyroides* Medic.) are poisonous. The poisonous elements are concentrated in various parts of the tree in each case. In the laburnum the seeds are particularly poisonous. In the yew the foliage and the seeds are poisonous, but, strange to say, the pink flesh or 'avil' around the seed is not. In a garden containing many rare trees and shrubs, it is possible that other poisonous kinds, introduced from overseas, might be found, but all the other common British trees are harmless."

So far I have dealt with the simplest form of feeding Budgerigars, having described a dietary which is alone capable of keeping our birds in good health all the year round; and I have, after much experimenting and a lot of study, almost come to the conclusion that, broadly speaking, Budgerigars do best on a comparatively simple diet without much in the nature of what can be termed "fancy" feeding. And yet there are some additional foods which can be utilised at different seasons with considerable advantage, judging by the results reported to me by other breeders.

SOAKED SEED

The feeding procedure, which our aviary manager, Mr. Albert Gregg, now follows, is this, in his own words: "Four parts canary seed, 1 part Pannicum millet, 1 part white millet, quarter part wheat and a small quantity of groats are mixed together, put into a bag and soaked for 24 hours in cold water, to which has been added four teaspoonfuls of Blue Label Deosan per bucket of water.

"After 24 hours the water is emptied out and the bag of seed thoroughly rinsed under the tap. Then it is hung outside to dry off; or if the weather is poor, the bag is hung over a tubular heater.

"Next day this seed is emptied into a bucket and laced with linseed, and a small amount of an emulsion rich in vitamins is mixed into it. On alternate days, the seed is sprinkled with a yeast product and the emulsion is left out.

"During the day grated carrot and crumbled brown bread is given to the breeding pairs at the rate of one tablespoon per pair. On leaving their parents the youngsters are housed in a double breeding pen which can accommodate a dozen birds, and they are also given grated carrot and brown bread mixed together.

"As an infrequent alternative to carrots greenfood is offered, and this is either spinach or seeding grasses.

"I like chickweed, but readers will appreciate that to supply five or six hundred birds regularly with it would require a full time collector!

"During the last breeding season in the hope of improving the development of the chicks at Lintonholme, we fed them a cake, but this was in the nature of an experiment. Until we have had more experience of its effects, I hesitate to recommend it."

VALUABLE DIASTASE

When grain is placed in water germination commences within one hour, and germination produces diastase, a nitrogenous ferment created from the digestive juices of the plant acting on the starch of the seed. Diastase dissolves starch into dextrine, which is easily digestible and quickly assimilated by the blood-stream. Dextrine is the basis of many proprietary baby and invalid foods. I am given to understand that diastase is so powerful that one part will dissolve or pre-digest 2,000 parts of starch, and one part of germinated grain will produce enough diastase to convert the starch in six times as much grain into sugar.

The value of the various malt products advertised rests, I am told, on the fact that malt, which is germinated barley dried and ground, is rich in diastase.

I think my readers, who have made use of either soaked or sprouted seed, will have observed how the parent birds when feeding chicks will show a preference for it over the seed in the hoppers, which would point to the fact that it provides something which is desirable.

There are on the market some excellent conditioners, and while a fancier cannot use all of them, he can select some.

Yeast is a first class addition to the dietary. Among its good properties is the provision of Vitamin B. It is on the market in a form suitable for Budgerigars. There are certain tonics on sale which are beneficial, and there are the synthetic vitamin solutions to which I have already referred. And this does not exhaust the list. Indeed, the fancier is catered for as he has never been before.

I must now leave it to my reader's own experience to guide him as to which feeding system to adopt; but I warn him not to be frequently changing his procedure and carrying out experiments with foods, possibly to his ultimate loss. A good, well-established simple feeding routine is preferable to one whose principal feature is its irregularity.

Nothing is more important in the feeding of Budgerigars than the provision of a suitable grit, which should be of such a nature that not only does it serve to grind the food and aid the process of digestion but also provides certain essential mineral constituents of which calcium or lime is the most important. Lack of calcium is injurious to the general health of any living thing and a deficiency of this mineral will cause weakness in bone and feather formation.

Other mineral substances which the system of a Budgerigar demands are iron, iodine, carbon, cobalt, magnesium, potassium, sodium, chlorine, manganese, etc. To both the Budgerigars and Pigeons we give a mineral mixture which contains all these, some of which our birds only previously obtained through green food or grits.

I believe some of the grits advertised are as near ideal for the purpose as man can make them. Personally so important do I consider the provision of lime that we use a grit containing 99 per cent. of it; the remaining 10 per cent. is flint.

Some people advocate shell grit with or without salt added. I do not consider this to be as good as the grit which we use and which I have described above because when it leaves the crop and passes through the provintriculous it comes in contact with the digestive juices which contain a high percentage of hydrochloric acid.

This starts to dissolve the shell grit before it reaches the gizzard, where it is wanted. Very soon the grit has almost completely dissolved and ceased fully to service its purpose as an assistant to digestion. Consequently, the bird eats more grit to compensate for the loss, which gives the fancier the erroneous impression that the grit must be good because his birds eat so much of it.

I have known owners give their birds only broken oyster shell, having formed the opinion that this was a very good natural grit.

Old mortar is valuable for the same reason, and it is undoubtedly because of its high calcium content, plus certain helpful salts, that cuttle fish bone is popular with most cage bird keepers.

It is claimed by many authorities that sea-sand will serve all the needs for which grit is used, but personally, whilst I agree that it possesses valuable properties, I do not think it can, alone, provide as much calcium as is required. It is essential that the grit should be finely ground, so that there is no danger of its injuring the birds' intestines as it can do if it contains large sharp-edged pieces.

Generally speaking I do not advocate the use of drugs and stimulants unless a bird is ailing. If Budgerigars come from healthy stock and are correctly fed and well managed they should retain good health without the aid of any artificial treatment, though, of course, illness can arise in an aviary, and for my views on this unpleasant occurrence I must refer my readers to Chapter 20.

A course of a suitable tonic can be beneficial, for instance, preparatory to the breeding season, during the moult, and in the case of those birds which are being prepared for exhibition.

HOW TO GIVE TONICS

Most fanciers give tonics in the drinking water, which can suffice, but I think a better plan is to give it by means of the millet spray or in the soaked seed if the owner concerned soaks seed in the way I have described earlier in this chapter. A good system is to put a sufficiency of the tonic into cold water and steep a millet spray in it overnight, giving it wet to the birds next morning.

It is essential that Budgerigars should always have food in front of them. Unlike poultry and pigeons they cannot safely be given a meal in the morning and another in the evening — just sufficient for them to eat up on each occasion. They must be able to eat when they want to eat. In actual practice it will be found that they themselves fix more or less regular mealtimes, their largest feed being before they retire to their perches for the night.

If a Budgerigar is deprived of food for any length of time it displays signs of distress, and it will quickly succumb if seed is not provided before it is too late. I have known pigeons live for days when through accident there has not been any corn available to them, whereas a Budgerigar cannot last twelve hours. Therefore the only safe course to pursue is to be meticulous in carrying out the injunction never to have the food pots or hoppers empty.

Figure 9-1   A Nest Box and Eggs

CHAPTER 10

MANAGEMENT IN THE BREEDING SEASON

EARLY OR LATE START?

In the Budgerigar Fancy there is a wide difference of opinion between those who believe in very early breeding, and those who advocate delaying the mating of the first pairs until after the middle of February. In principle I support the latter school of thought, though at Lintonholme we have in the last few years put together a limited number of pairs in January, really as a defensive measure in order to have some youngsters ready for the early Patronage shows.

No doubt the fact that the majority of these events are now held in August and September has brought forward the commencement of the breeding season—a regrettable situation in my opinion.

Every year I have disastrous results reported to me in aviaries where the temptation to have chicks in the nests soon after the bells have rung in the New Year has been too strong to resist. I admit that I also receive good reports, but I still contend that very early breeding is a chancy business, and I do know that in the old days before the early-breeding craze had started the number of youngsters bred was on average higher than it is now.

It is a question which individual fanciers must answer for themselves according to their circumstances and desires, and particularly the condition of the parent birds at the time of mating, which is undoubtedly the most important factor of all.

Those who commence to breed in early January must ensure that the birds mated are old enough to commence parental duties, as the second round youngsters of the previous season will certainly not be. Artificial heat must be provided. It must be thermostatically controlled, with the thermostat set at 45 degrees.

While, as I have indicated above, I favour later rather than earlier breeding, I do not go so far as those who advocate not starting until April (except unavoidably in the case of birds bred late in the previous year); and I like to see all the nest boxes down and the season finished before, at the latest, the middle of July. The end of June is even better.

An early March beginning provides sufficient time for the second round youngsters to complete their baby moult before the nights are long and the sunshine and warmth of summer are no more.

If the last clutches are not hatched until late August or early September the chicks miss in the earliest days of their lives — when their future health can be made or marred — those advantages which are enjoyed by the older youngsters, the sunshine, the longer hours of daylight and their genial warmth.

Chicks which have their first moult in late autumn or in the winter usually change their feathers slowly, and a slow moult is never as satisfactory as a normal one.

Youngsters born in the fall of the year are often slow in their development and it is not advisable to breed from them in the following season.

All this provides an argument against those who are opposed to making a commencement before April, and those who even advocate deferring putting the next boxes up until May is in.

But, as I have already stated, of much greater importance than the date when the fancier commences the season is the condition of the birds when they are mated. It is absolutely necessary that they should be ripe for breeding before they are provided with nest boxes. If this rule is strictly observed, the possibilities of egg binding, infertility, and eggs being cast out of the boxes by the hen, are reduced to a minimum.

Budgerigars are only in the desired state to go to nest when they are in perfect health, alert and full of life and activity, free from any sign of moult, with their feathers tight fitting and carrying that bloom which denotes physical fitness, with their wattles bright in colour, and when they are displaying obvious signs of desire to breed.

It is true that if birds which have reached this high point of condition are not then mated they may go out of form, probably start an unseasonable moult and not be again ready for breeding for a considerable time.

I may be asked why in principle I prefer rather later to very early breeding, which I do, with the qualification that the condition of the birds at a given date is all that it ought to be. My answer is this: that from March onwards the days are getting longer, the sun a little more powerful, and the severe weather of winter has passed. The climatic conditions are, therefore, more suitable for rearing chicks, as the activities of the wild British birds indicate to us. Spring closely approaches, and it brings with it those natural conditions of higher temperatures and more hours of sunlight, for which in January the early-breeder fancier had to find substitutes in the form of artificial heat and leaving the lights on in the aviaries until it is time for him and his family to go to bed.

Further, because of the improving climatic conditions it is natural to expect that Budgerigars which have enjoyed them and had ample exercise

118

in flights since the end of the show season should normally be in a better breeding state in late February or early March than they can be expected to be in late December or early January.

But in the case of the Budgerigar, compared with other birds, their condition is so non-static that for me to tell any fancier just when he should put his breeding pairs together would be presumptuous. In any case it is unlikely that all the pairs will be ready at the same time either as regards condition or age.

BREEDING AGES

There are differences of opinion as to the minimum ages at which cocks and hens respectively should be mated, but I think it can be accepted that the average view of the breeders as a whole is that cocks should not breed until they are eleven months old, though in our own aviaries we do not lay down quite such a hard and fast rule. We allow the actual development of the individual to govern the matter to a certain extent. Some birds seem to mature more rapidly than others, and one can exercise a little licence in such cases. All the same, the figures I give above are safe ones, and I advise my readers to adhere to them approximately, bearing in mind that as a general rule it is preferable for the birds to be older rather than younger than the minimum ages stated, if the fancier can so arrange matters.

Some authorities fix the minimum breeding age for cocks at eleven months and that for hens at twelve months; and there are, to my knowledge, a few fanciers who do not mate their hens until the second year after their birth. Personally I do not consider there to be any wisdom in suppressing a hen's natural instincts for so long after she has attained her full sexual development.

As to the maximum age at which Budgerigars can be employed satisfactorily for the breeding of high-class stock, this is to a great extent dependent on the vigour and condition of the individual. Some specimens are still hale and hearty at an age when others have become almost decrepit. Cocks can be used for more years than can hens, because the propagation of the species is not so demanding of the male as it is of the female.

When I am asked to express the maximum safe breeding age for cocks and hens respectively my answer is six years for cocks and four years for hens, but, as I have indicated above, these figures are subject to variation governed by the state of particular individuals, and I have had reported to me quite satisfactory results from cocks older than six and hens as old as six.

YOUTH AND AGE

I do not advise ever mating two quite old Budgerigars together. They should each be provided with mates younger than themselves.

Before the pairs are put into their breeding quarters they should be ringed with open, coloured celluloid rings. On each bird of a pair you place a ring of the same colour, on the opposite leg to that carrying the metal ring, of course. Before the youngsters from that pair are taken away from their parents you put on to their legs celluloid rings again of the same colour. Thus if the adults are ringed with blue rings, all their progeny of that season will also wear blue rings. This is a great advantage when later young birds of different breeding are flying together in an aviary, because one can tell at a glance without catching it just how any particular youngster is bred.

This is not an essential procedure, but it is one which most fanciers adopt.

Under every occupied nest box there should be pinned a card bearing the following wording, and with ample space provided for entering the various particulars indicated by the headings which I have had printed in capital letters:-

AVIARY No.2.   COLOURED RING: Red.
PAIR No.6.
COCK: Dark Green/blue, W50/34/ XY Year
HEN: Cobalt, W50/117/
FIRST EGG LAID: March 9th.
DUE TO HATCH: March 29th.
NO. OF EGGS: 6.
NO. OF YOUNSTERS: 5.
RING NOS.: 42.
          43.
          44.
          45.
          46. Transferred to pair No. 7.
REMARKS: Hen broke one egg.

These Breeding Cards should be used in conjunction with a Budgerigar Breeding and Show Register, which I describe fully in Chapter 11. The Breeding Cards are for rough notes, and Breeding Register for a more permanent record. The Breeding Register can be utilised alone, without the cards if the owner so desires—and this will certainly save his time—but the Breeding Cards cannot be satisfactorily employed without the Breeding Register. The latter provides for the recording of the following essential information:-

Pair No.; Cock; Hen; Theoretical expectation (that is the colours of the youngsters which the pair can produce); Date mated; In Aviary No.; Coloured Ring; Date first egg laid; Due to hatch; No. of eggs; No. of chicks; Ring numbers; Colour; Sex; Remarks.

At a Glance

As in the Register there are spaces for the recording of all the particulars set forth on a Breeding Card; in addition to other important particulars, it will be understood that the only advantage of using the Cards as an auxilliary to the Register is that as the owner goes round the breeding compartments they tell at a glance the progress of each pair of birds.

Also of importance during the breeding season are those other sections of the Breeding and Show Register which I shall deal with in Chapter 11, viz.: *Descriptions of Parent Birds* and the *Young Bird Register.*

Where more than one pair of Budgerigars are to occupy the same house, each pair should be kept in a show cage for a week or more prior to their being allowed into the aviary. The object of this preliminary caging is to induce the cocks and hens constituting the respective pairs to become so attached to each other that they will keep to their own mates when they are in their breeding quarters.

But even when "courtship" has been conducted in the manner I have described, there is no guarantee that mate changing will not occur. The fewer pairs there are in one place, the less the risk of the pedigrees of the youngsters not being as the owner wishes them to be; but even when there are only two pairs it is not uncommon for the two cocks to change wives. And where more than one pair are housed together, so unfaithful are Budgerigar cocks on occasions, that one bird may actually be the sire of all the youngsters in the different nests! All this is, of course, the strongest possible evidence in support of the one-pair breeding system as compared with colony breeding.

But there is another danger in keeping more than one pair together which is even more serious than that of cocks which are not faithful to the hens which we have selected for them. I refer to fighting hens.

Hens are at any time more pugnacious than cocks, although when kept together in the winter and separated from the cocks fights seldom occur; but when they are breeding their pugnacity is increased fourfold. Compared with hens at this season cocks are docility personified. If two hens select the same next box, both determined to retain it, there will be a fine old brawl between them. If one hen is sitting on eggs or nursing chicks, and another hen enters the next box, whether by accident or design, there will be a fight to the death, all the eggs or chicks being destroyed too, unless the owner discovers what is transpiring and separates the belligerents before serious damage is done.

I have known a hen to be so bellicose when mated that to allow her to breed in the same place as another pair was simply to court the death of the other hen. Without any cause whatever a hen of this disposition will attack another hen savagely, with often a fatal result.

I do not want it to be inferred from what I have written about fighting hens that battles in the aviaries are usual or frequent. They are not. In most cases all goes well, the birds live together in harmony, and each pair rears good clutches of chicks without let or hindrance. Nevertheless, the danger of the homicidal hen is one which must be guarded against, and the best preventative is the one-pair-per-place system, which also ensures perfect control of pedigrees, so essential where the breeder is establishing a strain on the lines to be described in Chapters 13 and 14.

If circumstances make the keeping of more than one pair in one aviary unavoidable, then the best protection against fighting hens is the provision of plenty of nest boxes, at least two to each pair. These should all be of one pattern and colour, and all hung well up on the walls of the aviary and all at the same height. When only one pair occupy a place, only one nest box is necessary.

It is very many years since I discontinued the erstwhile universal practice of keeping several breeding pairs together—known as the colony system. Practically no breeder of exhibition Budgerigars now follows any other method than that of keeping one pair in one aviary or cage, thus ensuring complete control of his pedigrees and perfect protection against pugnacity. And for this reason I feel sure that all the above advice, which relates to what is known as colony breeding is almost unnecessary, although it may be helpful to some of my readers who keep Budgerigars in garden aviaries and have no desire to breed exhibition birds.

In times past the arguments for and against cage breeding were great. Now it is the established method. Experience long ago taught me that cage breeding is superior to colony breeding, to which in many establishments it is the sole or partial alternative. Cage breeding can be conducted with complete success providing the cages are all they ought to be, and are in a suitable room, correct in every particular as regards light, ventilation and general construction. It is, however, imperative that the adults should be transferred to flights when they have finished breeding, to have plenty of exercise there and recover from the strain of producing their kind. And the young stock should be similarly treated.

When the now almost universal single-pair system (sometimes termed control breeding) is employed, it is not necessary to put the pair in a show cage for a preparatory courtship. They can go straight into cage or aviary. But it is not advisable to hang up the nest box for a day or two, or at least until the pair have been seen to mate. The withholding of the nest box gives the birds time in which to settle down, and avoids the rather abnormal sexual excitement which the appearance of a mate and a nest box simultaneously sometimes engenders, with often undesirable results, such as the throwing out of eggs as they are laid.

One cause of infertility can be the hen making herself inaccessible to the cock by remaining in the nest box and depriving him of the opportunity of mating. At Lintonholme our aviary manager removes the nest box for a short time (up to twenty minutes) on the day following the laying of each egg, so that mating can take place regularly in order to increase the probability of fertilisation.

THE FIRST EGG

As soon as the hen is regularly going in and out of the nest box, it will not be long before the first egg is laid. I am not able to say how many days it will be after the nest boxes are put up before the hen will lay, as they vary in this respect according to their condition, but ten days is about the average length of time. It is not necessary to put anything in the box in the form of nest material, though many fanciers do place therein a little sawdust, and I have nothing to say against the practice. The hen will lay on the bare wood, though she and her mate frequently make a few small wood shavings by gnawing, which you will see in the basin of the nest box. These shavings serve no good purpose. When making them no doubt the birds are obeying an old instinct of wild Budgerigars which have to make or improve their nests by boring into the trees.

The hen lays on alternate days until she has completed the clutch, which may consist of any number of eggs up to nine, though larger clutches have often been recorded. But even a nest of nine is above the normal, and an average of five may be considered to be perfectly satisfactory. An average of four in the first round and five in the second is normal. Hens usually have larger second clutches than first clutches, particularly maiden hens.

The period of incubation is eighteen days. The hen does not always commence sitting with the laying of the first egg. Sometimes she waits until the second egg is laid. Therefore, I always calculate the date of hatching at twenty days from the appearance of the first egg.

The hen does all the sitting, and the cock feeds her. She feeds the chicks in the box. Both feed the chicks for a time after they have left the nest.

The method of feeding is that of regurgitation, which means the pumping into the crops of the babies food which has been eaten by the parents, mixed with gastric juices, and made to just that right consistency for the youngsters' digestive organs to deal with it efficiently and for them to obtain the maximum amount of nutrition from it. The babies are at first fed on what is termed crop-milk provided by the hen.

Sequence of Hatching

As the eggs are laid on alternate days, it naturally follows that the chicks hatch on varying dates, and in a clutch of five, for example, we can have one youngster ten days old when the last chick has only just hatched, and there is a marked difference in the sizes of the babies. This is not really desirable,

123

even though with the Budgerigar it is perfectly natural. It cannot be disputed that when one dies in a nest containing chicks of uneven size, it is usually the smallest and therefore the weakest and the most likely to suffer if there is any lack of attention on the part of the parents.

To overcome this objection to the Budgerigar's natural system of laying its eggs on alternate days, and the chicks, therefore, varying in age and size, some fanciers have tried the experiment of lifting the first one, two or three eggs that are laid, placing them carefully in suitable boxes in sawdust, replacing them with pot eggs, and only allowing the hen to commence incubating her eggs after, say, the laying of her third egg. This system is that adopted regularly by Canary breeders, and, apparently, with complete success. This practice is not followed with my wife's birds, and I do not advise it. Obviously in the case of an establishment of some size, the extra work entailed by conducting this procedure will be no small amount.

Those who have sent me reports on their experiments in this direction have told me that they have not found it safe to lift more than two eggs. In many instances where they have extended the procedure to three eggs the first egg to be removed has failed to hatch.

DISTRIBUTING THE CHICKS

It is a good practice to equalise the sizes of the chicks as much as possible by changing them about from nest to nest, putting large ones with large ones and small ones with small ones. Further, as it is inadvisable to allow a pair to rear more than four chicks at one time, or at the most five—and then only when unavoidable—if we have, say, three in one nest and five in another we give the pair with three one youngster from the nest of five, leaving them with four each. By the exercise of a little thought changes can usually be made without difficulty which will leave the position of all the clutches in the establishment as we desire it.

Fortunately, Budgerigars are most accommodating in this direction. They do not object to the appearance of a few strange babies in the nest box, and if they have an eye for dimensions and if they do discover that some of the children are not their own, so strong is their parental instinct that they simply don't care, and carry on blithely as though the family was all their own!

There are recorded cases when a cock has died at the time when there were youngsters in the nest box, of a new cock being introduced and of his having carried on as step-father without hesitation and with complete success. At Lintonholme we have done this on two occasions. Once it was quite successful, but in the other case, the youngsters were killed. We shall not do it again!

RECORDS ESSENTIAL

In changing chicks about from nest to nest either for the purpose of equalising sizes, equalising numbers, or because, as sometimes occurs, the adults are proving to be bad feeders, the owner must keep a complete record of all the transfers so that he does not lose trace of the actual parents of the youngsters moved — in other words, does not run the risk of being unable to record their pedigrees accurately.

This danger can be completely avoided by ringing the chicks before they are changed, leaving the ring numbers on the Breeding Card of the real parents, but writing thereon "Transferred to Pair No.-." An accurate account of all transfers must be kept in this way.

I have found that occasionally there arises the necessity to transfer a little baby when it is really too small to ring. In this case in order to ensure that the record of its parentage shall not be lost, it has to be placed under a pair which are of such a colour that the colour of the transferred chick when it is fledgling will indicate that it is the stranger. For example, you can change a youngster from a pair of Light Greens to a pair of Lutinos without any fear of losing track of it. The appearance of a Light Green in a nest consisting of Lutinos will tell you all you want to know.

When the hen is sitting on eggs I think it is advisable to disturb her as little as possible except for an occasional glance in the nest box prior to her having completed her laying to ensure that she is not suffering from egg-binding, a trouble which I shall refer to more fully later in this chapter.

After hatching I believe in looking inside the boxes every other day or, still better, every day. Most hens soon become accustomed to the owner inspecting their babies, and I do not see how these periodical examinations can do any harm. On the other hand, they can be a definite advantage.

For one thing they lead to the discovery of any chick which may have died, and, which if it were not removed would decompose and emit an offensive smell which would be injurious to the other youngsters.

In Chapter 8, I referred to those particularly dirty nests which sometimes occur with frequency when certain birds are occupying them. These would not receive the attention which they should have if regular inspections of the nests were not conducted.

And then a box containing young birds has to be opened in any case whenever one or more is at the age for ringing.

HOW TO FIT RINGS

The closed metal ring authorised by the Budgerigar Society can be slipped on to the chicks' legs without the slightest pain in less than a minute at approximately four or five days after hatching. The method of ringing is as follows:-

Take the bird from the nest box, place the ring over the two front toes and pass over the ball of the foot; then with a match, pointed by burning, insert under the small toe and pull through. In the same way the other toe is passed through the ring.

Another way is to pass the three long toes through the ring, then slip the ring over the ball of the foot, and pull through the remaining toe with a match pointed by burning.

The rings are ordered from the Secretary of the Budgerigar Society and supplied by officially appointed ring makers. The marks on each ring consist of a code number, serial number, and the numbers indicating the year of issue, e.g. H11−121−81. H11 is the code number, 121 the serial number, and XYthe year number. The rings are anodised with a different colour each year.

Every member of the Budgerigar Society and the Area Budgerigar Societies is allotted a code number and this gives him or her the right to have it stamped on all rings purchased. Thus the name of the breeder of every bird so ringed can be traced. It is usual for a member to instruct the ring maker to commence the serial numbering of his or her rings at 1 every year.

PROBLEMS IN BREEDING

"Dirty" Feeders

I have referred above to those particularly dirty next boxes which occur with some pairs of Budgerigars. These birds are what we know as "dirty feeders." They distribute seed all over the inside of the boxes, it becomes mixed with excreta, and there is a fine old mess visible to the owner when he is on his tour of inspection.

The nest box can be easily cleaned, of course, but a worse evil of these dirty feeders is that they plaster the chicks' faces at each feeding with almost as much regurgitated food as they pump into their crops.

This, often mixed with a quantity of excreta, sets into a cement-like substance, which, unless it is removed *very frequently,* has a most damaging effect on the beaks of the youngsters. It definitely retards the growth of the upper mandible, which at that tender age is weak and sensitive. The lower mandible, being stronger, continues its normal development, outgrows the upper mandible, and the result is what is known as an undershot beak, which is very unsightly and a blemish which makes a bird absolutely useless for exhibition.

The owner should clean the beaks of the chicks whenever he discovers the cement-like substance adhering to their faces.

126

Distorted Beaks

Sometimes, due to the same cause, the beak does not actually become undershot, but the upper mandible develops a thin and corrugated appearance, and in some cases the tip of the beak is distorted. These beaks may come right in time, but often they never acquire their natural strength and shape.

Some authorities contend that undershot beaks can also be inherited. I have never been able to convince myself of the accuracy of this statement, although I admit that I have no proof that *some* undershot beaks are not due to the cause I have above described but are an inherited characteristic. And it may be that some undershot beaks are attributable to a rickety condition.

It is certain that theorectically there is no reason why parents or brothers and sisters of youngsters which have undershot beaks definitely known to be attributable to "dirty feeding" should not be used for breeding purposes. In fact, the bird itself with the undershot beak caused in this way will not necessarily breed chicks with undershot beaks, because it is a proven genetic truth that *acquired* characteristics are not handed down. Nevertheless, I have always taken the absolutely safe course—and I advise my readers to do likewise—of not breeding from or selling a bird which has, or ever had, a malformed beak. It is true that undershot mouths are inherited in dogs, and in some cases in Budgerigars they may be due to inheritance. I still have an open mind on the subject.

A dirty nest box is also a positive danger to the feet of the chicks. They become clotted with the cement-like substance to which I have referred, it sets hard, and can have most damaging effects. If the attatchment is discovered before it becomes solid it can be detached without much difficulty with the fingers. Later the toes have to be carefully soaked in warm water and the adhering material removed. If this is attempted without soaking, there is a grave risk of one or more toe nails being torn away. When the adults are fed on the right kinds of seed, dirty nests do not often occur, which is fortunate. Some fanciers practically never experience them.

Egg-Binding

Some people look incredulous when I tell them, quite truthfully, that I have never personally experienced a case of egg-binding in Budgerigars—in other words, the inability of the hen to dispel the egg at the moment when it should normally be laid—yet it is a danger for which the breeder must ever be observant. If a hen is egg-bound and immediate and successful action is not taken, she will surely die. Maiden hens laying their first egg are probably the most likely subject for eggs binding, although cases often occur with unfit or very old hens—and it is not always the first egg of a clutch which becomes bound.

As soon as a case of egg-binding is discovered, the hen should be placed in a cage and put before a hot fire, olive oil being applied to the vent by a feather.

If these measures fail, there is a more drastic treatment, but I do not advise it except as a last resource and after heat and olive oil have been given every opportunity of succeeding. It is the pigeon fanciers' method and consists of putting a piece of muslin over a small basin containing boiling water. You hold the suffering hen over the muslin, the steam ascends from the boiling water, and, if all goes well, the egg is dropped on to the muslin. She must not be suspended over the steam for more than a few seconds at a time.

Egg-binding is often due to the hen not really being in good breeding condition. A general opinion is that a course of cod liver oil feeding, as described in Chapter 9, up to the time when the hen lays her first egg is a most effective preventative.

Neglected Chicks

Although Budgerigars are as a rule exceedingly good parents, just as they are comparatively prolific breeders, occasionally a pair of birds neglect their chicks either by ceasing to feed them or only half feeding them. Non-feeding means a quick death; half-feeding means retarded growth and a badly grown youngster, which will never mature into a vigorous, healthy adult. Therefore, it is clear that as soon as the discovery is made that the parents are not giving proper attention to their offspring, the chicks must be removed to another pair, consisting, if possible, of birds on which the owner knows he can rely to do their work as it should be done.

Although I am referring here to those troubles which infrequently occur when young Budgerigars are in the nest box, I do not want any of my readers to get the impression that normally they have many of these difficulties to contend with, because such is not the case. In fact, Budgerigar fanciers have but few worries compared with breeders of many other kinds of livestock. Nevertheless, we have to tackle problems as they arise in a cheerful, philosophic way, and with the determination to overcome them. It is well, therefore, that I should describe the most common obstacles which have to be combated on occasions, so that the novices who read this book may be prepared for them.

Infant Mortality

Great breeders and rearers as Budgerigars are, the beginner must not expect *too* much. In any season there is no such thing as a large number of eggs in every nest, 100 per cent. fertility, 100 per cent. hatching, and 100 per cent. rearing. For instance, we all lose some chicks, particularly when they are very young, without any apparent cause.

There are (say) five young ones in a box, all as far as can be seen equally strong. One morning we find that two are dead, yet the others go on and prosper. Why did those two die? If I could dogmatically reply to that question I should have solved a riddle which has perplexed me all my fancier life. Sometimes we can supply the answer. Frequently we cannot do so. The problem of mortality in young birds and animals is a formidable one, and the greatest authorities have not been able to discover a complete solution.

Budgerigar breeders have the satisfaction of knowing that with these birds the infantile mortality percentage is low compared with the percentage in some other species of livestock, and so long as the deaths of chicks do not become abnormal, they can rest content and realise that most of their contemporaries are faring no better, many of them probably worse.

It is when deaths are numerous that a serious review of the situation has to be made. Steps must be taken to discover, if possible, what is wrong with housing, feeding, management, or the parent birds, to cause the excessive mortality.

Usually when chicks die through not being fed, this apparent neglect on the part of the parents can be explained by the fact that the babies are too weak to "ask" for food in the natural way. Then the old birds do not bother about them.

Normally in Budgerigar keeping everything runs along smoothly, but it is surprising how breeding seasons vary. One year nothing goes wrong, the next year unexpected difficulties arise and the result of our efforts fails to satisfy. We all have our good cycles and our bad cycles, in spite of their being no change in our management or feeding or the condition of the parent birds, which makes us agree with Shakespeare that there are more things in Heaven and Earth than are dreamt of in our philosophy.

Be of Good Cheer

It is the fancier who accepts reverses with equanimity and a determination to overcome all obstacles who ultimately achieves his or her ambition as a breeder. We must ever use our failures as the teachers of lessons which will serve us well in the future, benefit by our errors, and turn our misfortunes into blessings in disguise.

I am digressing, but I desire to cheer those novices who may be discouraged by any of those untoward occurrences which I describe in this chapter.

Now to return to more practical matters. I have on occasions known Budgerigar cocks die through an excess of zeal in feeding the hen and chicks. They have literally fed themselves to death, feeding away each evening all the food in their crops and going to their perches for the night without retaining any seed for their own nutrition.

When we catch a cock pining in this way we take him away from the hen until he has had time to have a few good meals and recuperate from his deprivation. The hen attends to the wants of the family in the meantime. After the cock has been replaced in the breeding compartment we keep a watchful eye on him to see that he is not repeating behaviour which but for our timely intervention would probably have caused his death. A cock which is starving himself in this manner loses his tightness of feather and his alertness and has a mopish appearance.

That defective feathering which is described as French Moult can usually be detected before the youngsters leave the nest box, though sometimes it is not until the chicks are out in the aviary that this displeasing condition asserts itself. As I propose dealing with this trouble in Chapter 20, nothing more will be said about it here, and I will pass on to another annoyance which occasionally occurs, viz., that of feather plucking.

This practice on the part of one parent—I think it is usually the hen—consists of the deliberate plucking or biting off of the feathers as soon as the babies begin to fledge. Sometimes the feathers are pulled right out, sometimes they are nipped off close to the skin.

The best thing to do when a pair start feather plucking is to remove the youngsters to another pair, if possible. If this cannot be done, then put the chicks into another nest box close to the original box. Make sure that the cock finds them, which as a rule he will do soon. Then the hen will confine her attention to the old box, in which she will lay her next clutch of eggs, the cock will attend to the babies in the adjoining box and they may well be saved from further plucking.

In some cases after the first moult of a feather-plucked youngster the feathers grow naturally on the bare parts, but this is not always the case; in fact, I think that in most instances these birds are never normally feathered. At least, I have noticed for over twelve months after the date of hatching a deficiency in both the length and the quality of the feathers which have grown on plucked areas.

As to whether the tendency to feather plucking is inheritable or not, I am not prepared to say, but it is a possibility which must not be overlooked. If it is proved that feather-pluckers can transmit this unfortunate nervous practice to their offspring, then birds bred from them must neither be bred from or sold; and, of course, it is unwise in any case to allow a feather-plucker to rear any more youngsters when once the pre-disposition has been discovered, because a repitition of the offence is almost a certainty. Some fanciers, when they find that a clutch of chicks is being plucked, and they are unable to transfer them to foster parents, smear them with some offensive-smelling oil. Cod liver oil is sometimes used for this purpose. Oil of Geranium is another remedy. But this oiling of chicks is a messy business, and I do not advise it, unless absolutely unavoidable.

There is now advertised by a reputable firm an anti-feather plucking solution, which appears to be the answer. It is used as a spray.

There is an old theory that in excessively hot and dry summers lack of humidity in the atmosphere is calculated to cause chicks to die before hatching, due to the membranes in the egg becoming so tough that the chick cannot break through them to chip the shell. It is to counteract this condition that moisture is artifically provided by poultry fanciers when eggs are being incubated, the object being to prevent excessive evaporation of the natural moisture in the egg.

Lack of humidity on very hot days can be counteracted to a certain extent by spraying the walls and floors of the aviaries with cold water. At Lintonholme we neither provide moisture in the nests or spray water about the houses.

Although as I have indicated "dead in shell" may be attributable to dryness of the atmosphere, I do not think it is so frequently responsible as it is usually alleged to be. The natural weakness of some chicks is, in my opinion, more often than not the reason for their inability to hatch, and in such cases it is better that they should die rather than be born and be for ever weaklings.

To summarise I am convinced that cases of "Dead in Shell" and addled eggs are due to one of the following causes, as given by Prof. Taylor in an article in *Cage Birds:* A weak germ due to weakness in the sperm; abnormal position of the chick within the egg preventing satisfactory hatching; bacterial infection of the yolk sac (which can also be a cause of infant mortality); eggs plastered with excreta; an excessively dry atmosphere; parents suffering from malnutrition and responsible for lack of nutrition in the egg yolk; parents not in full breeding condition; chilling of the eggs by the hen leaving them for any fairly lengthy period.

Red Mite

Red mite is the most difficult of all parasites to eradicate completely from an aviary. They will make their presence felt at times even in the cleanest establishment. They dwell in cracks and crevices in the woodwork. They are not to be seen by day but they come out in myriads at night, suck the blood of the birds, and change in colour from grey to red. By daylight they have disappeared, only to commence their marauding again when darkness arrives.

Paraffin brushed in freely in all the likely places for red mite to inhabit is a useful preventative. So is creosote, but unfortunately some time after it has dried it seems to lose its offensiveness to the mite, which blithely ignore it; and it is not advisable in any case to have creosote where the birds can reach it. I can recommend some of the strong proprietary mite destroyers advertised in *Cage and Aviary Birds* from practical experience. They are much superior to paraffin.

At Lintonholme we use a red mite destroyer that also destroys the red mite eggs, which all the recommended treatments do not do. It is applied with a spray gun.

As far as nest boxes are concerned, immersion in boiling water is the best procedure, and always before nest boxes used in a previous season are again placed in the aviaries they should be thoroughly scrubbed, soaked again in boiling water and disinfected. The use of cardboard nest boxes obviates this task, except that the wooden bases have to be so treated. Every precaution should be taken by the adoption of such means as I have described to prevent a serious invasion of these parasites because they can adversely affect the health of Budgerigars, their constant blood-sucking conducing to a debilitated condition.

I have advisedly warned the novices who read this book of the difficulties with which they will have to contend at times, yet I again emphasise the fact that the majority of young Budgerigars flourish exceedingly well from the moment they are hatched, and when they are 30 days old, or thereabouts, they leave the boxes and fly into the aviary—beautiful little creatures— clean, tight feathered, lively, and a delightful sight for any bird lover to behold.

The parents continue to feed them for a week or more, but very soon they commence to pick, and are able within a few days to consume daily sufficient food to fully satisfy their appetites. But the adults do not then cease to feed the babies, and I consider it advisable to leave them with the old birds for eight to ten days, that is until they are about 40 days old. No first-round youngsters must be left with their parents after the second-round chicks have commenced to hatch, and I do not like to see chicks still with their mother and father when the eggs of the second clutch are being incubated. Particularly when the birds are breeding in cages do some young ones develop the habit of going back into the box, to the discomfiture of the sitting hen.

Before transferring young ones to the "nursery" keep them for at least three weeks in the bird room in training cages.

This early training gives to the youngsters a steadiness which does not desert them for the remainder of their lives, and which makes it all the easier to train them later to comport themselves gracefully in the show cages when they are at the shows.

Nursery Days

From these training cages the young birds are transferred to the "nurseries," which are reasonably large aviaries, in which they can secure an abundance of fresh air and exercise, which assists their development enormously. It is advisable to introduce a few old birds to guide them to their food. After three or four days these adults can be removed if the owner so desires.

I have previously indicated the evils of overcrowding, which is never more undesirable than when the young stock is in a "nursery."

A careful daily inspection should be made to see that all the youngsters are progressing satisfactorily. If any appear weakly they should be removed; otherwise their more vigorous fellows may "chivy" them off the food and generally make their lives unpleasant.

And this reminds me of an important instruction to which I must give expression, viz: all "bad doers" either in the nest box or "nursery" must be carefully recorded in the Breeding Register, because these birds must never be bred from—however satisfactory they may be in appearance later—for all those good reasons on which I have expounded at length in Chapters 13 and 14.

TWO FAMILIES ONLY

In several places in this book I stress the golden rule of not taking more than two nests per season from each pair. The temptation to rear the extra clutch of chicks can be great, but it should be resisted with determination.

The third nest is asking too much of the physical capacity of the adults. It takes so much out of them that it makes them unreliable for breeding purposes in the following season, and if they are exhibition specimens, the strain which the third nest involves makes it more difficult to get them into show condition.

Further, third-round chicks are almost invariably less vigorous than their older brothers and sisters, and, therefore, themselves less suitable as parents when they in turn attain the age for breeding. These birds sold to other fanciers will probably fail to give satisfaction, and the spread of such specimens throughout the aviaries of this country can actually damage the whole race of domesticated Budgerigars, just as similar injury can be done by the sale to unsuspecting purchasers of birds which have been "bad doers" as babies or which have suffered from illness and have merely been "patched up."

Now the implementing of the two-nests-only rule calls for further explanation. Its real implication is that a pair of Budgies should only be allowed to *feed* two nests. It is the feeding which taxes the systems of the parents and not so much, in the case of the hen, the laying and the sitting. Therefore, if you find that every egg of a clutch is infertile, or if all the eggs are addled or the chicks "dead in shell", or if for any other reason no young are forthcoming, you need not count that as one round. In due course the parents will throw out the eggs and prepare to go to nest again, which you can let them do.

The fact that it is the feeding which puts the most strain on the adults gives the clue to the reason why some exhibitors make a practice of holding over a

133

number of young birds without breeding from them in the season following the year of their birth. This can be a particularly desirable procedure in the case of second-round youngsters.

The birds selected for the purpose are usually those which show the most promise of developing into good exhibition specimens. Undoubtedly by not having to feed youngsters in the first full year of their lives they mature more rapidly and are the more likely to be successful show birds earlier in their careers than otherwise would be the case.

Of course, it is almost a practical impossibility for an owner to keep unmated all his promising young cocks for an entire season, but modifications of the principle can be applied to some yearlings from which one actually does obtain chicks in the first season.

For instance, from some, particularly those hatched in, say, late June or early July, one nest only may be taken in the following summer.

Sometimes it is wise to allow a young cock which has the appearance of being a prize winner to fertilise the eggs but not to feed the chicks. This is avoided by transferring the eggs to another pair of birds, if, of course, there is a pair available; or they can be divided between two pairs.

FOSTER-PARENTS OR "FEEDERS"

In order to ensure always having birds so situated that the fancier is able to place in their nest eggs lifted for the reasons above described, or chicks which are being unsatisfactorily tended by their own parents, or chicks which have to avoid pairs having to feed too many youngsters and thus break "the not more than four or five" rule, the most efficient method is to use birds kept specially for the purpose of serving as foster-parents or "feeders." This system is operated extensively by pigeon fanciers, and I know of no reason why it should not be of equal assistance to Budgerigar breeders.

A number of pairs of Budgerigars, which must be strong and healthy but which can be inexpensive and of no merit when judged by exhibition standards, is all that is required. The actual quantity of these "feeders" to be mated simultaneously with the mating of the pedigree stock will be governed by the number of pairs of the latter and, of course, by the accommodation at the owner's disposal. In fact, the only possible objection to the use of foster-parents is that the fancier whose aviaries are limited in size and number may not be able to spare the additional space to house these birds satisfactorily and, of course, extra cost of feeding is involved. The more pairs of "feeders" kept, the greater the chance that there will always be pairs ready to take charge of eggs or chicks when they are required to do so. Modified colony breeding can be practised in the case of feeders, though it is essential for them to have settled down and be living together in harmony before eggs or chicks from the pedigree stock are transferred to them.

I have written about the feeding of adult birds in the breeding aviaries and the youngsters in the "nursery" at length in Chapter 9 and, therefore, there is no need for me to repeat my opinions here, beyond saying that feeding when Budgerigars are breeding is of paramount importance, probably more so that at any other season of the year.

I have already explained that owing to the varying condition of the birds one cannot start them all off breeding simultaneously at the commencement of the season and, therefore, it automatically follows that they will not all have completed rearing their two clutches of eggs at exactly the same time.

Novices sometimes describe to me a difficulty which they have when they want to bring breeding operations to a close, due to the fact that before the last chick of the second nest has left the box the hen has almost invariably laid again. It is the sacrificing of these eggs which is repugnant to the owner. He finds it difficult to resist the temptation to let the hen continue sitting, and almost before he realised what is happening he is allowing the pair to rear a third batch of chicks, which is entirely contrary to wise policy.

However unsentimental and sacrificial the action may appear to be, these third-round eggs should be destroyed, or put under another pair, as soon as the last chick has left the nest. Then the boxes should be taken down and the pair of birds left to feed the second-round youngsters for eight to ten days, when the cock should be separated from the hen.

In our own aviaries we often avoid the hen laying before the second clutch of chicks has left the nest by taking the cock away when the youngest chick is about a fortnight old, leaving the hen to complete the rearing of the youngsters entirely by herself. Anyone who adopts this practice must observe closely if the hen is feeding properly, and if any lack of attention is noticed the cock must be returned immediately, though rarely, if ever, will this necessity arise.

Figure 10-1 A Modern Breeding Room showing on the left a humidity indicator, centre the thermostat, and right, a thermometer.

CHAPTER 11

KEEPING RECORDS

KNOW THE FACTS

Although the hobby of breeding and exhibiting Budgerigars for exhibition cannot be considered to be a business, the commercial-minded fancier usually likes to know at the end of each year whether his birds have more than paid their way or if they have been an expense to him. Therefore, he adopts a simple system of book-keeping.

Some breeders will not go to this trouble, especially those who are well placed financially and to whom it does not particularly matter how much their Budgerigars cost them.

Whether the fancier keeps accounts of income and expenditure or does not trouble to do so is entirely a question of personal desire. But, on the other hand, the recording of pedigrees is, in my opinion, a duty the carrying out of which is essential to continuous success, as will be well understood from what I shall have to say about the importance of parentage in Chapters 13 and 14.

I compiled a Budgerigar Breeding and Show Register some years ago. This is divided into the following sections:- Descriptions of parent birds; Adult birds not mated; Breeding Register; Young Bird Register; and Show Register.

The Show Register provides for the recording of the following essential particulars:-Name of Show: Date: No. of entries: Prizes: Specials: Colours and numbers of successful birds.

In the sections of the Register headed "Descriptions of Parent Birds" and "Adult Birds not Mated" there is written the ring numbers, colours, sexes and pedigrees of all those specimens which the owner is holding over for a season without breeding from them, but which he does not intend to sell.

Descriptions of all the youngsters reared are, for the sake of easy reference, eventually transferred from the "Breeding Register" to the "Young Bird Register," in which the following separate columns are ruled:- Ring No.: Colour: Sex: From Pair No.: Name of purchaser, if sold.

The "Breeding Register" is utilised in the manner which I have described fully in Chapter 10.

This Register should be kept carefully so that there cannot be the slightest risk of error in so far as pedigrees are concerned. These Registers are for one year's use only, and a new Register has to be purchased at the commencement of each season. It is, however, important that many of the particulars entered in the Register, and particularly pedigrees, should be retained permanently and for this purpose I advocate the card index system in preference to the old-fashioned pedigree books.

In evolving the method which I describe below I did not lose sight of the great desirability of retaining for all time not only the pedigrees of birds employed in the breeding aviaries but also a written record of their good and bad properties. My contention that it is necessary to keep in one's possession written knowledge of the appearance of Budgerigars from which one has bred but which may have died or gone to other aviaries, will be well understood in view of the principles of breeding I shall describe later.

TRACING FAULTS

It will be gathered from what I say in Chapters 13 and 14 that information as to the failings and excellences of ancestors can be invaluable when one is formulating a breeding plan. By means of these records of good and bad points of birds bred from in former years, one can frequently trace the origin of a fault which suddenly makes its appearance without any recent cause.

At Lintonholme we apply the card index system to the keeping of permanent Budgerigar records in the following manner:-

The index cards and guide cards measure 5 in. x 3 in. These are kept in a small inexpensive filing cabinet. The guide cards are used for dividing the colours—Light Greens, Violets, Cobalts, Mauves, Skyblues, Opalines, Greys, Lutinos, Grey Greens, and so on.

On the face of each card we write the colour, sex, ring number, date of hatching and, if a bought bird, the name of the breeder and the name of the fancier from whom the bird was purchased.

The following is a fictitious example of the front of an index card:-

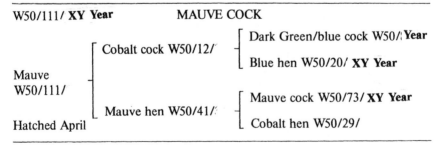

If the bird has won prizes these are described on the back of the pedigree card in the following way:-

1   Derby (16) Ellwood
2   Birmingham (10) Addey

(The number in parentheses is the number of entries in the class). There is always a card made out in this manner in the filing cabinet for every Budgerigar in the establishment.

I will now explain what happens if a bird is sold. If it is a specimen from which we have never bred we take the card out of the cabinet and send or hand it to the purchaser, but if we have bred from the bird or it has won prizes then we send the purchaser a copy of the card and retain the original, writing on the back the name of the purchaser. This card is put into another filing cabinet which we call the "Sold and Dead Index."

In the event of a bird dying exactly the same procedure is adopted, except that we write on the back of the card the date of death. If a bird which has never been bred from or exhibited should die, we simply take its card out of the index and destroy it, because it is of no further use to us.

When writing on the face of the card we use it broadside; when writing on the reverse side we place the card in the upright position because this gives more room for wins if they should be numerous.

All index cards in both filing cabinets are placed behind their correct guide cards in numerical order according to the ring numbers.

INCOMINGS AND OUTGOINGS

To keep an account of income and expenditure is a simple matter. Use a book on each page of which a series of cash columns are ruled, in the manner exemplified later in this chapter.

On the left of each two pages record income—on the right expenditure. The headings on the income side are: Total; Birds Sold; Prize Money; Various—and on the the Expenditure side: Total; Birds Purchased; Food Purchased; Entry Fees; Labour; Various. Of course these headings can be changed to suit a fancier's own circumstances and requirements. The items which come into the "Various" columns of the income and expenditure books have to be analysed at the end of the year for the purpose of the profit and loss account.

When *one* of the two pages is complete the columns on *both* pages are totalled and carried forward overleaf.

The advantage of this system in addition to its simplicity is that when the

INCOME

Date	INCOME	Total	Birds Sold	Prize Money	Various
		£	£	£	£
Jan. 15	Prize Money	5.00	—	5.00	—
18	W. Jones: — Violet ck. W50/80/ **XY Year**	10.00	10.00	—	—
20	York Judging Fee	5 .00	—	—	5.00

EXPENDITURE

Date	EXPENDITURE	Total	Birds Purchased	Food Purchased	Entry Fees	Labour	Various
		£	£	£	£	£	£
Jan. 6	F. Jones	3.50	—	—	—	3.50	—
8	XYZ Ltd., Seed	30.00	—	30.00	—	—	—
11	J. Smith — Blue ck. S999/30/	30.00	30.00	—	—	—	—
12	Birmingham Fees	8.00	—	—	8.00	—	—
13	Rings	3.00	—	—	—	—	3.00

additions are made at the foot of each page the total of the column headed "Total" must be equalled by the sum of the totals of the other columns. If they do not balance in this way it is proof that an error has been made, and this can be found and duly corrected.

At the end of the year when the accounts are balanced, a profit and loss account is prepared. The items on one side of this account are the following:-

Stock as on 1st January, XY (or whatever the year may be); Birds Purchased, Food Purchased, Entry Fees, Labour, Carriage, Advertising, Printing, Insurance, Sundry Expenses, Accounts Owing, Depreciation— and on the other side:- Stock as at 31st December, XY (or whatever the year may be); Birds Sold; Prize Money; Various. The difference between the two sides represents the profit or loss for the year.

QUESTION OF DEPRECIATION

With reference to the item "Depreciation" this is, of course, depreciation written off the aviaries, cages, etc. I advise depreciating the aviaries at 10 per cent. and the cages and similar appliances at 33 and a third per cent., taking this off the original cost every year, by what accountants call the "straight line" method, in preference to depreciating off the diminishing values.

In taking stock it is advisable in order to be safe to undervalue rather than overvalue, as business men who read this book will well understand.

When making a valuation of the birds, the best system is to fix an average price and multiply it by the number of birds in the aviaries. In valuing such things as Budgerigars, where there is no market price, one has to say to one's self "How much could I reasonably expect to get per bird if I offered the whole stud for sale?" The answer to that question supplies the average price which you want for your stocktaking purpose.

You must also take into stock at cost or lower any seed, etc. in your possession at the close of the year.

The account-keeping system which I have described is by no means elaborate but it has the advantage of simplicity, and it secures just the same results as a more complicated method of accountancy would do. And, after all, Budgerigar keeping is a hobby, not a business.

Figure 11-1 A Modern Range of Aviaries

CHAPTER 12

COLOUR PRODUCTION

MENDELISM

Although the Mendelians (all honour to them) have provided us with accurate knowledge as to colour expectations, they cannot—and do not claim to be able to do so—tell us how to breed birds with better markings, birds of better type or birds of greater size. In other words, they do not tell us how we can apply Mendelism in such a manner as to produce superior show specimens; and I am not suggesting that they can or should.

For advancement in this direction we have to rely upon the old livestock breeders' methods — and they are extraordinarily reliable — commonly referred to in the terms "selection," "line-breeding," "in-breeding," "out-crossing," and so on, and the owner's intuition for mating his birds to the best advantage.

So, therefore, that is all I shall have to say about Mendelism in this chapter, because my object just now is to assist my readers in the improvement of colour and markings in the Budgerigars kept by those who desire to win more and more prizes.

In attempting to give advice on colour production I am setting myself a task as difficult as that of giving advice to a young man in love. Just as no one *knows* the very best methods of winning a maiden's affection, so no one *knows* the perfect system of producing the different colours *in excelsis*.

Good and Bad Matings

We all naturally praise those colour matings which have provided us with the best results in the past or which have given great satisfaction to those of our friends who have told us how their best specimens have been bred, but I know of nothing in connection with Budgerigar culture about which one can be less dogmatic than this subject of matings calculated to improve colour in the different varieties. There seems to be no royal road to success in all cases, yet there are some matings which I think one can say without hesitation are definitely bad and other matings which one can assert are definitely good. And those who have had experience can be emphatic about these proved good and proved bad crosses respectively because of their own experience of them, coupled with the experience of many other people who have pooled their knowledge for the benefit of breeders generally.

Many Possible Pairings

We can therefore, be positive as to these particular colour matings — the proved good ones and the proved bad ones — in the light of actual practice, the outcome of trial and error as distinct from mere theory. But these extremely good and extremely bad crosses are few compared with the very numerous ways in which Budgerigars can be mated. And it is when we come to those pairings about which opinions differ, and the results of which are often inconsistent, that he would say this or that cross is the best to produce this or that colour would indeed be likening himself unto the gods.

In view of these facts it might well be said, how can I attempt, as my readers may have thought I intended to do when they commenced to read this chapter, to describe all the absolutely best crosses to produce the best coloured birds in the different colour varieties? I shall most certainly not do so. I should be happy if I were able to print such a chart here as that would mean. All I can do is to describe what I think are the best methods by observation of the results in my wife's aviaries and in other successful establishments with which I am familiar.

GENERAL PRINCIPLES

I must content myself by describing a number of general principles relative to colour production in the hope that my readers will be able to apply them to their own requirements to their ultimate advantage. I will refer to matings which I consider should be avoided and matings, which, in my own experience and the experience of the very successful breeders who have given me valuable information about their breeding results, have proved satisfactory *when the birds used have been the right birds for the purpose.*

How much more simple would this problem of colour production be if it were possible always to achieve the best results by mating birds of the same colour together — Cobalt to Cobalt, for example.

There is apparently some kind of linkage between type and colour. Inspection of Budgerigars in the aviaries and at the shows makes it clear that, generally speaking, different colours differ from each other in type. Although individual Budgerigars provide exceptions to the rule, taking the birds as a whole there are differences in type between Greens and Cobalts, Cobalts and Blues, Lutinos and the marked varieties, Greys and Opalines, and so on.

144

We have an example in the Cobalts, and Blues bred in the same nest from Cobalt x Skyblue. They often differ in shape. The Blues and Light Greens/blue produced from Light Green/blue x Blue frequently display a similar distinction and so do the Violets, Cobalts and Mauves from a pair consisting of a Violet and a Mauve. Numerous other cases could be cited.

This apparent linkage is not confined to type. It often applies also to size. It is not unusual for birds of one colour to be smaller than birds of another colour when bred from the same parents.

The advice which I shall give in this chapter will not only be devoted to improvement in the colour itself but to improving colour simultaneously with the production of Budgerigars of better type in the respective varieties.

Type Variability

Those who study this engrossing subject and who read what I have to say must also appreciate the fact that we have to essay to overcome that type variability in the different colours to which I have referred above. In short, our ambition is not only to improve the coloration of our birds but also to standardise the type throughout all our colour varieties; and the type which is our objective is that described in Chapter 3.

The writer on colour production also experiences difficulty in being dogmatic as to which are the best matings to produce certain desired results because so much depends on the ancestry of the birds to be mated. Each case has to be dealt with on its merits, and the skill of the breeder when deciding on his matings therefore bears a more important relationship to success than can any theoretical exposition. And here we have another reason why I can but generalise when describing the best crosses to produce the various colours.

Importance of Ancestry

I have said that much depends on ancestry as to which are the best matings to employ. I will be more explicit.

Many fine Cobalts of the most desirable shade of colour have been bred from Mauve x Blue, but that fact would not justify the statement that Mauve x Blue will invariably produce good coloured Cobalts, as so much is dependent on the parentage of the Mauve and the Blue respectively.

I will describe an actual experience in our own aviaries at Lintonholme to demonstrate my meaning more clearly:-

We mated two pairs, in each case a Mauve cock to a Blue hen. The cock in Pair No.1 had a Cobalt ancestor within the two previous generations of the more desirable colouring; and exactly the same remarks applied to the two hens. The result was that the youngsters bred from Pair No.1 all failed in colour, being of the bluey Cobalt shade, and the Cobalts from Pair No.2 were all of the desired shade in colour.

Now what are we taught by these results? It is that the Mauve cock in pair No.1 had inherited from his Cobalt ancestor the undesirable Cobalt colour and the Mauve cock in Pair No.2 had inherited the more desirable shade.

I only quote the Mauve x Blue cross for the production of Cobalts as an illustration of the point I am endeavouring to make. Innumerable other examples could be put forward.

Hereditary Colour

What it all amounts to is this: *A bird of any colour which is so genetically constituted that it can breed youngsters not only of its own colour but also of other colours will possess the ability to produce those other colours and its own colour good or bad in shade and depth according to the shade and depth of the colours of its progenitors.*

I will give you another example. Good Cobalts are frequently the outcome of mating Cobalt x Dark Green/blue, but you must not expect to see good coloured Cobalts among the offspring of this combination if the Cobalt parents or grandparents (we should possibly go even further back in the genealogical tree) of the Dark Green and the Cobalt were bad in colour; in fact, the danger will be present if the Cobalt ancestor of either of the members of the pair failed in colour.

I hope I have already written sufficient to convince young fanciers that the simple action of crossing the different colour varieties with the object of producing youngsters in accordance with the Mendelian expectations irrespective of the quality of their own colour and the colours of their parents and grandparents, will not alone necessarily give them those good coloured Budgerigars which it will be their desire to breed in order to win prizes.

It is obviously an utter impossibility for me or any other writer in a book of this character to comment on the good or evil of each of the thousands of different colour matings which can be made.

The fact that there is this multitude of combinations shows the scope which the breeder has available to him, although it is unnecessary to put into actual practice anything but a minority of these crosses in order to achieve success. Therefore, I feel that I can with safety confine my remarks to a number of colour matings which have proved satisfactory in my wife's aviaries and in the aviaries of others who have generously enlightened me as to the manner in which their best colour production results have been achieved.

When the breeder is actually deciding upon his matings before the breeding season commences, much more important than the description of different crosses to give the various colours is the application with common sense of those principles described above relating to individual birds and their pedigrees, the breeding theories which I will expound in Chapters 8 and 9, and of two other principles with which I will now deal.

In the earlier editions of this book in this chapter, "Colour Production", I stressed the virtues of what I termed "dipping into the Green" — that is, crossing the other colours with Light Greens in order to fix the type of the latter on other varieties. I did this because at the times when the previous editions were published the superiority of the Green in type combined with size, in spots and in other features, was marked. It was unusual in those days for winning Light Greens not to be awarded the premier specials at the shows.

But today other colour varieties are quite as good — in fact, as a general rule, superior — to the Light Greens, and my slogan of "dipping into the Green" has consequently outlived its usefulness.

Do not misunderstand me: There are still some excellent Light Greens in the land, but high-class Opalines, for example, are even more numerous as are Greys and Grey Greens.

In certain cases mating of a bird of another colour with a Light Green or a Dark Green can still be valuable, as you will learn to appreciate from what I say later.

Light Greens

In the second edition of this book in writing about Light Greens I said in effect that Light Green x Light Green was the best way to breed exhibition specimens, and that there should be no variation in this mating when Light Green youngsters were the sole objective. In short, I advocated keeping Light Greens pure.

This is a striking example of the mistake one can make in giving expression to predictions in so far as livestock breeding is concerned. Within a few years circumstances caused me to have to "eat my words", as I had to do in the third edition.

All was going normally and well with Light Green breeding in this country until we suddenly realised that some of the best strains of this variety were ceasing to produce an adequate number of chicks. There was an obvious decline in fecundity, the reason for which has never been discovered. It became clear that the situation was becoming worse season after season, that it could not put itself right, and that the urgent need to outcross to other colours presented itself.

At Lintonholme we mated some of our best Light Greens with Opalines. Fortunately they blended well, and soon by using selected Light Green/ Opaline cocks and Light Green hens with one Opaline parent fertility showed signs of improvement, and the advantageous effect of the blend in so far as fertility was concerned became apparent.

In addition we mated Light Greens to Skyblues, and, again, there was improvement in fertility.

As in the days before the craze for purity in Light Greens had got hold of us all, it has been discovered that some excellent show Light Greens are split for Blue, for Opaline, or for something else.

The development in Light Green culture which I have described has, of course, made it more impossible than ever before to give anything approximating to a guarantee of purity to a purchaser; but people now fully realise that it is not essential to have complete purity in a Light Green family as we used to think it was.

Now please do not jump to the conclusion that, because of what I have just written, I deprecate the old pairing of Light Green to Light Green. I do not. Provided the birds are suitable in every respect as mates, when judged by visual properties and pedigrees, and there is no reason to think they will not produce other than a full quota of youngsters, then, of course, Light Green x Light Green is a correct mating, and we who breed this, the oldest variety of them all, will annually use it (in addition) to pairing Light Greens with other colours.

Those who compare what I have written now with what I wrote in 1948 will rightly say that this is complete *volte face,* and so it is; but I am not alone guilty of making this change of advocacy in so far as Light Green breeding is concerned. Many of us who once cherished the purity of our Light Green families have had to alter our attitude, not because of any particular desire to do so but because of circumstances beyond our control. And the experience we have had of out-crossing has taught us that we were too dogmatic when we affirmed that Light Green x Light Green was much the best way in which to breed birds of the highest class in this colour.

As to which are the best colours for mating to Light Greens for the purpose described, my experience has mainly been with Opalines and Skyblues, and I have not found any better, though I do not assert that these are the only suitable out-crosses.

Dark Greens

Dark Green x Dark Green gives us Dark Greens, Olives, and Light Greens. In recent seasons we have bred some pleasing Light Greens from this mating, and a few Olives, which while not carrying the deep body colour which the best possessed in the days of this variety's popularity, have been pleasing. We have also bred some nice Dark and Light Greens from Dark Green x Light Green.

For Skyblue and Cobalt breeding Dark Greens are at times valuable and they have become an integral part of our Violet breeding plan, about which more anon. If they are to be used for Cobalt breeding, for instance, and they are bred from Cobalts, the latter must have been good in colour if they, in turn, are to breed good coloured Cobalts; and the same principle applies, though I think to a lesser degree—there being less variation in shade in

Skyblue to that which obtains in Cobalt—if they are to be used for Skyblue breeding.

Dark Greens fall into two categories, Type I and Type II, a genetical distinction described in Chapter 16. Type I Dark Greens are the best for Blue breeding and Type II Dark Greens are the best for Cobalt or Violet breeding.

Many fanciers have found that correctly-bred Dark Greens have a most beneficial influence on the colour of Cobalts and Blues. They seem to brighten and deepen it, and when the Dark Greens used are very good in type, they can effect improvement in that direction also.

Although, as I said in Chapter 4, the Olive is now a *rara avis,* for the benefit of those who may wish to revive the variety, I will repeat what I said about their breeding in the earlier editions of this work.

The object of the breeder of Olives is to produce birds deep and level in colour and free from any signs of green. The principal matings are Olive/blue x Mauve, Olive x Mauve, Olive/blue x Olive/blue, Olive/blue x Olive, and Olive x Olive.

These I will divide into two sections to simplify consideration of the question, viz.: Olive x Mauves and Olive in appearance x birds Olive in appearance, ignoring for the moment the Olives' invisible colour factors, if any.

Whilst it is undoubtedly correct to say that some of the best and darkest coloured Olives have been bred from Olives (split or otherwise) x Mauve, I have come to the conclusion that providing you have in your possession several Olives of the correct shade and depth of colour, you can maintain these qualities by persisting in the mating Olive x Olive, thus founding a strain of pure Olives.

Actual practice has proved that when Olives are rather light in colour one can deepen the colouring in the offspring by mating to a deep coloured Mauve, but even so it would seem that the introduction of a sufficiently good deep coloured Olive, if procurable, would be just as satisfactory an enterprise.

Sight must not be lost of the fact that an Olive and a Mauve are one and the same in coloration except that the latter is void of yellow pigment, and as the Mauves are quite as patchy in colouring, if not more so, than many Olives, it becomes theoretically difficult to recognise why a Mauve should be any better as a cross to an Olive than an Olive itself, assuming that the Olive and the Mauve are equal in depth and evenness of colouring. On the other hand so few are the good Olives available today that anyone who might decide to found a family of Olives on the lines I have described would have to resort to Mauves, of which good ones are more numerous. Incidentally, I do not know of anyone who is considering this enterprise.

In the old days when good Olives were plentiful I used Olives/blue in

Cobalt, etc., production with much success.

When using the cross Olive/blue to Mauve for both Olive and Mauve production, I prefer to use an Olive with one Mauve parent instead of an Olive with one Cobalt parent. We have bred pleasing Olives in recent years from Dark Green x Dark Green.

Another method of producing Olives is Dark Green/blue x Mauve. Anyone who wishes to breed some good Olives, should not overlook the virtues of the Opaline cross. There are a few quite good Opaline Olives in the country. We have bred some from Opaline Dark Green x Opaline Dark Green and Opaline Dark Green x Dark Green.

Light Yellows

Pure Light Yellow to pure Light Yellow is the only mating which one need seriously consider when the production of high-class exhibition Light Yellows is the sole objective. Light Yellows/white, Light Yellows/Lutino or Light Yellows bred from Light Greens/yellow, Light Greens/white or any other Green Series are no use for Yellow breeding. These birds carry more green suffusion than do the best Light Yellows, and their youngsters inherit it.

As the Standard indicates, the ideal colour is that which the term "buttercup" aptly describes, and it should be as free from pencilling and green suffusion on the rump and elsewhere as possible. Unfortunately, depth of body colour is often accompanied by heavy pencilling on the wings, whereas the lighter coloured birds are frequently more pure. The Cinnamon Yellow is usually more free from green but lighter in shade. If the cross with the Cinnamon had accomplished one thing only, viz., purification, it would have proved a blessing, but, unfortunately, it simultaneously robbed us of colour depth. Nevertheless, it might be wise to lose something in colour and improve type (for which there is a great need in Light Yellows) by founding a family of Cinnamon Light Yellows. I know a fancier in South Africa who has successfully accomplished this.

Another problem which besets the breeder of Light Yellows is associated with size. The bigger birds are often less deep and bright than the smaller ones, and it would seem that the "Yellow" and "Buff" theory comes into the story here.

Be all this as it may, up to the time of the obvious decline in the general quality of Light Yellows, many good show birds were regularly produced by the method adopted by successful breeders of Light Yellows, namely the continuous mating of pure Light Yellows to pure Light Yellows without the introduction of any alien blood whatever; the meticulous selection of the birds of the best type and the best colouring; the ruthless elimination of those faulty in shape or faulty in colouring.

Mr R.J. Watts produced his famous strain—the foundation of the buttercup Light Yellow—by these methods.

Unfortunately, the Light Yellow has declined so much in shape of body and head and in size that to persist with Light Yellow x Light Yellow cannot bring about any general improvement. There are not sufficient good birds available for the purpose.

Some may ask if crossing with the Dark-eyed Clear Yellows might improve the situation. The answer is no, because the Dark-eyed Clear Yellows are no better shaped, if as good, as the Normal Light Yellows. Certainly they are superior in colour, but it is in type that Light Yellows are inferior to other varieties today.

Dark Yellows

It is inadvisable ever to mate any Budgerigars with the primary object of producing Dark Yellows for exhibition purposes for the reasons fully explained in Chapter 4. In fact, Dark Yellows cannot really serve any useful purpose, either as show or breeding birds.

Olive Yellows

As indicated in Chapter 4, Olive Yellows are now very scarce, and they are often not sought as an out-cross for other colours. I know of no fancier who is actually breeding Olive Yellows with a view of producing specimens in this variety worthy of competing in Any Other Colour classes. If anyone decides to do so, Olive Yellow x Olive Yellow would appear to be the best mating if the birds used are sufficiently good in type.

Skyblues

Skyblue x Skyblue is an orthodox and good mating, providing both birds of the pair are large, typical and well marked. With specimens of this quality one can make straight pairings of Skyblue to Skyblue for several generations, if so desired. Therefore, it will be seen that the number of Skyblue x Skyblue pairs in an establishment will be governed by the general merit of the Skyblues in the stud.

Skyblues which are somewhat deficient in size, lacking in fullness of body or at all weak in head, even though not deserving of being described as inferior Budgerigars, should be mated to a good big Light Green/blue excelling in those points in which the Skyblue is rather deficient.

If, in a stud, the continuous mating of Skyblue to Skyblue season after season eventually leads to the production of smaller birds rather lacking in substance crosses to other colours must be made. Hence I am convinced that if we are to improve—nay, even if we are to maintain—colour and size in Blues we must at intervals cross our Skyblues with birds of other colour varieties, of which very good Light Greens/blue can, on the whole, prove to be the most beneficial though not more so than Opalines, which have given us splendid results.

By employing the Light Green/blue in the manner described one need not interfere with an in-breeding plan, because by simple control an owner's Light Green/blue can be related to his Skyblues, as can other colours to which the Skyblues are mated.

Many good breeders wishing to lay the foundation of a good strain of Skyblues have made their own Light Greens/blues in the first place. Not being able to purchase a suitable Light Green/blue they have obtained a high class Light Green and mated it to one of their best Skyblues. All the youngsters from such a pair are Light Greens/blue and no Skyblues will be bred in this line until the second year; but events may prove the time was not wasted.

When selecting a Light Green/blue for Skyblue breeding it is always advisable to ensure that its Skyblue parent was satisfactory as to size, colour and shape. It is also necessary, of course, for the Light Green parent to have been a good one.

Some of the best Skyblues ever bred have come from Light Green/blue x Skyblue.

I have seen some magnificent Skyblues which have been bred from Dark Green/blue x Skyblue, and I cannot do other than express approval of this cross, which would no doubt be used more often if there were more suitable Dark Greens/blue available.

Type I Dark Greens/blue are the most useful for Skyblue production because they give us a higher Skyblue expectation than when a Type II is employed.

Cobalt x Cobalt on the average produces 25 per cent. Skyblues, and these are often very good in colour though frequently inferior in size to the Cobalts in the same nest. I do not, however, favour the mating of a Cobalt to a Cobalt, for reasons which I shall give later.

Theoretically one might form the opinion that Skyblues so bred might show that Cobalt shading which is a minor fault, but this does not always follow. Nevertheless, having got your Skyblue from Cobalt x Cobalt it is inadvisable to mate that bird to a Cobalt if Skyblues are your objective. It is far better to put it to a really good Skyblue, a Light Green/blue or a Dark Green/blue. The same remarks apply to Skyblues bred from Cobalt x Skyblue.

With reference to Cobalt x Skyblue, theoretically one may assume that there is a risk here of producing Cobalts of the blue Cobalt shade, and Blues showing a trace of Cobalt, but the fact is that we and others have bred excellent coloured Blues and rich coloured Cobalts from this cross *but always when the Cobalt has come from Cobalts of the correct shade and likewise the Skyblue ancestors of the Skyblue used have been desirable in colour.* Never mate Cobalt to Blue unless the requirement just described is fulfilled, and never use this cross unless the two birds are entirely suitable for each other in so far as type is concerned; in fact, when we mate our birds in the first place we always consider whether or not they are a perfect fit as regards size and type, because, as I indicate more than once in this book, shape is with me the first consideration in a Budgerigar.

A Perpetual Problem

As in the mating Cobalt x Cobalt so in the mating Cobalt x Skyblue do we often see a dissimilarity in size and type between the Skyblues and the Cobalts so bred, and here we have striking examples of that difference in type between colour varieties to which I referred at the opening of this chapter and which presents one of the problems with which Budgerigar breeders have to contend. We often note a similar variation in Light Greens/blue and Skyblues of the same clutch.

Many other matings are there, of course, by which one can produce Skyblues, but, as I have already said, I am not attempting the impossible task of describing the advantages and disadvantages of all the different methods of producing all the different colour varieties, and there are undoubtedly good birds in the country bred by crosses to which I do not refer at all. What I *am* trying to do, as I indicated previously, is to give those matings which, from information I have received from other breeders and from results in my wife's aviaries, have given the most satisfactory results.

The moral of the Skyblue story which I have just written is this: Whether you breed good Blues at times from the cross Blue x Blue, Light Green/blue x Blue, Cobalt x Blue or from any other similar pairing, you must endeavour to maintain size and shape and depth and brightness of colour by periodically "dipping into the green."

Breeders of Skyblues must not overlook the value as an out-cross of the Opaline, as described by me later in this chapter, while Greys and Grey Greens are also valuable in colour out-crosses for Skyblue production.

In our aviaries the Skyblues are a part of our "Blue Series Breeding Circle", which consists of Violets, Cobalts, Mauves, Violet Mauves, Skyblues, Violet Skyblues, Opalines of these colours, with the introduction here and there, now and again, of Dark Greens/blue, Violet Dark Greens/blue, Light Greens/blue, and Opaline Greens/blue. We are always more concerned with the type of the two birds constituting a pair than with their colour variety.

Cobalts

The Cobalt is patent proof of my statement that there is no *best* method of breeding the majority of colour varieties in which Budgerigars are to be seen, and just as there are so many different shades of Cobalt so there are so many systems of producing them. The maintenance of colour simultaneously with the retention of good size and type in this variety is exceedingly difficult and the matter is not simplified by the fact that the Cobalt is heterozygous as distinct from a bird like a pure Light Green which is homozygous. In other words, two Cobalts mated together, unlike the pure Light Green, the Skyblue, the Mauve, and the Olive, do not give us youngsters all of their own colour. Actually, when we mate together two Cobalts we breed Mauves and Skyblues in addition to Cobalts.

If we had before us at the beginning of a breeding season two Cobalts of the most desirable colour and fulfilling our demands as to type and size, if we knew that every chick would be a Cobalt, we should be more inclined to mate them together than we often are, because those two birds, whilst being just what we might require for Cobalt breeding, owing to their ancestry, may not quite meet our desires for Mauve or Skyblue production. On the other hand, it may be that they are a pair of birds capable of bringing into the world not only good Cobalts but Skyblues of merit, and Mauves which, although they may not be suitable for Mauve breeding in the future, may be of great value to us for breeding Cobalts in the mating Mauve x Skyblue for instance.

I must admit that I have failed to find a reason why Cobalt x Cobalt should be unsatisfactory and, therefore, I cannot completely condemn this mating, but I do not advise anyone to use it unless the two members of a pair excel in colour and in shape and whose Cobalt ancestors were of the desired shade of cobalt colouring. Cobalts bred in the same nests from a pair of Cobalts often vary surprisingly in colour. We do not seem to be able to control this variation and the only thing to do is, of course, to select the best coloured Cobalts out of a clutch for our future breeding operations.

In any case Cobalts bred from Cobalt x Cobalt must not themselves be mated to Cobalts. They must be paired to birds of other colour varieties. The Cobalt breeder is happily situated if every season he has a number of pairs constituted of Dark Green/blue Type I x Cobalt and/or Dark Green Type II x Blue, always providing that the immediate Cobalt ancestors of the Dark Greens were of good cobalt colour and with the further proviso that the Dark Greens are of good size and shape. To achieve success in the exhibition world never use birds which come below a certain standard of excellence.

Light Green/blue x Mauve serves a double valuable purpose. The expectation from this mating is 50 per cent. Dark Greens/blue Type II and 50 per cent. Cobalts. The Dark Greens/blue Type II, as previously set forth, are most valuable for Cobalt production, for the reason that if they are mated to Skyblues they give us an expectation of no less than 50 per cent. Cobalts.

Mauve x Skyblue, providing the Mauve has a good Cobalt ancestor, is another serviceable cross; in fact some of the best coloured Cobalts I have seen have been bred in this way. From this pairing all the chicks are Cobalts.

In many aviaries there are a number of Cobalt-bred Mauves which have too much cobalt in their colouring to make them desirable either as show birds or as a force for the cultivation of Mauves. Yet these birds can be most valuable for mating to Skyblues or Cobalts with the primary object of their being the parents of very satisfactory Cobalts.

I have known good Cobalts bred from the mating Olive/blue x Skyblue when the expectation is 50 per cent. Dark Greens/blue Type I, 50 per cent. Cobalts. But it would not be so easy now to find an Olive/blue suitable for the purpose because there are so few of them.

Whether you select as mates for your Cobalts Light Greens/blue, Dark Greens/blue, Cobalts, Skyblues or Mauves, as in the cultivation of all Budgerigars for exhibition purposes, the results are greatly dependent upon the suitability of the mates in so far as size and type are concerned, and also upon the manner in which they themselves have been bred.

Mauves

A sound theory which I feel sure any breeder can apply to his birds with great advantage to himself if he desires to be the owner of home-bred winning Mauves, is to avoid using Mauves which show a considerable amount of cobalt colouring intermingled with the other mauve colouring — as, alas, so many Mauves do — desirable as such birds may be for Cobalt breeding.

In the days when there were good Olives in the land Olive/blue x Mauve gave us the best Mauves at Lintonholme, providing always that the Olive/blue had a good coloured Mauve parent and not a Cobalt parent. The principle is a simple one, viz.: keep as far away from the Cobalt as you can and the probability is that you will have less cobalt in your Mauves, although I have to confess that I have seen some amazing exceptions.

Several Budgerigar fancier friends of mine have told me that they have had unsatisfactory experiences with the cross Mauve x Mauve, alleging that continuation with this straight pairing season after season has resulted in deterioration in size. Nevertheless, I cannot see any reason to ban this mating completely. But when I mated Mauve to Mauve I should want both birds to reach a somewhat high standard as regards both colour, shape, and size. For instance, I would not mate together two Mauves both very light or patchy in colour, or, more important still, with a lot of cobalt flecking or suffusion. To do so would intensify such faults.

If, on the other hand, one becomes possessed of a number of Mauves bred correctly, nicely coloured, shapely and big enough, strict selection of the best and ruthless elimination of the worst should, one would imagine, lead to a gradual improvement. Nevertheless, in the light of my own experience and the experience of others, it would seem to be unwise to persist with the mating Mauve x Mauve season after season without any colour crossing, and immediately there is the slightest sign of any deterioration another colour must be introduced.

The course pursued by the old-time breeders of Mauves was to cross Olive/blue and Mauves, but the scarcity of good Olives would make this difficult today.

In these paragraphs about Cobalts and Mauves I have not referred to the pairing of Cobalt x Violet and Mauve x Violet, but I shall do so under the heading of Violets. Actually the development of the Violet birds has greatly changed the Mauve story, and very good Mauves and Violet Mauves are being bred in Violet breeding families. Many of them are much better in colour than one might have expected them to be.

Whites

Whites, as these birds are called, can be bred in all the different body colours in the Blue series with deep and light suffusions. Whites of Light suffusion are rarely seen nowadays but the birds with a deep suffusion are quite often appearing in nests from Normal and Clearwing pairs that are carrying the White character. They are mostly shown in the Any Other Colour classes unless special classes are scheduled for them.

Greywings

My readers cannot fail to have noticed that in no case so far have I advocated the use of the Greywing as an out-cross. I have avoided this with deliberation, because I do not think our Greywings — again I am speaking generally and making an allowance for exceptional individuals — are capable of improving our older colour varieties in type, size or stamina, as no one can say they are superior to the Mauves, Cobalts, Blues, etc., for all-round excellence, although they had greatly improved up to the late 'thirties, since when they have declined in number and quality.

On the other hand, I feel that the Greywing breeder can, when occasion demands, make crosses to the Normal coloured Greens, Mauves, Cobalts, Skyblues, Greys, Violets, etc., with advantage. The fancier will have to use his own discretion as to when he makes these crosses. If he finds his Greywings are commencing to fail in size or shape in any degree, then he should make an excursion to the Normal colours. By doing so, he will breed a number of Normal colours split Greywing, but these birds will be of assistance to him in his Greywing breeding endeavours.

I can greatly simplify my advice on Greywing production by stating that in my experience and in the experience of others with whom I have been in consultation from time to time, generally speaking the remarks which I have made above in dealing with the Normal colours, and the descriptions which I have given of desirable and undesirable Normal colour matings, apply in principle to the same colours in the Greywing family. For instance, I do not like to persist too long with the mating Greywing Blue x Greywing Blue. But the dangers with regard to loss of depth of colour in the Normal colour varieties to which I have called attention if certain crosses are made continuously do not arise in the same way with the Greywings, for the reason that one does not fear loss of depth of colour on the body as one fears it in the Normals, although as in the Normals so in the Greywings one must ever keep a watchful eye on size and type.

To illustrate, Greywing Cobalt x Greywing Cobalt is a much more desirable mating than Normal Cobalt x Normal Cobalt.

The difficulty in breeding Greywings is maintaining the correct depth of markings, which, as I indicated in Chapter 5, to be ideal should be exactly midway between zero and black. Variation in depth of markings in the Greywing classes at our shows is repeated by a similar astonishing variation even in the same nests of chicks, when one often finds no two birds alike in this respect.

One likes to mate correctly marked Greywings together, but if one continues the youngsters often become so dark in markings and body colour that they are bordering on the Normal in appearance.

In the old days when we bred Greywings more extensively in my wife's aviaries than we do now, I out-crossed dark-marked Greywings in the blue series to Whites, and almost all our Greywings (other than Greywing Greens) were eventually split for white. Consequently every season we bred a number of Whites from our Greywing Whites. It did not matter much at that time because the Whites were showable. It was before the era of the Cinnamon White of light suffusion and the Whitewing. Now, however, Whites bred from Greywings would be of little value, and, therefore, if I were a breeder of Greywings nowadays I should avoid that White crossing in which we all indulged nearly twenty-five years ago.

To avoid the production of too many birds with markings so heavy that they approximate to the Normal, I should mate those with very dark wings to those with very light wings, and by selection and elimination hope to have at the end of each season a sufficiency of correctly mated birds to serve my purpose.

It will be clear from what I have just written that Greywings too light in markings for exhibition can, if of good type, be serviceable as breeders.

However he crosses his birds, however good the material, the breeder of Greywings will always be having to fight variability in depth of wing markings. Only by judicious selection and skilful breeding generally, and the able use of colour crosses at the right times, will the breeder be able to produce annually Greywings of the most desired coloration.

In dealing below with particular Greywing matings I shall not refer again to crosses with the marked Normal varieties, but it may be taken that what I have said above on this subject applies to all the colour varieties in which Greywings are cultivated.

Greywing Greens, Light and Dark

Greywing Light Green x Greywing Light Green gives splendid results, always providing the birds mated are suitable not only in type but also in colour in general. If they are too dark in markings and not of the correct body colour but of a darker hue, then the youngsters are likely to be darker still.

If one member of the pair is somewhat dark and the other rather light, or if they are both a little light, there is no reason why they should not be mated together; in fact if they are both just right as regards markings and body colour, whilst some of their chicks may be too heavy in markings, a number of them will most probably be of the correct shade and these can again be mated to Greywing Light Greens in the following season. By skilfully adopting this process with all Greywings one can breed Greywing to Greywing — always using specially selected birds — indefinitely without an out-cross; and this is not confined to the Greywing Greens but applies to other colours of Greywings also, but in all cases only if the type is not deteriorating; and it is a fact that Greywings generally are neither so good nor so numerous as they were once upon a time.

In the old days we used to mate Greywing Greens, which were too dark in body colour and markings, to Light Yellows. Thus in the course of time we bred some Light Yellows very unattractive in colour, however good they might be in shape and size, and their only use to us was for further Greywing Green mating. Consequently, we did not make the Yellow out-cross except when we considered it to be absolutely necessary. This is similar to the Greywing Blue and White story, and I advise the Greywing Green breeder to keep his Greywings together except when he thinks an out-cross to a Normal is desirable.

Some years ago there was a family of Light Greens in this country that was split Yellow. It was a very good family, and produced many winners. The Yellow out-cross had probably been made a number of years before the time of which I write, without being repeated, but the latent Yellow factor was still carried, and occasionally when two of these Light Greens/yellow were paired together, Yellow youngsters made their appearance.

These were big, fine birds of the type of their Green brothers and sisters, father and mother. I used some of them as mates for some too-dark Greywing Greens, and produced Greywing Greens/yellow, which pleased me immensely.

This was an exceptional opportunity of "dipping into the Green" without actually using a Light Green. The great advantage was that I bred in the first generation Greywing Greens/yellow instead of Light Greens/yellow. Of course, I bred more Yellows from subsequent matings in the new line which I had started, and these were useless as show Yellows or for Light Yellow breeding. Some of them were used in later Greywing pairings. There was some wastage here, but in this particular case I considered it to be worth while.

Greywing Dark Greens have considerable value as a breeding force in the production of Greywing Cobalts, Greywing Blues, and Greywing Mauves, just as good Dark Greens render valuable service when used in the cultivation of Normal Cobalts and Normal Blues.

Greywing Olives
Greywing Olives, like the other colours of Greywings, if they are becoming too dark in body colour and markings, can be crossed with other Greywing Olives of a lighter hue, and they can be used for crossing to Greywings in the "blue" series. It's a long time since I saw a Greywing Olive.

Greywing Blues, Cobalts, Mauves, Greys and Violets
As stated earlier in this chapter, the principles which apply to colour matings in the Normal colour varieties apply to a certain extent to the colour matings in the Greywing colour varieties, subject to those important modifications which I have referred to at length in regard to depth of markings, and the advisability of mating to Normal coloured birds occasionally if necessary to maintain size and type.

Cinnamons
The breeder of the Cinnamon varieties cannot do better than follow those general principles which I have described for the production of the Normal colour varieties, except that he has to adapt his breeding plan to those rules governing sex-linkage which are explained in Chapter 16.

The Cinnamon breeder must also pay more attention to the colour of the markings than does the breeder of birds with black markings, because there is a much greater possibility of variation both as regards shade and density.

The Cinnamon has been improved in type through the years mainly as the outcome of, in the first place, out-crossing to the Normals.

I have written briefly about the production of Cinnamons because what I have said about the methods of producing Normals and Greywings equally applies to these birds. Generally speaking, the Cinnamons we have today are of better quality than the Greywings and they are more popular.

Fallows
Comparatively few people now breed the Fallow variety. They never enjoyed more than a passing popularity. At one time it was thought that the

judicious use of Fallows improved colour in some of the Normals — Cobalts, for instance — but I think this was more theoretical than practical. With exceptions, they have never been as good as the old varieties in size and shape, and I am afraid that *if* one did improve colour by crossing them into Normals, that which was gained would be but poor compensation for a deterioration in type which would be likely to occur. Be this as it may, the suggestion that Fallows were useful to Normal breeders was not carried out by many fanciers, and nowadays it is rare for anyone even to refer to the theory.

It is possible to breed a White Fallow and a Yellow Fallow, but few specimens of either kind have ever been exhibited. Of those I remember the Whites were in no way better than Albinos, and the Yellows were inferior to Lutinos.

The breeding of Fallows in their different colours should be conducted on similar lines to those recommended for the breeding of Normals, Greywings, etc.

Pure Yellow Red-eyes (Lutinos)

I have put the word "Lutinos" in parentheses to distinguish these birds from the red-eyed Yellow Fallows to which I have just referred, although fanciers when speaking of these birds almost invariably use the word "Lutino".

In a sex-linked variety the colour gene is on the sex chromosome. In a non-linked variety it is on a different chromosome. A Lutino is masking some normal colour (say Light Green) as explained in Chapter 4.

Let us imagine, for the sake of illustration, that you mate a non-linked Lutino cock masking Light Green to a sex-linked Lutino hen masking Light Green. The genes for albinism being on chromosomes which cannot pair (viz., an ordinary chromosome and the sex-chromosome) albinism will not occur in the youngsters.

Therefore, the result will be exactly the same as if the parents had not been Lutinos, but externally of the colour which was masked; and all the offspring will be black-eyed Light Greens, in appearance like any other Light Greens, but the cocks will be split for Lutino.

The earliest Lutinos left much to be desired. They were often small, narrow in body, nipped in neck and mean in head; and in colour they varied considerably. It has to be recognised that although, theoretically, a Lutino is pure yellow in colour, there is often, even now, a green sheen to be seen — usually on the hind parts of the bird. Complete absence of this sheen is desirable. Believe me, there was a lot of it on most of the first examples of this beautiful variety.

It was obvious at the outset of Lutino culture that skilful out-crossing to the Normal was necessary in order to improve type and size, and increase depth and brightness of colour.

Fanciers, not unnaturally perhaps, conceived the idea that the best Normals for the purpose would be those carrying one dark or two dark factors, e.g., Dark Greens, Olives, Olive Yellows and Dark Yellows.

Yellow Pigment Only

As I have already told my readers, the Lutino is that form of albinism which is void of all pigment except yellow. Our object was obviously to have that retained yellow as bright and deep as possible.

As the beneficial effect of skilful Normal out-crossing built-up, Lutinos advanced amazingly in shape and colour, and straight Lutino x Lutino crosses became desirable. Whereas not long before the war one could rarely find two Lutinos which one dare mate together—so faulty was the variety —now in the best studs there are many high quality specimens which one can select for Lutino x Lutino pairings. There is, of course, less wastage from Lutino x Lutino, because all the youngsters are Lutinos and has been for some years the almost universal pairing.

Some of the birds mated have been very good, some not so good, and others bad. I have, therefore, feared that what has happened to the Light Yellow might happen to the Lutino, but the fact is that this attractive variety has maintained its quality well. Even so, the danger exists, and there is a need for colour out-crossing in some families. At Lintonholme we have mated Lutino to Light Green with some success, and Opaline Light Green is also well worth consideration as an out-cross. My advice on this subject is the following:

If in your stud of Lutinos size or shape of head or body is falling off introduce a shapely Light Green or Opaline Light Green hen—not a small one—and mate it to a Lutino cock. This can restore size and type, but the colour of the youngsters will probably be inferior to the pure Lutino father and his relations. Having secured improvement in shape of head and body, your task is to restore colour by selection. It will not be advisable to mate any of the offspring to Light Green or Opaline Light Green, as you do not want a double dose of the out-cross.

Clear White Red-eyes (Albinos)

To tell the complete story of Albino production would be to repeat much that I have written about the Lutino. There are the following points of similarity:–

(a) I use the term "Albino" because I am not referring here to the White Fallow. ("Albino" is the word by which fanciers refer to them in conversation.)

(b) They mask Normal colours in the "blue" series, whereas the Lutino masks Normal colours in the "green" series.

(c) Out-crossing to Normals is absolutely necessary to improve and maintain size and type.

(d) Only exceptional Albinos should be mated together; and there are fewer available than there are Lutinos.

When a Lutino is mated to an Albino, Albinos can derive the benefit of any improvement effected in the Lutino if they are bred from Lutino × Albino.

But fanciers who have good Lutinos usually hesitate to mate them to Albinos, because owing to the general inferiority of the latter, Lutinos so bred are likely to be inferior specimens; and the owners concerned wll not wish to spoil a good and improving stud of Lutinos.

Albinos can be crossed to any Normal in the "blue" series, the Normal Albinos so bred being used are Normal/lutino production. The dark factor provides no argument here, because, of course we want neither depth nor tint in the body colour, which should be pure white, though it does often show a blue sheen in the same way that Lutinos show a green sheen.

There is scope for someone to set himself the task of providing a stud of Albinos equal to the modern Lutino. This could be done.

Violets

The genetic formula of the Violet, as compiled by some eminent authorities on Budgerigar genetics when the earliest Violets made their appearance, is rather complex. If a thorough understanding of it were essential to the practical breeding of Violets, then I am afraid but few non-scientific fanciers would undertake Violet breeding. They would decide that the problem presented to them was too intricate to be faced with confidence and equanimity, and even the undoubted beauty of the Violet would probably not be sufficient to persuade them to make this variety one of their specialities.

I am pleased to be able to say that my own actual experience with Violets has proved to me that Violet production is no more complicated than is, say, the breeding of Cobalts.

In the first place, the Violet character is one that causes a variation in the body colour, and in so far as the true Violet is concerned, it is nothing more or less than a variant of the Cobalt. Therefore, in your breeding operations treat the Violet as though it were a Cobalt and mate on the general lines which I describe above for Cobalt production.

The Violet character is not sex-linked but Dominant and it is not essential for it to be carried by both parents for Violets to appear among the offspring.

Leaving Greens out of the question for the moment, we can have Violet Blues, true Violets (Violet-Cobalts if you like) and Violet Mauves.

The Violet Blue has no dark character, the true Violet has one dark factor, the Violet-Mauve has two dark characters. Although Violet-Blues and

162

Violet-Mauves are valuable for Violet breeding, it is the Violet with one dark character (the variant of the Cobalt) which is the show bird, and the one which we are out to produce.

To achieve this we should obviously, whenever possible, so arrange our matings that there is a high expectation of breeding many youngsters possessing only one dark factor. And this is exactly the same procedure which one follows when desiring to breed a goodly number of Cobalts.

Owing to the need to improve type in Violets, there has been, and still is, much out-crossing to the Normals. Mauves and Cobalts have been used extensively for this purpose. The Mauve, in particular, has helped to increase the number of Violets in the country, because of its possessing the dark character in double dose.

Mauve $\times$ Skyblue, for instance, gives us birds all carrying one dark character, whereas from Cobalt $\times$ Skyblue the expectation is 50 per cent. one dark character and 50 per cent. no dark character. Cobalt $\times$ Cobalt provides 25 per cent. two dark character, 50 per cent. one dark character and 25 per cent. no dark character.

If we substitute in the above pairings Violet for Cobalt, Violet-Mauve for Mauve, and Violet-Blue for Skyblue, in some or all cases, the dark character expectation as set out is unaffected.

In our own aviairies we have found that from our Violet-breeding pairs we get both ordinary Mauves and Violet-Mauves, Cobalts and Violet-Cobalts, Skyblues and Violet-Blues.

We have proved that Dark Greens/blue and even Light Greens/blue can be used for improving type and size in the Violet, in accordance with my advocacy of their use in the breeding of Cobalts, and, therefore, those Green crosses which I recommended earlier in this chapter for Cobalt production can be employed in a Violet breeding plan when necessary. There are certainly such birds as Violet-Dark Greens/blue, Violet-Light Greens/blue, and there can be Violet-Olives/blue. Although these three varieties do not show violet in their plumage, a difference in shade from the normal is noticeable. In Violet-Mauves violet can usually be seen in the rump. Violet-Blues are much deeper in colour than Normal Skyblues; in fact, they border on the Cobalt.

Many years ago there took place in the columns of *Cage Birds* a most interesting discussion on Violet breeding, the controversialists being Mr. E. W. Brooks, who viewed the problem from the more scientific angle, and Mr. Fred Garvey, who approached the matter solely as a practical breeder. Mr. Garvey contended that the breeding behaviour of the Violet was no different from that of the dominant Grey, and that when preparing a breeding plan it should be treated as such. Actually it can, so breeders may safely use their Violets in this simple way.

But Mr. Brooks would not completely accept Mr. Garvey's statement, and he pointed out certain differences between Violet breeding results and Grey breeding results. Realising that both were right from their respective viewpoints I contributed an article to *Cage Birds* in which I summarised the position as I saw it. I said in effect that both Mr. Brooks and Mr. Garvey were right, but both were approaching the matter on different lines. I said then, and I repeat, that the Grey is a dominant which can impress its colour on a youngster with no dark character, one dark character, or wo dark characters. Thus we have Light Greys, Medium Greys and Dark Greys, Light Grey Greens, Medium Grey Greens and Dark Grey Greens.

On the other hand, although Violet is also dominant the only Violets which are really violet in colour are those with one dark character. Consequently birds which theoretically are Violet Blues, Violet Mauves, Violet Light Greens, Violet Dark Greens, and Violet Olives cannot by any stretch of imagination be termed true Violets (that is the Violet with one dark character) than one does Greys when Grey breeding.

In actual fact Mr. Brooks, Mr. Garvey and Mr. Watmough were all correct in their ideas of how the Violet character worked only they expressed it in different ways. In fact Violet is a character just like Grey as it alters the visual colour of all birds whether carried in a single or double quantity in both the Green and Blue series.

Since the earlier editions of this book were published great strides have been made with Violets. In our own private aviairies (as in others) we have created a family which regularly produce Violet Cobalts (Visual Violets), Violet Mauves, Cobalts, Violet Blues, and Opaline Violets, Cobalts and Mauves, and all of good colour and equal in type.

The Dark Green/blue played its part in establishing this line, as did also Cobalts, Normal Mauves and Skyblues and Opalines of various colours, which were introduced into the family with great satisfaction to ourselves Therefore, no longer do we produce our Cobalts and Mauves just as we did in the old days, because now that the Violet has come into the picture and the Opaline has proved its breeding value in this connection, our choice of matings is wider than it was when the Violet was unknown.

Opalines

As Opaines are sex-linked the usual rules with regard to sex-linkage apply. (See Chapter 16).

I know of no variety that attained good exhibition standard so rapidly after its first appearance. It was comparitively soon after they were first being regularly seen at our shows that Opalines of quite outstanding merit were being staged.

Two properties in which many of these birds excelled were heads and spots. Their large, round skulls were most appealing, and in spots they were quite the equal of the best Light Greens. This laudation does not, of course, apply to *all* the earliest Opalines, nor does it to-day. Yet the fact remans that amongst Opalines we have seen, through the years since they were first exhibited, specimens of really excellent merit.

The need for out-crossing to Normal varieties, as in the case of all new colours when they are being established, could not be disregarded; and undoubtedly the Light Green then proved to be the most valuable bird for this purpose.

Out-crossing to other colours has been pursued with good and bad results, mainly according to the quality of the Normals introduced. Years ago the position arose that instead of the Normal improving the Opaline the Opaline improved the Normal; and so it is to-day.

The development of the Opaline was so satisfactory that much sooner than in the case of the Lutino, for instance, it was desirable to mate Opaline to Opaline extensively.

Above I have described how Opalines have helped in Violet breeding, and I also refer to them as an out-cross in this chapter under the heading of "Light Greens". In our aviaries we have found the Opaline one of the most valuable out-crosses we have ever employed. For instance, they have had much to do with establishing our strain of Violets.

When Opalines are crossed with Normals, all those principles of colour crossing which I have described earlier in this chapter can be employed.

The mating of Opalines to Cinnamons and to Greys has provided us with the Opaline Cinnamons, Opaline Greys and Cinnamon Opaline Greys to which I referred in Chapter 4.

In selecting mates the fancier has to consider one property much more seriously than has the breeder of, say, Light Greens or Sky blues, viz., the markings on the wings and on the mantle, or saddle.

One problem with which he has to deal is that of achieving the desired colour on the wings. As I said in Chapter 4, when one gets a clear saddle there is a danger of its being accompanied by a shortage of black on the wings. This has to be borne in mind by judges as well as breeders, but the latter must strive by skilful selection to breed a bird with a V as clear (or as clear as possible) of black, and at the same time with an equal distribution of colour on the wings.

Greys and Grey Greens

Because the Grey is dominant it is quite easy to produce them in quantity. In the earlier days of the variety, they were mated to Light Greens to improve size and type, and as Grey is dominant to the wild type this gave in the first generation Grey Greens. Greys of the light, medium and dark shades (erstwhile named Grey blues, Grey Cobalts and Grey Mauves) were mated to Skyblues, etc., and they still are, although there is no objection to pairing Grey Green to Grey or Grey to Grey, providing the birds suit each other as to pedigree, shape, etc.

Generally speaking, I prefer the light and medium Greys and Grey Greens to the dark shade; in fact, I do not know of anyone who is deliberately trying to produce Dark Greys. The darker shades are not much, if at all, handicapped in competition.

If the breeder wishes to avoid breeding Dark Greys he must take care not to put together two birds which can have any youngsters possessing the dark factor in double dose. A few examples are: – Medium or Dark Grey × Mauve, Medium or Dark Olive, Medium or Dark Grey × Dark Green; Medium or Dark Grey × Cobalt; Medium or Dark Grey × Medium, or Dark Grey. Other matings of a similar nature will readily suggest themselves to my readers.

The practice followed by many Grey breeders is whether to mate Light Grey (occasionally Medium Grey) to Light Grey, or Light Grey (very occasionally Medium Grey) to Skyblue. All this, of course, applies equally to Greys and Grey Greens.

The mating of Light Grey to Blue is good, and by this method one can build up a family of related Greys and Skyblues, and breed winners of both varieties. But if the owner has a good strain of Skyblues, it might be advisable to continue to treat this as a separate line altogether. Thus he will have two families of Blues, viz.: *(a)* his ordinary Skyblue family, and *(b)* his Grey-Skyblue family. When founding his line of Greys and Skyblues linked therewith, there is no reason why he should not select some birds from line *"(a)"* for crossing but it might be disadvantageous to him to mate their youngsters back into his ordinary Skyblue line.

The system I have just described can be employed equally well in Grey Green production, Light Greens and/or Light Greens/blue being utilised as the colour cross. There is no objection to pairing Grey Green or Grey Green/blue to Grey.

Actually Greys and Grey Greens are now so good in show properties that there is no reason why a family should not consist of these two varieties only, probably improved if Opaline Greys and Opaline Grey Greens are also utilised.

Yellow-face Type I and Type II.

These birds really belong to the Blue series because their ground colour is white but have varying areas of yellow suffusion. It is the Type I birds that are most desirable for exhibition purposes as their yellow suffusions are more or less confined to specific areas, namely, mask (face), tail and wing butts.

With the Type II birds the whole body has a strong yellow wash giving the birds a sea green colouring. They can always be identified from Greens as the colour of the feathers on the underside of the wing butts is always a blue shade.

Both kinds of the Yellow-faced character can be carried in split form by Green series birds but they cannot be split for both Yellow-faced and Blue at the same time.

Whereas the Yellow-face Type II birds follow the usual pattern of inheritance the Type I have a different manner of reproduction. When two single character Yellow-face Blue Type II are mated together the theoretical expectation is as expected 50% single character, 25% double character and 25% Normal Blue. In actual fact that is the result but with a difference as the double character Yellow-face Blue Type II birds do not show any yellow on their plumage and look exactly the same as ordinary Blues. When one of these special double character Yellow-face birds is mated to a Normal blue all their young are Yellow-face Blues with a single character. It took breeders quite some time to fathom out this unusual way of passing on the character; therefore with the Yellow-face Blue Type I mutation it is only the single character birds that actually show the yellow markings on their plumage.

Whitewings and Whites of Deep Suffusion

I do not propose to write about the breeding of Whites of deep suffusion, because now no one sets out with the deliberate intention of breeding these birds, as explained in Chapter 4. Therefore, I will deal here only with the production of Whitewings.

When the Whitewing first made its appearance at our shows the contrast between its deep body colour and almost pure white wings was much admired, as it still is, but the size and shape of the original specimens left a lot to be desired.

It was obvious at the outset that extensive crossing with the Normals would be necessary. Thus there were many matings of Normal x Whitewing, which brought into existence numerous Normals/Whitewing, as Whitewing is recessive to Normal.

These Normals/Whitewing laid the foundations of what are now the best strains of Whitewings. In fact, in my opinion, crossing to the Normal is still necessary, and I doubt if any fancier has available to him all the Whitewings (or Yellow-wings) of sufficiently high merit that he requires to complete his pairings with Whitewing x Whitewing or Whitewing x Yellow-wing only.

It is quite sound to mate Whitewing to Yellow-wing, thus obtaining Yellow-wings/Whitewing.

Apart from such variations as the above, and providing the cock and hen to be put together are satisfactory as regards type and coloration, Whitewing X Whitewing is good. And so long as size and shape are maintained, no colour cross is necessary. But the owner need not hesitate to digress from this simple system as soon as he sees the need arising. And I am afraid the need is there now in all the Whitewing and Yellow-wing Green families with which I am acquainted.

When we bred Whitewings we found that there was great variation in the colouring of the youngsters, even from the same nest, particlarly in the darker coloured birds, e.g., Mauves and Cobalts. Sometimes no two were alike, either as regards body colour or purity of wing. Some, in fact, differed but little from the old-time Whites of deep suffusion.

The breeder's object is, of course, by selection to overcome this inconsistency and breed more and more Whitewings conforming to show standard.

Yellow-Wing Greens

All that I have written about the breeding of Whitewings applies to the production of Yellow-wings, with the exception that here one can, if so wishing, dip straight into the Green.

An outstanding Light Green can be mated to a Yellow-Green. This should produce valuable Light Greens/Yellow-wing, which when put to Yellow-wings will breed Yellow-wings. These can be paired to other Yellow-wings or to Whitewings, when Yellow-wings/Whitewing will be the outcome. These birds can, in turn, be mated to Whitewings. And so there may come into being both Yellow-wings and Whitewings showing the beneficial effect of the out-cross to that outstanding Light Green.

Incidentally, and as I have already indicated, just as we mate our Normal Skyblue to our Light Greens/blue, so it is quite permissible and often wise to provide Whitewing mates for Yellow-wings, and in due course found a strain of Yellow-wings and Whitewings all of one family.

As with Whitewings so with Yellow-wing Greens, generally speaking there has not been that improvement which was once expected, and I am certain that only by judicious out-crossing to the old Normal varieties will progress be made.

CHAPTER 13

HOW TO BREED WINNERS

IMPORTANCE OF STRAIN

If I had headed this chapter "How to Establish a Strain of Your Own" the advice which follows would have been unchanged. If an owner desires to form a stud of Budgerigars which can consistently produce winning specimens, then he must evolve a strain, unless he be content, and has the means, to expend goodly sums of money annually on birds capable of breeding high-class youngsters for him.

If the latter is the procedure adopted, then the fancier is not depending on his own abilities as a breeder. He is obviously making use practically always of material provided by those from whom he purchases his birds.

Although the buying of good foundation stock is essential, and although the introduction of fresh blood to improve certain qualities in one's own birds may be necessary from time to time, the ambitious Budgerigar breeder should set out with the intention of eventually founding a strain of his own and then being able to produce virtually all the birds he requires in his aviaries both for breeding purposes and as exhibitis at the shows.

Such a person will discover that the need for introducing new blood will diminish as the standard of excellence of his own stock increases.

He who strives to establish a strain places the greater reliance when breeding on home-bred birds. He who makes no attempt to found a strain has to pin his faith mainly to those specimens which he buys, which, truly, we all have to do in the first or second year after commencing in a livestock hobby, though this reliance should not persist indefinitely.

The apex of a fancier's ambition should be to own a collection of home-bred specimens practically all possessing high merit and all bearing a family likeness to each other, in fact, all distinguishable as being of a certain ownership.

When a breeder has reached this point in his operations, then his strain will become linked with his name in the public mind, and people will talk of Mr. So-and-So's strain of Greens, or whatever colour (or colours) the birds of this family may be produced in. But even though you may not be honoured to that extent — and few are — it does not follow that you will not gradually evolve a magnificent winning collection of Budgerigars, all bred in your own aviaries, if you apply intelligently the methods which I describe below, and if reasonably good luck attends your efforts.

Great success in exhibiting does not alone warrant an owner to claim to have a strain of his own. He may have won most of his prizes with birds which he has bought, or he may have frequently won with home-bred specimens: but ones which differ greatly in characteristics and which probably are not even slightly related. In other words, they are not members of a family evolved to a high standard of excellence by the owner's own efforts as a breeder for a number of years.

In livestock circles few Fancy terms are more erroneously employed than is "strain". Stock is frequently advertised as being of Mr. —'s strain, when the advertiser does not own a strain to which other breeders place his name, as in the Racing, Homer world, for example, we refer to Gurney's, Barker's, Gitts's, Logan's and other lines, which were founded by their originators through years of highly skilful breeding and whose names pass on to posterity.

I appreciate the fact that many of my readers will not desire to own very large establishments, possess several hundreds of Budgerigars, or become so famous as to have their names handed down to future generations. Well satisfied are the majority of people who pursue our hobby to own small or medium-sized studs – just as many birds, in fact, as they can look after themselves in their spare time without assistance – breed a number of good specimens, exhibit occasionally and win prizes. This type of fancier is most desirable and there is none more worthy of encouragement. And it is such breeders as these who often breed some of the best birds in the country.

THE SMALLER BREEDER

I refer to these owners of medium-sized collections at this juncture because I want to point out that although this chapter aims so high as to apply to those who wish to earn undying fame by establishing strains which will bear their names, the princples which are enunciated are just as applicable to the "smaller" people. Similarly all that I shall say in Chapter 14 on in-breeding and line-breeding should be as valuable to them as to those who may breed several hundreds of chicks per annum and who keep practically every known colour variety in which the Budgerigar is bred. The small stud owner should not come to the conclusion that he cannot evolve a strain. It is quality not quantity that is the touchstone. Some of the best families of Budgerigars have materialised in small establisments, but they have always been produced when the owners have specialised.

I must emphasise the fact that the founding of a strain of one's own is a difficult proposition and it takes years of skilful endeavour to accomplish it. In the first place the owner must be a man of unlimited patience and great determination to overcome difficulties, which he must always face cheerfully. He must be a genuine livestock lover. He must be continuously observant. He must use common sense, and he must develop in the course of time something of an intuition as to how to mate correctly and to know at a glance those birds which will be of assistance to him and those which will in no way serve his purpose.

He will have acquired what is known as a "fancier's eye." No written instruction can alone provide any of my readers with this trait. Some men and women develop it quickly. To others it never comes.

I cannot claim that the methods which I am about to describe are complete. In a contribution of this character one can only deal with basic principles and tendencies. There are exceptions to all livestock breeding theories. In dealing with the production of living things we have to contend with influences which are not fully understood even in these enlightened days when so much biological information and the written teachings of the experience of many breeders are available to us. We are not considering a problem so concrete as, for example, a problem in engineering. Living things do not function with the precision of a machine. And the individual's application of the theories of breeding has a great bearing upon results. Some do the job properly; some do it badly.

KNOWLEDGE OF THE IDEAL

At the outset the fancier must have a thorough understanding of that which he is aiming to obtain. In other words he must have a perfect knowledge of what is required in an ideal Budgerigar. His interpretation of the standard must be absolutely accurate, and the ideal must be ever kept in mind. He must, in short, know perfectly well just what kind of birds will win prizes under the best judges, and similarly he must be familiar with those cardinal faults which make a specimen unworthy of a place in his aviaries. It is his ambition as year succeeds year to produce more and more Budgerigars approximating to the ideal as he visualises it.

It is obvious that the better the Budgerigars purchased as foundation stock the better will be the youngsters produced, and the sooner will the owner be on the road to great achievement. Therefore, as I have said elsewhere in this book, if your means and accommodation are limited, it is far better to buy a few really good birds than a large number of inferior birds. In short, quality before quantity must be the maxim, although, naturally, the more birds of good quality the breeder can afford to buy, the more chances he has of breeding both show birds and desirable stock birds.

The Real Test

It is frequently stated that the fancier with small or moderate financial resources is at a disadvantage compared with the wealthy man. I agree with this assertion if the wealthy man concerned couples with his money ability as a breeder. But in the long run a working man armed with correct knowledge as to how to mate his birds will beat the man of money who lacks this skill and who has to rely on his cheque book to keep his name in the forefront at the shows.

Many fanciers in different sections of the livestock world, who have won for several years with valuable specimens purchased at high prices, have then ceased to lead the classes because they have got tired of writing out cheques and have not established strains capable of continuously producing animals or birds worthy to maintain their reputations.

In livestock culture it is an axiom that one gets out of it what one puts in — plus a little more – and the fewer the faults and the more numerous the good properties in the original pairs, in fact in all the birds used on all occasions when mating, the sooner will success be achieved. Obviously, therefore, it is most desirable to buy the best specimens procurable when laying the foundations of a strain.

"Something Behind Them"

It goes without saying that not only must the original purchases be birds of good quality but they must be healthy, and they must have "something behind them" — in other words, bred themselves from good parents and not what are termed "flashes in the pan." Occasionally an inferior pair of birds will breed a winning youngster even though all its brothers and sisters may be bad ones. When such a product — an oasis in a desert — is used for breeding purposes it is usually a disappointment.

The beginner must realise that he cannot buy perfect specimens, and naturally owners will not often be willing to sell their very best birds except at fantastic prices. All that the beginner can do is to obtain the best procurable for the money which he can afford to spend.

Obviously a great deal depends upon the fancier's ability, or the advice which is given to him when buying his foundation stock. If he buys badly more ruthless elimination will be necessary later, and time will have been lost.

Whenever one procures birds or animals it is always very helpful if one can not only have an *authentic* pedigree supplied with them but also knowledge as to the properties of the parents and even the grandparents, though this is, of course, not always possible.

As time rolls on the disadvantage of not knowing all about antecedents disappears because the owner is using mostly, if not entirely, birds bred by himself and he is, therefore, *completely* familiar with their pedigrees. In my opinion, pedigree plays almost as important a part as does the appearance of the birds themselves, and, of course, in applying the principles of in-breeding ancestry is of vast importance, as my readers will learn from Chapter 14.

Sources of Trouble

I have referred above to the "flash in the pan" and its being often valueless for breeding purposes. Such a specimen is the outcome of luck. Budgerigars in this category are occasionally to be found in consignments intended to be sold as pets or they are produced by unskilful breeders who merely mate birds together haphazardly. These are not the sort of birds with which to establish a strain. The introduction into an establishment of these flukes is often followed by the production of faulty offspring and the retarding of the breeder's progress towards the attainment of his ideal.

For the purpose of this chapter I am assuming that the original pairs are not related, though I should not have the slightest objection to purchasing related specimens if I knew that the owner was a skilful breeder, bred his own winners with regularity, and had an established strain of the colour variety concerned. In fact, I should prefer them.

As I shall explain more fully in Chapter 14 an out-cross, even when birds of merit are employed, frequently brings together latent failings which come to the surface in the progeny. Therefore, great care has to be exercised in examining the first season's youngsters when one has to decide which birds to breed from in the following season and which to dispose of.

Because several of the chicks bred are obviously inferior to their parents and disappointing to the eye, the young fancier should not instantly come to the conclusion that the sellers have not treated him properly. He should realise that this is only his first season, that distinct out-crosses may have been made, and that second season results may cause him to form a very different opinion as to the breeding abilities of his foundation stock.

Towards the end of the first year when all the chicks are in adult plumage the owner should bring into his bird room all the young stock and their parents. Each pair of adult birds should be put into cages, and alongside them there should be caged all the youngsters which they have bred.

The owner's task is to select those birds which he must retain for use in the following breeding season and those which he must dispose of. It is necessary for him to set a certain standard of excellence, only birds attaining that standard to be retained; all the others to go. In the first year this standard will not be set so high as it will be in subsequent years. Every year a higher standard should be fixed. Thus every year better and better breeding pairs will be employed, until the time arrives when all specimens which are bred from are of very high quality.

The selection of the breeding team for the following season should not be left until the time for breeding is actually at hand. It is a good idea to "mate on paper" many weeks before breeding commences. In other words, make a list of the cocks and hens (there should be more hens and cocks) to be retained, and how, broadly speaking, you will mate them together. By adopting this method the breeder knows exactly if his breeding stud is complete or if it is necessary to make any new purchases to fill up gaps.

I admit that bringing in new birds in this way, unless they are related to one's present stock, will cause further out-crossing in the second season (with the consequent efforts of out-crossing as a possibility) but this may be unavoidable, and it is better to act in this manner than to in-breed with inferior stock merely for the sake of in-breeding, as I emphasise in Chapter 14.

Although I believe in in-breeding I never in-breed unless the birds mated are essentially suitable both in appearance and pedigree. Therefore, it naturally follows that in the earlier seasons after commencing, in only a proportion of the pairs are the members related. If all goes well, as year succeeds year more and more pairs will consist of birds related to each other, and as the stud develops so the necessity for out-crosses will diminish. The sooner it disappears altogether so much more pleased should the owner be.

In the early stages of the development of a team of Budgerigars it is absolutely essential to have in your possession individuals possessing all the good properties which you ultimately desire to combine in the majority of the birds you produce; and if you do not bring in all these points with your original purchases, then you must do so with later purchases.

I have already said that you get out what you put in. Therefore, obviously, you must ensure that all the qualities are there before you blend them together by *sensible* in-breeding. Without in-breeding it is impossible ever to reach a stage when all your birds possess the same family characteristics to which I have referred earlier in this chapter.

Now to return to our breeder standing in his bird room in the early winter following his first breeding season with the birds in the cages before him which he has been breeding from and the youngsters which they have produced.

I postulate that he has a good understanding of the ideal Budgerigar, is familiar with the faults which occur in these birds, and has acquired the necessary knowledge as to what is good in-breeding and what is bad in-breeding. He must also decide there and then — and this determination must never leave him — that he will not be tempted to make use of any bird "just to complete a pair" if if does not reach the required standard.

RUTHLESS ELMINATION ESSENTIAL

So his first step is obviously to put on one side all those specimens which are not capable of assisting him to progress. Ruthless elimination in this manner is essential to success, because whether one is in-breeding or not in-breeding the keynote of successful livestock production is undoubtedly **Selection.** *The whole story revolves round the breeder's ability to select mates wisely and never to mate two birds together unless there is a definite purpose for so doing.*

Our first-year enthusiast, who has now to decide how he will mate those birds which are in the cages in the following season, should take the best cock and select *the* most suitable hen for it, then the second best cock and the best available hen for it, and so continue to the end of the matings. In other words he should not, as some breeders do, "average the pairs". This practice consists of mating a very good cock to a hen of inferior quality, or a valuable hen to a moderate cock, based on the theory that the bad properties of one bird should be set off by the good qualities of the other. This system is only likely to yield youngsters of *average* merit and will never improve the stud.

A really good cock is wasted on an inferior hen, and vice versa. To put it simply, if a bird is high-class then its mate should be high-class. It is only then likely that the progeny will be as good or better than the parents.

To apply my remarks to actual major properties, a cock with a large head, for example, should be mated where possible to a hen with a large head with the object of breeding birds excelling in head. Now if we made use of the "averaging" method we should mate that cock to a hen with a small head to correct her failing in that property. The chances are that the outcome would be moderate-headed chicks. The only method of consolidating good points is to have those good points in both mates, and if we can also have them on both sides of the pedigree, so much the better.

Mating on Appearance

I consider it wise to mate the birds on appearances only in the first place, and then consider if there is anything in their breeding which makes any of the "appearance" matings undesirable. We may find that we are mating daughter to father or son to mother. That is alright providing we have not the same faults on both sides of the pair; but even if we are out-crossing we must not have the same faults in both birds. Just as by mating the two good-headed parents together in the above example we expect better heads, so if we mate two parents nipped in neck (say) we shall be likely to breed youngsters nipped in neck.

Our whole object in selecting mates is to consolidate the good points and eliminate the bad points, and that is what I want to instil into the minds of my readers as the principle to which they must ever adhere, not only at the end of this first breeding season but **every** year when deciding upon the matings for the following year's breeding.

Discard Bad Specimens

With further reference to the ruthless elimination of birds which must not be used for breeding purposes, just as those which fall below a certain standard of excellence as regards their exhibition properties must be put aside, so must the owner discard any specimen which has suffered from an illness or which has been a "bad doer" as a chick. Ill-nurtured youngsters or birds which have been seriously indisposed, even though they may *appear* to have become normal, should never be used for breeding purposes however good they may be as Budgerigars. If all fanciers would adopt this advice without the slightest variation, constitutional troubles sometimes encountered would almost cease to exist.

It is impossible to maintain good health and continue to produce strong, virile stock if we fall to the temptation of employing in the breeding aviaries birds which we know cannot be physically sound.

After the Second Season

At the end of the second season the fancier is once again in his bird room and has in the cages all the birds from which he has been breeding and all the youngsters which he has bred from them, the latter in adult plumage.

Even more ruthless elimination is now necessary than that which was exercised in the previous winter. In fact, every year the test which the birds have to pass in order to qualify them for retention has to be made more severe.

The owner will not now find his task of mate selection so difficult as he did after the first season, and in the third year it will be easier still. The position will have become clarified. The breeder will be able to observe from which lines the best youngsters are coming and he will have more knowledge as to the predominant good properties and faults in the different families.

A procedure which is most helpful at the end of the second breeding season, and which should be carried out annually afterwards, is the grading of the parent birds and their progeny in the following manner:-

Take a sheet of paper and classify all the breeding pairs and all the youngsters from them into first grade, second grade, and third grade.

The adult pairs in the first grade will be those which have bred your best youngsters and the fewest inferior youngsters. The second grade adult pairs will be those which, judged in this way, have been moderately successful. The third grade adults will be those whose offspring as a whole do not satisfy you. In this grading the appearance and pedigrees of the parent birds themselves must also be taken into consideration.

Grade all the best youngsters, too, according to the grades in which you have put their parents, their own merit, and the quality of their brothers and sisters. It is possible that in the third grade there is a pair which has bred a most attractive youngster but whose brothers and sisters entirely fail to satisfy. This odd swan amongst the geese would not cause me to place its parents in a higher grade, and whilst I might retain that youngster for breeding I should not have the same confidence in it that I should have in one that had better nest mates.

Having finished this grading, if you have in the first grade sufficient adults and youngsters to complete the number of breeding pairs which your aviaries will accommodate, so much the better. Failing this, select the best birds in the second grade, and you can include—with the reservation I have made above—that very good youngster which may have come from grade three parents.

In practice, we sometimes put the cock of a pair in one grade and the hen in another. This is done in cases where we come to the conclusion that the failings in the youngsters are due to one of the parents and that if the other parent had a more suitable mate it would breed much better chicks.

FOUNDATION BIRDS

Some Budgerigars which not only excel in show properties but which consistently produce high-class youngsters are "starred". Such birds are worth their weight in gold and become "foundation" birds. In livestock breeding establishments these "star" specimens appear from time to time; for example in racehorses there was long ago the mighty *St. Simon* and in more recent times that wonderful stallion, *Solario*. The progeny of these sires have made racing history. Correctly employed, a Budgerigar of this kind can itself found a famous family. It is a bird of this quality which occupies a key position in a line-breeding or in-breeding scheme.

You want to breed as many relatives of a "foundation" bird as you possibly can, because your aim should be to consolidate its own good visible properties and, which is even more important, the power to reproduce them consistently.

If it becomes quite obvious that your Budgerigars generally are failing in any particular property, and it is clear that you have nothing in your own stock to correct the weakness, then, in my opinion, the proper procedure is to purchase a number of birds excelling in that point. If, for instance, too many of your youngsters are coming regularly small in head, some big-headed out-crosses must be brought in. Later, when there are in the stud , all the good properties in abundance, and few, if any, even minor failings, then indeed it is a rare occurrence for there to arise the necessity for a new purchase, for the breeder has all that he requires in his own aviaries. Sometimes the stage is reached where a new purchase is practically never necessary.

When buying the original pairs, when introducing new specimens later, when preparing breeding plans, and when "mating the birds on paper," the greatest thought should be given to the qualifications of the hens. In all livestock culture, important as are the sires, the dams are more so. I hold the view that the female has usually a greater influence on the quality of the progeny than has the male. Whilst in Budgerigar breeding it is folly to mate a good hen to an inferior cock, it is even more foolish and wasteful to put a high-class cock to a mediocre hen. The fancier who buys an expensive cock and who does not provide a hen for it of at least equal merit, is definitely crippling his chances of breeding youngsters worthy of their sire.

All the most successful livestock breeders I have known have been those who have paid great attention to the female members of their studs. I am acquainted with some breeders of Budgerigars who have bought valuable cocks at the shows and elsewhere, but who do not turn out home-bred winners simply because the hens in their possession are greatly inferior to the cocks.

Every year as the time for mating approaches the process of skilful selection and ruthless elimination must be repeated. If progress is maintained, after a few years so well established will the stud become, so many good Budgerigars will it contain, and so well bred will they be, that—except in a few cases—in so far as pedigree is concerned, almost any bird can be mated to any other bird, providing there is not *too intensive* in-breeding. When this pleasing position has been arrived at, pedigree can then receive less consideration, and the visible properties can, to all intents and purposes, become almost solely the guide when the mating scheme is being prepared.

Useful to Others

I have stressed the necessity for ruthless elimination of birds not considered to be suitable for the breeder's own requirements. I wish to make it clear, however, that the specimens thus set aside for disposal may be valuable to those who purchase them. Although they may not fit into one fancier's breeding plan, they may be just right for another man's purpose. In fact, birds produced in a stud which is being correctly evolved will be more valuable to novices and others than will those which are the outcome of mating at random. Therefore, a breeder who is establishing his collection of Budgerigars on good lines can sell his surplus birds with confidence, providing they have been well reared and are healthy, and the buyers have equal faith.

Neither in business, livestock breeding, nor any other human endeavour do I place much reliance on the Goddess Luck, and yet the fact remains that the breeder can have a share of either good luck or bad luck in his breeding operations, and he does need some of the former if he is to breed many

178

famous birds.

I shall refer at some length in Chapter 14 to the consideration which must be given when mates are being selected to latent faults, not necessarily apparent in the birds themselves but which we know were possessed by some of their antecedents. But, as I have indicated, of even more importance than pedigree are the actual visible properties. So first of all we must decide each mating on appearances, and then consider whether the pairing remains suitable after parentage has also been considered. The maxims which I am about to describe concern visible qualities. The application of them, conjointly with possible latent weaknesses, will be explained in the next chapter.

Never mate together two birds with the same failing. If the cock fails in head and the hen fails in head, the probability is that the youngsters will fail in head, and the same remarks apply to every fault of which a Budgerigar can be the possessor.

In order to improve any particular point you should have it good in both the cock and the hen, e.g. if you wish to fix spots, and breed youngsters with this marking *in excelsis,* have them good in both sire and dam.

If one member of a pair excels in depth of chest (say) and the other member is very deficient in chest, the likelihood is that their progeny will only be moderately deep in chest.

Correcting Minor Faults

If you have a bird which is rather cloudy in wing markings, for instance, but which is so good in other respects that it earns its place in your breeding team, you must select a mate for it which is perfect in wing markings. By doing this the chances are that the youngsters will be better in markings than one parent and inferior to the other. This is the only way to correct minor faults; you should endeavour not to breed at all from Budgerigars with major faults if your object is the breeding of winners. In the following season you will select the best-marked youngsters from the mating and pair them to perfectly marked birds. This selective process is continued until the failing is eradicated.

Of course, the properties I have referred to above are merely given as examples.

I am sure that after perusing what I have written above, and shall write in Chapter 14, my readers will realise quite clearly that the whole story of success in the production of winning animals and birds can be condensed into two words—*selection* and *elimination.*

My friend, Lt.-Col. J.Y. Baldwin, who erstwhile was a famous breeder of Nun pigeons and who later made history with Alsatian dogs, adopts a method of mating which, judging by the extraordinary results he has achieved, is worthy of the serious consideration of all breeders of livestock.

Briefly his system is this:-

In the first place when breeding Nuns—which I will take as my example for the benefit of the readers of this book—he set himself a standard of excellence and any bird falling below that standard would not be used by him for breeding purposes under any circumstances.

He adopted the plan which I advocate of keeping, in addition to pedigrees, a detailed record of all the failings and good properties not only of the birds at one time in his possession and which were of sufficient merit for him to use for breeding purposes, but also of birds which had died or which he had sold and from which he had obtained youngsters, so that in all cases he had a description of the appearance of parents, grandparents, and great-grandparents.

When deciding upon his matings, any bird which failed in any major property was provided with a mate which was not only good in that property itself but whose parents, grandparents and (if possible) great-grandparents were also good in that particular point. By adopting this plan he was definitely consolidating the property in which the bird for which he was selecting a mate was deficient.

The wisdom of this procedure will be obvious, particularly to those who agree with the advice which I have already given in this chapter. Of course it will not always be possible for a breeder to carry out Lt.-Col. Baldwin's system to the letter, because he may not always have knowledge of the properties of antecendents for three generations, especially in those instances where the birds have been purchased. After a few years of breeding the fancier will possess a description of all the home-bred stock which comes into the breeding plan and it will therefore be easier as time goes on to adopt the method described almost fully.

In-breeding was automatically indulged in by Col. Baldwin, and I can well remember his Nuns being all of one pattern. There is nothing in this procedure which is contrary to the breeding systems which I advocate in *The Cult of the Budgerigar*. On the contrary, I consider that Col. Baldwin's success achieved by the application of the theory which he evolved is further proof of the soundness of the methods advocated in this chapter and in the next.

CHECKING THE PLANS

I have referred above to "matings on paper" and the wisdom of knowing how you propose to pair your birds on a date well in advance of the commencement of the breeding season. In the case of Budgerigars, unlike other forms of livestock, you will find that you will have to change many of your "paper" matings when the time arrives for you to put the pairs together, and for the following reason.

In a number of cases you will discover that both members of a chosen pair are not in breeding condition at the same time; and in other cases after the nest box has been put up one member of a pair, almost invariably the hen, will let you down, and another mate has to be provided. To control these possibilities it is advisable to have alternative mates for every cock, which is the reason why it is desirable to retain for breeding purposes more hens than cocks.

The situation described is capable of upsetting a breeding plan to some extent, but it is one of those things which in Budgerigar culture we have to grin and bear.

I wish Budgerigars were like racing pigeons in so far as breeding condition is concerned. After pigeons have completed their moult in the autumn you know that they will remain in full feather until the following breeding season is over, and that when they once attain good breeding condition they will retain it until the time comes to break the pairs. Consequently, when our Modena pigeons are "mated on paper" I know full well that the pairs will stand as I have written them, and that there will be no changes such as are forced on the Budgerigar breeder. This assists greatly in the devising and carrying out of a breeding plan.

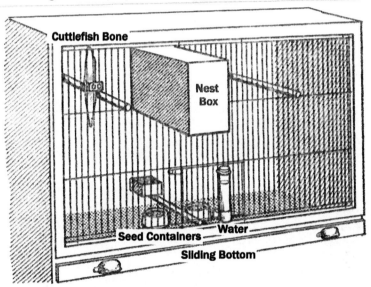

Figure 13.1 Breeding Cage (Designed by Cyril Rogers)

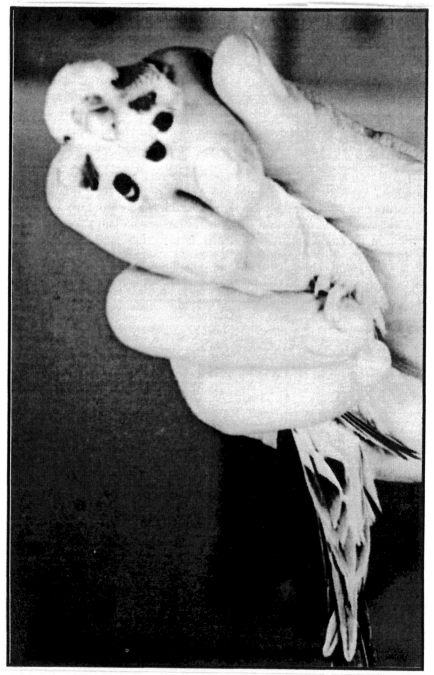

Figure 13-2   Holding a bird correctly

CHAPTER 14

IN-BREEDING

BASIC DEFINITIONS

Different authorities give different definitions of the distinctions between **line-breeding** and **in-breeding.** Personally I have always found it impossible in practice to differentiate completely between the two. Some say that in-breeding is the mating of very close relations and line-breeding the mating of more distant relations, and in a rough-and-ready way there may be wisdom in these definitions. But if we adopt this dictum the difficulty is in knowing at what point in-breeding ceases and line-breeding commences, or vice-versa.

Myself, I lean to the idea that the in-breeder is one who mates relations to fix good properties possessed by the birds which he is employing in his breeding aviary, and that the line-breeder is really establishing families based upon particular "foundation" sires or "foundation" dams. In other words, he is endeavouring to reproduce particular birds with any improvements he can make upon them by skilful selection as he goes along.

If this is accepted as a broad principle it will be seen that breeders of horses and breeders of cattle using outstanding sires or dams and breeding back regularly to those sire or dams and their progeny without in-breeding so closely as father to daughter or mother to son, except maybe on isolated occasions, can claim to be more line-breeders than in-breeders.

But the breeder of Budgerigars who is not opposed to the mating of relations, whilst he, too, will use "foundation"birds as does the line-breeder in cattle and horses, will also put together specimens very closely related and which in themselves cannot be termed "foundation" birds. Consequently I, personally, am unable to say that I am definitely a line-breeder or definitely an in-breeder. My method is really a combination of the two, which I think is satisfactorily covered by the more comprehensive term "in-breeding."

Some advocates of line-breeding prepare rather elaborate charts to show how the descendants of a given pair of birds should be mated in order to produce that ideal after a number of generations which was the objective at the commencement.

The birds are treated as units and selection does not play such an important part as I consider it should do. Personally I have not a lot of faith in these charts, because I do not believe that one can ever bring the breeding of winners down to a mathematical process. It it were all so simple as these charts would lead us to believe the uncertainty of breeding pedigree animals and birds, which is one of its greatest charms, would disappear and we should all produce high-class individuals with almost monotonous regularity and ease.

The breeding of superior exhibition specimens cannot be accomplished by the application of anything in the nature of mathematics.

PURPOSE OF IN-BREEDING

In-breeding is the mating of relations but the in-breeding which is advocated by so many successful livestock breeders does not mean breeding from a pair of related birds merely because they are related. The in-breeding to which this chapter is devoted is the pairing of related birds with a specific object, viz., that of fixing and producing *in exelsis* good properties of the particular Budgerigars which are being used and the good properties possessed by their ancestors, and at the same time avoiding as far as is humanly possible intensifying faults or constitutional weaknesses.

Although sensible in-breeding is the near cut to success and whilst the capable in-breeder will beat the man who never in-breeds, in-breeding can be a short road to failure, because it is just as easy to in-breed faults as it is good points; and it is the avoidance of the in-breeding of faults and the knowledge of the right moment at which to bring in an out-cross, if one is required, where the skill of the breeder is proved.

As I have already indicated, the in-breeder's object is to fix in the members of a strain all the good properties and none of the bad ones. If reasonable and well-applied in-breeding is employed that object can almost be attained — there is no such thing as perfection — but if it is unskilfully and carelessly applied then in-breeding can fix more of the bad points in a strain than it can good ones.

Correct in-breeding not only produces birds which are good exhibition specimens but it produces birds which are capable of breeding younsters as good or better than themselves, something which the continuous mating of unrelated stock cannot be relied upon to do.

The outcome of in-breeding will be satisfactory or unsatisfactory according to the quality of the birds used in the breeding aviary – in other words, the quality of the relations mated together and their suitability to each other. It is better in every way to breed from unrelated stock in

184

preference to putting relations together without any known reason for so doing. Such reckless in-breeding as this obviously conducted by one lacking in knowledge of the principles of in-breeding can do irreparable harm.

Consistent and intensive in-breeding should only be undertaken by one who thoroughly understands what he is about. I do not advise novices owning small studs of birds of only moderate quality to in-breed extensively in their early years. It is advisable for them to rely upon birds which they have purchased and the advice as to mating which is at their disposal by the person who sells them their stock or by experienced fanciers to whose opinions they have access.

No fancier should in-breed with two birds unless he is perfectly satisfied with both their appearance and their pedigrees. He must be familiar not only with the good and bad qualities of the birds themselves but also of their parents, grandparents, and even farther back still if possible. All families have their good points and their bad points. The best families have the fewer faults, the worst families the most faults.

A pair of birds can, as we all know, breed a Patronage Show winner and a very bad youngster in the same nest. The Patronage Show winner may be said to be representative of the best in the family, the bad youngster representative of the worst in the family.

To in-breed with that very inferior specimen would obviously be the way to produce further inferior specimens. In chapter 13 I advised that when deciding upon a mating the first thing to take into consideration is the appearance of the two birds which the owner proposes to put together, and that, having become satisfied that they are a good match in so far as appearances are concerned, he should proceed to consider their parentage, if knowledge of the quality of their parents is available to him. Information about antecedents is of great importance when one is in-breeding, because in-breeding is calculated to bring to the surface latent failings handed down from a previous generation. I will take a hypothetical case: —

We have before us two related birds. We desire to fix, and improve upon, their own good points, and for which properties their family are generally noted. Because they are related they are both more likely to possess the ability to reproduce those good properties. If they were not related one might have the factors for the good properties. If they were not related one might have the factors for the good properties but not the other, which is the reason why in a case of this kind it is wiser to mate related birds than unrelated birds.

Let us assume that one of the good properties concerned is head. Both excel in skull and our knowledge of their parents and probably their grandparents is such that we are aware of the fact that good heads are a characteristic of this particular family. Obviously, then, in so far as head is concerned these two birds are perfectly suitable.

Consider all Properties

But when deciding upon a mating every property has to be considered. So we now turn to spots. We know that although this family is productive of most excellent Budgerigars, it is rare for a really good spotted youngster to come from them. They are all inclined to be small in spots. That being the case we must ascertain most carefully that neither of the two birds possesses that weakness. If both are small in spots they must not go together or we shall definitely still further engender the production of small spots; in fact, in such circumstances if *one* is reasonably good in spots and the other poor in spots it would not be wise in-breeding to produce youngsters from this pair of birds.

This is a definite rule to which all in-breeders must adhere in regard to all major weaknesses and as far as is humanely possible as regards all minor faults as well. In a word, it is of vital importance that one should never in-breed with two specimens if one of them possesses a weakness which occurs with any frequency in representatives of that particular family.

Do not overlook the fact that a serious failing in an ancestor may not show itself for a number of generations, hence the great desirability of keeping accurate descriptions of the properties of any birds which have been bred from and which may have died or have been sold.

When an old fault recurs unexpectedly it must receive immediate attention with a view to its elimination; otherwise in-breeding will consolidate it.

Constitutional Weakness

What I have written with regard to the possibility of propagating property faults applies with equal force to the dangers of weakening constitution in the strain if the greatest care is not always taken to avoid in-breeding from any stock which is not absolutely constitutionally sound. You must be convinced of the health of every bird which you breed from. Adopt this plan religiously and you need not fear that well-controlled in-breeding will cause weakness of constitution.

In the last few paragraphs I have deliberately stressed the dangers of continuous in-breeding if proper care is not exercised by the owner. I have done this because I know that many of those who condemn in-breeding do so because of results which it is not fair to attribute to the practice of in-breeding but which should have been rightly ascribed to the improper methods of the breeders concerned.

But before my readers proceed to study this subject I want them to have well fixed in their minds the idea that the natural expectation of producing a good property in a youngster is all the greater if the factors governing the production of that good property are possessed by both parents, and that obviously the probability of both parents possessing those factors is increased if the two birds are related.

That, in a few words, sums up the value of in-breeding and gives the reason why it can be the short cut to success in the production of exhibition Budgerigars of high quality, providing – and here I am repeating myself for the purpose of emphasis — the greatest care is exercised in ensuring that two birds used will not instead of propagating good properties propagate bad properties or constitutional weaknesses. These dangers can be avoided only by the continuous exercising of careful selection and ruthless elimination.

Why Results Vary

When two good, unrelated birds are mated together they often breed some attractive youngsters because it so happens that they suit each other as mates not only as regards appearances but as regards their concealed qualities. On the other hand, as often as not when two unrelated specimens are paired they breed youngsters which are not so good as themselves or which, in fact, may be really inferior specimens.

This is because they do not *both* carry all the factors for the most desirable properties of their species, and which diversity would probably not exist if they were related. To put is simply, these parents are good in themselves but they do not blend well.

In-breeding brings "the dirt to the surface" and discloses to the owner the failings he has to contend with — in other words those points which by selection and elimination he has to eradicate from his stock. Without in-breeding those weaknesses might have remained hidden for a lengthy period only to come forth and cause trouble in later seasons.

When we know how we stand as regards the good properties and the bad properties which we have available to us in our breeding team we know better how handle the situation. Therefore, on many occasions we should not blame in-breeding for the appearance of failings but bless it for having brought the trouble to our notice. It is as well that we should know all about weaknesses in our birds, and, armed with such knowledge, proceed to eliminate them, it being, as I have already stated, our principal object to consolidate all the best qualities in the stud and dispel the worst.

Breeding Back to One Parent

In actual practice it often occurs that one in-breeds back to one parent and not to the other. Here is an example. A cock with an extraordinarily good head and with, so far as can be ascertained, ancestors and brothers and sisters also very good in head, is mated to an unrelated hen only fair in head and not coming from a particulary good-headed family. Both the cock and

187

the hen are shapely and pleasing in other points. The youngsters from this mating are satisfactory in all their qualities except head, in which they are deficient. It can be decided that they have inherited the weakness of head from the dam. Therefore, it would obviously be a mistake to mate one of the young cocks back to its mother, as we should only be fixing weakness in head. On the other hand, it would be wise to pair one of the young hens back to her sire in order to fix his good properties, plus the other good properties which we have secured from the dam (apart from head); and at the same time we should be improving head in the next generation.

However skilful the in-breeder may be, however great the care he may exercise in the avoidance of fixing in his strain any faults of structure, colour or markings, any weakness in constitution, or any tendency towards sterility or other inheritable characteristic, sometimes after a number of seasons of in-breeding with a particlar family, failings unexpectedly begin to appear. Suddenly, almost without warning, some of the youngsters bred may fail somewhat in a particular point. As soon as such a sign becomes apparent the breeder must realise that the time has arrived when an out-cross has to be made.

For the purpose of example let us imagine that the birds are declining somewhat in size. We must bring in at least one unrelated specimen excelling in size and not deficient in any of the points which we have already established *in excelsis* in out stock. If possible we must convince ourselves that the relatives of the out-cross do not fail in those properties and are also big birds. If the out-cross also comes from a strain in which correct in-breeding has been employed, it is all the more valuable, because it is more likely to be prepotent for its own good properties.

Having purchased the out-cross (which, for the sake of explanation, we will presume to be a cock), what now has to be done is to graft his good qualities into our own in-bred family. We take the best of the young hens bred from him and mate her back to her father. Thus we secure a dose of the father on both sides. Some people, having introduced an out-cross, go so far as to mate brothers and sisters from the pair of which the out-cross is one member, but I do not advise this *unless both birds are of exceptionally high quality.*

I have known brother X sister produce splendid youngsters, but, as a method of very close in-breeding, I prefer father X daughter or son X mother. Actually when pairing brother to sister you are only re-assembling the properties of the two parents, which theoretically may not seem to be progressive, though where two birds of outstanding merit and breeding are concerned, there are occasions, as above indicated, when this pairing can be made with gratifying results.

It is an excellent plan to mate the out-cross to two birds in the first season in order to breed a number of half-brothers and sisters.

By pairing these half-brothers and sisters you get the blood of the out-cross on both sides, which is what you aimed to do. From the progeny of the out-cross in the first generation you can by systematic in-breeding and selection impress the good quaities of the out-cross upon the family with which you have orginally merged it.

It must be agreed that you always stand a better chance of fixing a property if you have the factors for that property on both sides of a mating. Now if you buy a bird for the purpose of improving a particular property, how can you ever have a dose of that property on both sides of a mating if you do not mate relatives? Without consanguinity you would always have that bird's influence on one side only. A moment's thought will prove to you that this statement is correct.

I have referred to the mating of half-brothers and sisters. I consider this to be one of the best forms of in-breeding at any time. It is particularly useful when utilising one of those "foundation" sires or dams to which I referred in Chapter 13. These "foundation" birds are usually the outcome of skilful in-breeding. They are prepotent for their properties; they are homozygous for all that is best in a good exhibition specimen. I have known such valuable breeding forces in pigeons and other livestock which would stamp their pleasing characteristics on all their progeny no matter to what they were mated, although naturally for "foundation" birds one selects high-class mates.

Having proved you are the owner of a bird of this character, half-brothers and sisters bred from it are invaluable for carrying on the line.

You want to spread through your stud all those qualities in which a "foundation" bird excels. Therefore, you breed back again and again to that bird or its progency. Call this system line-breeding or in-breeding, it is undoubtedly the method which has brought into existence some of the most successful birds and animals of all kinds that have ever been seen. It is only by in-breeding or line-breeding, whichever you term it, that you can consolidate and improve upon the properties of a "foundation" bird.

OUTCROSSING

Indiscriminate out-crossing can ruin a strain. Externally the out-cross birds introduced may appear to be capable of effecting the improvements desired, but all the owner gets for his pains is a crop of unexpected faults not previously occuring extensively amongst his own birds, and not necessarily observable in the birds of the out-cross or in their parents. The seller of the out-cross is not to blame; neither is the purchaser. It is just a case of two unrelated families being unblendable.

I am, of course, taking an extreme case. It by no means infrequently occurs that quite unrelated specimens do blend and winning youngsters are produced in the first generation. But here again luck has much to do with the matter for one can never be perfectly confident of the *first* results when a complete out-cross is brought in. Nevertheless, I am not one of those who dogmatically asserts that it should *never* be necessary to introduce an unrelated bird into a good in-bred family.

But in view of the risk attendant on the mating of unrelated stock the wise breeder looks for some method of modifying the dangers of out-crossing when out-crossing of some kind has become completely unavoidable if progress is to be maintained or improvements effected. I will describe two systems which have proved most efficacious. Their employment is not really true out-crossing; it can be better described as semi-out-crossing.

The Two-Line System

The first plan is to have two (some have more than two) inbred strains in the same colour or group of colours in the one establisment. The birds of one line are distantly related to the birds of the other line.

When an out-cross is required in Family A it is taken from Family B, or vice versa. Such matings are only made when absolutely necessary, and any youngsters which the owner retains from this semi-outcross are carefully transferred to Family A or Family B, not being used first in one line and then in the other. This assists in keeping the two families so apart that they do not become one family only, which is the danger when the dual (or maybe treble) family system is in operation.

Some years ago I was talking to the late Charlie Thompson, of Darlington, who bred more champion English rabbits than any other breeder. He told me that he adopted the two-line method, which I have described, and that in 25 years he never introduced an unrelated animal into his rabbitry.

The second semi-out-crossing system is to buy birds from another owner who has been breeding skilfully with stock originating from the same source as one's own strain, and, therefore, related to it. It is, of course, not by any means always possible to do this. When it is practicable, however, it often has most desirable effects. The fact that the birds have been kept in a different part of the country, or for some other reason not easy to ascertain, seems to make these relatives capable of bringing into another establishment a new vigour – equivalent to what is known as hybrid vigour – usually associated only with the complete out-cross. And these new birds brought in from a distance sometimes give better results than do birds bred within the establishment. Here is an example:-

When we first started with Light Yellows at Lintonholme we bought our initial breeding stock from Mr. R.J. Watts. The late Lady Bromley Wilson also laid the foundations of her winning team of Light Yellows with birds bred by Mr. Watts. Years later we introduced some of Her Ladyship's birds into our stud. They blended immediately, and the combination had a lot to do with the success that followed. Mr. Watts, by the way, as I say elsewhere in this book, had evolved his strain of Light Yellows by means of in-breeding.

Usually when an out-cross is introduced its purpose is to improve certain properties in which a particular family is lacking. The object is to absorb the good points of the out-cross without simultaneously absorbing any undesirable features.

Very occasionally the process is reversed, and the owner's own family is blended to the out-cross. I will explain this more clearly by describing an imaginary case.

A fancier, Mr A., owns a collection of Budgerigars which are all mostly in-bred. He is not satisfied with their general quality. They are alike in type, but winners are not forthcoming with any regularity. The owner has not had sufficiently good material with which to work. When he has brought the best out of his stock by careful selection, elimination and in-breeding (to a large or small extent), that best has just not been good enough. And, believe me, this can often happen.

Now a competitor of his, Mr B, is beating him at the shows. Mr B is persuaded to sell one, or at the most two, of his better quality specimens to Mr A. Mr A cannot get more of Mr B's strain in order to breed himself more of this successful family. What can he do?

He can make the best of his own and mate them to birds he has purchased from Mr B. The first generation youngsters will be mated back to Mr A's birds. In the second year, birds with more of Mr B's blood in them than Mr A's blood will be mated together. And so it will go on until the pedigrees will contain a lot of Mr B's strain and little or none of Mr A's. The birds purchased originally from Mr B will have been used as the foundation of a new family.

NO STRAINS OF THEIR OWN

Those fanciers who will never mate relations and who avow that they are entirely opposed to in-breeding, unless they have a very large Budgerigar establishment, cannot possibly avoid regularly buying a number of birds in order to prevent consanguinity; and those who have to depend on making extensive purchases annually obviously have to rely as much upon the ability of the breeder or breeders from whom they buy as they have upon their own capability. This seems to me to be contrary to what should be be the ambition of every owner, viz., to build up a strain of his own capable of producing the majority of his winners and stock birds.

I have already indicated that I am not opposed to making purchases to bring into a stud that in which it is lacking if there are any signs of decline in one's own in-bred strain; but I consider that if a breeder has *continually* to being in new blood in an attempt to maintain his position, he is not only putting himself to what should be unnecessary expense but he is running a grave risk of bespoiling that which he should already have accomplished by his own efforts. The risk he runs is that of introducing birds the latent characterstics of wich are an unknown quantity.

I should not write with such confidence about the virtues of in-breeding if correctly pursued, and I should not have been able with any authority to say what I have said in this chapter and also in the last one if I had not proved in actual practice all that I have said.

It is not with any desire to be egotistical that I mention the fact that my father and I built up studs of English Owls and African Owls respectively which were supreme in their day by the applications of those principles which I have enunciated. During the last ten years I have established a stud of Modena Pigeons, members of which are winning many prizes in the hottest competitions, and I have in-bred these birds more closely than I have ever in-bred before.

I have a family or Red Chequers which have been in-bred for eight years without an out-cross. They are recognised as being the best Modenas of their colour in the world. They have won the highest honours at the leading shows including the Esquilant Trophy at the Dairy show. They are all exactly similar in type. Their vigour is unimpaired. There fertility is excellent, better, in fact, than in some other colours in the loft which are less closely in-bred.

I do not refer to these successes vain-gloriously but only with the purpose of proving my own sincerity. Scores of examples could I bring forward of achievements with all kinds of exhibition animals and birds to bear testimony to my contentions. And I can assert that our own Budgerigars would not have gained much success if there had not been any in-breeding in our aviaries.

THE CRITICS ANSWERED

Now I will deal with the objections to in-breeding which are at times expressed. I contend that in-breeding is often blamed unjustifiably when it is not the in-breeding that is at fault but the manner in which it is applied. I have admitted that in-breeding is a two-edged sword. Just as in-breeding can bring high success so can it be the cause of dismal failure, and it is the failures which have given rise to those objections with which I am now about to deal.

A stock criticism is that in-breeding is contrary to nature. This is absolutely wrong. There is undoubtedly a tremendous amount of in-

192

breeding amongst gregarious wild birds. This is uncontrolled in-breeding. The birds mate as their fancy dictates and not as a fancier decides. I have indicated that uncontrolled in-breeding can lead to disaster. Therefore why does it not do so well in wild life? The answer is because of that world-old rule, the survival of the fittest. The health and vigour of wild birds and animals are maintained because of the ruthless elimination of the unfit, which cannot survive climatic conditions and destruction by natural enemies.

This is like unto the law of the jungle and it assures the maintenance of the vigour of the race. On the other hand, the fancier keeping livestock in domesticity protects them from all those handicaps with which wild creatures have to contend and he has himself to enforce that ruthless elimination of the undesirable which is so essential to ultimate success.

Another criticism levelled against in-breeding is that it reduces vigour. I have already agreed that it will do so *if it is allowed to* but I think I have shown you how this can be avoided. Numerous examples could I bring to show that skilful in-breeding can increase vigour, just as I could bring evidence to prove that the indiscriminate mating of related stock can reduce vigour; and contrary to the contention of many people, the same remarks apply to size.

LINE-BREEDING OF JERSEY CATTLE

A striking example of how health and stamina have not only been maintained but actually improved by the continuous mating of related animals is provided by Jersey cattle.

In Jersey it has been illegal since 1862 for cattle of any kind to be allowed on to the island except for immediate slaughter. Consequently there must have been continuous line or in-line breeding, and yet the quality and health of the Jersey cattle has improved and the milk yield and the butter-fat content of the milk has increased. There has, however, been the strictest control by the Royal Jersey Agricultural Society of all breeding operations, and no cow or bull can be used for breeding purposes until it has passed a test for both appearance and pedigree conducted by the Society's inspectors. It will thus be understood that there obtains in Jersey that strict elimination and selection which I have emphasised in the course of this chapter *must* be carried out if in-breeding is to achieve its object and not be in any way harmful.

And then we have those people who tell us that in-breeding is unscientific. To contradict this I will quote at length from some of our leading students of biology:-

The late Chritian Wreidt wrote of the virtues of in-breeding in his book,

Heredity in Live-stock*. He proved that in-breeding consolidates the good properties by producing birds in greater numbers homozygous for such good properties. A specimen which is homozygous for a property has the factor for it in double dose. Wreight wrote:–

"The Mendelian law teaches us . . that in-breeding results automatically in homozygous constitution. Experiments show that in-breeding in itself is not detrimental, but the genetic factors of the animal used in in-breeding alone determine whether the results are good or bad."

Wreidt demonstrated conclusively what I have already stated earlier in this chapter — that when faults and constitutional weaknesses appear by in-breeding, that is actually a point in favour of this practice it has brought to the surface weakness which are latent and which without in-breeding we should not be able so quickly to eliminate.

According to Wreidt, by skilful in-breeding we decrease the numberof birds heterozygous for bad properties and increase the unumber homozygous for desired properties.

Wriedt asserted that the genotype (the genetical constitution) of an animal or bird can be even more important than its actual shape and colouring. Specimens which consistently produce good offspring (the foundation birds which I have referred above) even with different mates, and which stamp their excellence upon their descendants are (*vide* Wreidt) homozygous dominants and such birds are produced by in-breeding, and continued in-breeding the number of homozygous offspring is also increased. Other quotations from Wreidt which support my arguments are the following: –

"There is no sire of any breed so prepotent as an in-bred sire."

"By in-breeding it is possible to determine whether a breed contains general defects which will have . . . bad consequences. If a breed has remained sound and strong through several generations of in-breeding there is every reason to believe that there are no defects hidden in that breed . . ."

"By careful in-breeding and careful selection through four to five generations a breed will be found which is constant for those factors selcted as a basis, and at the same time free from hidden defects."

"The basis on which breeding must rest is the homozygosity to be obtained by intensive in-breeding in conjunction with strict selection."

And here is a quotation from the late Mr E.C. Richardson, who was a scientific correspondent to *Fur and Feather:*-

"The leading authority is *The Effects of In-breeding and Cross Breeding on Guinea Pigs,* by Sewell Wright, published by the United States Dept. of Agriculture in two small volumes.

"Wright's experiments involved the breeding of about 30,000 pigs, and

* Wreidt — *Heredity in Live-stock* (Macmillan & Co. Ltd.).

194

the description of them, together with his commentaries, brings out clearly why in-breeding, accompanied by rigorous selection, should be the general rule, whilst an occasional out-cross may be desirable.

"Very briefly, in-breeding, unaccompanied by selection, brings to the surface all characters good and bad. Hence in-breeding, plus selection, tends to preserve the good qualities. Owing, however, to the fact that mutations sometimes occur in stock, and to the fact that mutations tend, as a rule, to be harmful, there may be a tendency to deteriorate with which selection inside an in-bred stock is not powerful enough to combat and in such cases an out-cross may be desirable."

A Single Line

Eugene Davenport in *The Principles of Breeding** wrote:-

"By 'line-breeding' is meant the restriction of selection and mating to the individuals of a single line of descent. The purpose of this system of breeding is real breed improvement—to get the best that can be gotten out of the race, and better than ever before if possible.

"Experience has shown that if the purpose be breed improvement carried to its limits, it is not enough to confine selection to the limits of the breed. All breeds are exceedingly variable, and real results aiming at anything more than mere multiplication can follow only closely drawn lines within the breed—breeding in line, or line-breeding.

"Line-breeding excludes everything outside the approved and chosen line of breeding. It not only combines animals very similar in their characters, but it narrows the pedigree to few and closely related lines of descent. This 'purifies' the pedigree rapidly and gives the ancestry the largest possible opportunity. The system is eminently conservative. It discourages variability, and rapidly reduces it to a minimum. Moreover, whatever variations do occur will be *in line with the prominent characters of the chosen branch of the breed.*

"The nature of results secured by this system (line-breeding) can almost certainly be predicted; and when they do appear, and improvement is at hand, it is backed up by the most powerful hereditary influence obtainable, because of the simplicity and strength of the ancestry, which, if the selection has been good, all 'pulls' in the same direction. The records of all breeds will show the pronounced results that have followed judicious line-breeding. A volume could be filled with pictures of famous animals so produced . . .

"No other system of breeding has ever secured the results that line-breeding has secured, and if the present state of knowledge is reasonably sound, no other system will ever be so powerful in getting the most possible out of a given breed or variety, and this with the greatest certainty as we go

* Davenport — *The Principles of Breeding: Thremmatology* (Ginn and Company).

along. The only requirement is *not to abandon individual selection*. A pedigree is not a crutch on which incompetence can lean; it is a guaranty of blood lines — a field *inside* of which breeding operations and selection may with confidence be confined.

"The word 'confined' is used advisedly, for, after line-breeding has been practised for a few generations, the ancestry become a kind of pure breed of its own — a breed within a breed, so to speak — and any attempt to introduce blood from other lines is likely to be followed by the pains and penalties of hybridisation; for a departure from line-breeding is a kind of crossing in a small degree, and so rapidly do blood lines become intensified that line-bred animals assume all the attributes of distinct strains, as they in truth are, and they will be likely to behave as such ever after.

"In saying that line-bred animals tend to behave like pure strains, and that their progeny from union with other strains behave like hybrids, it is not meant that such unions should never be made, or that such behaviour is as persistent as with real crosses. In truth, many lines are so stubborn as never to blend with others afterward (behaving like the most strongly established races), but, on the other hand, most of them will yield to well-directed and persistent effort; that is to say, a line-bred herd *can* be modified, and in time made to assume the characters of another family, but the process is attended with a struggle and not a few failures. It has been fashionable at times to decry line-breeding, but the fact remains that a few generations of good breeding soon bring the herd and its career to a point where *line-breeding must be practised* or a worse alternative must be accepted, for with well-selected strains all out-breeding is mixed breeding . . .

A Close Relation

"Line-breeding carried to its limits involves the breeding together of individuals closely related. When it involves the breeding together of sire and offspring or of dam and offspring or of brother and sister, it becomes in-breeding, or 'breeding in and in'. It is line-breeding carried to its limits, and of course possesses all the advantages and disadvantages of that form of breeding carried to their utmost attainable degree.

"Three forms of in-breeding are possible amongst animals, namely:–

"1. Breeding the sire upon his daughter, giving rise to offspring three-fourths of whose blood lines are those of the sire – a practice which, if followed up, soon results in offspring with but one line of ancestry, thus practically eliminating the blood of the dam. This form of breeding is practised when it is desired to secure all that is possible of the blood of the sire.

"2. Breeding the dam to her son or sons successively, thus increasing the blood lines of the female side. This form is practised when it is the dam's blood lines that are to be preserved and condensed. Both systems are necessarily limited to the lifetime of the individuals involved. Either system can of course be approximated by the use of granddaughters or grandson, which would by common consent be called in-breeding, but relationship more remote would generally be regarded merely as line-breeding.

"3. Breeding together of brother and sister – a from of in-breeding which preserves the blood lines from both sire and dam in *equal* proportions. It is inferior to either of the others as a means of strengthening previously existing blood lines, but it is freely employed when the *combination* has proved *exceptionally successful,* virtually establishing a *new type*. It has all the dangers of the other two, and in a larger degree, because we have practically no acquaintance with the *new* combination, whereas in strengthening the proportion of one line of ancestry over another, whether it be that of the sire or that of the dam, we are dealing with previously existing blood lines known to be harmonious. . . .

"Nobody claims advantage of in-breeding *per se,* but it is the acme of line-breeding, and when superior individuals are at hand it is the most powerful method of making the most of their excellence. It is the method by which the highest possible percentage of the blood of an exceptional individual or of a particularly fortunate 'nick' can be preserved, fused into and ultimately made to characterise an entire line of descent on both sides.

"If persisted in, the outside blood disappears by the same law that governs grading, and the pedigree is speedily enriched to an almost unlimited extent by the blood of a single animal. ... A large proportion of the really great sires have been strongly in-bred.

Only Worthwhile System

"An in-bred animal is of course enormously prepotent over everything else. Its half of the ancestry, being largely of identical blood, is almost certain to dominate the offspring. In-breeding is, therefore, recognised as the strongest of all breeding, giving rise to the simplest of pedigrees – an advantage quickly recognised when we recall the law of ancestral heredity. In this respect it is all that line-breeding is and more. ... All things considered, no other known method of breeding equals this for intensifying blood lines, doubling up existing combinations, and making the most of exceptional individuals or of unusually valuable strains. ...

Plenty of examples of successes can be instanced, and every breeder is familiar with them. ..."

Davenport then went on to show the dangers of in-breeding if it were not accompanied by strict selection and ruthless elimination.

In *The Basis of Breeding* * Leon F. Whitney, when referring to in-breeding says: –

"In-breeding is the great means at the disposal of the breeder to originate new breeds or purify old. ...

"In the past any breeder might shudder to think of mating brother to sister once. But if we select for excellent traits and discard the weaklings, I see no reason why we cannot secure strains which are not only pure for the traits in question, but which will suffer no harm from in-breeding . . . .

"Dr. Charles B. Davenport has in-bred mice for fifty and more generations. After less than half of this number had been produced he might almost have said that every mouse was the twin of every other, so identical were they. The reason is that they inherit the same assortment of genes in uniform pairs, and there are no longer genes left which produce defective characteristics.

No Harmful Effects

"Dr. Castle has in-bred rabbits for many generations without harmful effects when the rabbits were selected for desirable traits as the in-breeding continued.

"Take the Laverack strain of Setters for instance. They were originated by breeding brother to sister for five generations, and Mr. Laverack selected the best from each litter and tested them for hunting ability as he in-bred them. Thus only the best were selected and used. He must have approached making the strain very nearly uniform in their genes. ...

"The great role of in-breeding should be the elimination of undesirable traits and the doubling-up of desirable ones. If young from in-bred animals are so weak that they cannot survive, they show beyond a doubt that within the germ plasm of the parents there are genes which, when combined, actually kill the offspring. Therefore, is it not highly desirable to rid the breed of them?

"I prefer to think of in-breeding as an eliminative process rather than as a strengthening process. ...

"In-breeding is a real art, one which demands a high degree of courage. Not every man wants to face the facts. Altogether too many people would prefer to have an animal which appears to be a splendid individual on the surface, but which is likely to pass on undesirable traits, than to have one which may not be so good to look at, but will never pass on germ plasm which will create another less desirable specimen than itself.

* Whitney — *The Basis of Breeding* (Fowler Printing Co.).

"An in-bred individual which is also a good type of animal itself is the truly great sire or dam, and the prize winner which is untested is not to be compared with him or her in genuine value to the breed. So here again we see that the truly great breeder is not the man who goes about buying show specimens, but rather the man who in-breeds and tests and tries his animals until he knows how to combine this with the germ plasm of others to produce the desired ideal type."

Figure 14-1   A Bird Room Set Up At The Start of the Breeding Season. Note that all of the nest boxes are outside the cages, therefore allowing a single cage be be used for each pair

Figure 14-2   A Modern Type of Ventilator (Fresh air is essential)

CHAPTER 15

THE "YELLOW" AND "BUFF" THEORY

SIZE AND COLOUR

It was the late Dr. M. D. S. Armour who first applied what is generally known as the "yellow" and "buff" theory to Budgerigar culture. Its principles are not, as at first might be assumed, confined to the breeding of Yellows but are extended to the cultivation of other colour varieties.

This contention is based on the principle that variation in form and size often accompanies variation in colour.

Birds which Dr. Armour described as "buff" are larger, coarser in feather, have smaller throat spots and generally less distinct wing markings. He was also of the opinion that they lack type, particularly in head, although he expressed the further view that this apparent failing in head may be merely due to the comparatively large body of the "buffs".

Those birds which come into the "yellow" class ("not necessarily yellow in colour but of the colour of the variety: 'yellow' here meaning the darker shade," to quote the Doctor's own remarks) are usually smaller, have compact well-formed bodies, good heads, good throat spots, very distinct wing markings and a sheen on the plumage. Whereas the "buffs" appear to be slightly smoked, this is entirely lacking in the true "yellow," in which the colour is decided and lustrous.

In a contribution to *Cage Birds* Dr. Armour said:–

"Until we realise and accept the fact that in all colours we have to deal with two classes of colour, the dilute and the concentrate, we cannot hope to achieve all-round perfection? We must use both the 'yellow' and the 'buff' for our purpose, and we can afford to discard neither.

"If we breed 'yellow' to 'yellow' generation after generation, we shall maintain depth of colour, quality of feather and excellence of type, but we shall lose size. The 'Yellow' is the more desirable, but we cannot afford to disregard the 'buff.'

"This acceptance of 'yellows' and 'buffs' explains our lightly suffused and heavily suffused Whites, our deeply coloured Grey-wings, our pale Blues as against our dark Blues (not Cobalts).

"I am aware that, in making this assertion, I may be laying myself open to severe criticism, for many readers will not accept my explanation of the heavily suffused and lightly suffused Whites being due to the fact that the birds are either 'yellows' or 'buffs.'

"But if we look on the presence of 'yellow' in a bird being due to either the absence of a factor which inhibits the formation of pigment, or the presence of something which is necessary for pigment to be fully formed, we see that this explains the heavily suffused White or the lightly suffused White.

"But in the former, the 'diluting factor' is absent, whilst in the latter it is present, rendering the bird of the paler 'buff' shade.

"Until we realise, whatever the factor, that there is a distinction between a bird which carries deep body colour and one which lacks this depth, we cannot make any deliberate headway.

"We may unconsciously pair up a deeply coloured bird with a pale bird 'just to even things up', but this is not the best way consistently to maintain size, colour and type along with feather quality.

"Polish and high finish are not the result merely of spraying and conditioning; some birds will never acquire the finish of others, no matter how carefully they are treated. The finish and sheen depend on the feather texture to a greater extent than any conditioning.

"I am convinced in my own mind that the following theories hold good:–

"1. Breeding 'yellow' to 'yellow' continually will reduce size to an extent which is undesirable in an exhibition specimen.

"2. Breeding 'buff' to 'buff' repeatedly will produce big, coarse-feathered birds which are undesirable as exhibition birds.

"3. The pairing of 'yellow' to 'yellow' as far as possible, with the occasional introduction of 'buffs' is productive of the best results, birds which are *of reasonable size* carrying desirable features which are infinitely more important than mere bulk, namely good type, richness and lustre of plumage, good well-defined markings and shapeliness of head.

"Incidentally, the 'yellow' class of Light Greens, etc., carry the richest yellow in the masks and this is most desirable.

Further Comments

In response to a request from me Dr. Armour kindly supplied the following further comments on the "yellow" and "buff" theory:–

"I doubt if there is much to add to what I have already written on this subject. My experiences have been mainly with Light Yellows and Light Greens bred from Green × Green matings, and where we are dealing with the pure varieties, Greens which are homozygous for Light Green and Yellows which are equally pure there is a definite distinction between the two shades, 'buff' and 'yellow.'

THE "YELLOW" AND "BUFF" THEORY

"Recently a fancier asked me to pick out the 'buffs' and 'yellows' from his stock and, frankly, I was unable to do so. The birds were of so many shades and sizes that there was confusion, for when I thought I had at last got a big 'buff' Green, when I viewed it in another light it looked distinctly dark.

"The trouble I had here was that the birds were bred from all kinds of crosses. Some were crossed with Yellow, some with Blue, some with Cobalt, and so on. Where there is indiscriminate cross-mating one cannot rely on the 'yellow' and 'buff' distinction. We can certainly pair a 'buff' Green with say a 'yellow' Skyblue (a Blue which errs on the side of being too deep in colour) and we get good results in this way, but we cannot take a Green/yellow and discriminate between that and a Green/blue as to its being 'buff' or 'yellow'. Where we get cross-breeding we get variation of shade which is due to the cross and not to the presence of a dilution factor.

"There seems to be some confusion on the matter of 'buff' and 'yellow,' for some people imagine that a 'buff' Green is a Light Green and a 'yellow' Green a Dark Green.

"Some breeders are probably somewhat sceptical regarding the uses of 'yellows' and 'buffs' for the breeding of exhibition birds. I agree absolutely that this theory is of no use to the breeder whose pedigrees are all over the place. I have no interest whatever nowadays in the crossing of various colours for only the most elementary Mendelism is necessary to allow of accurate prediction of the *colours* of the progeny.

A Wider Field

"The field is much wider when we come to the study of the variations in one colour variety, for Mendelism alone does not account for such things as feather texture and there is no dominance, but in its place possibly what is entirely different – prepotency. Again, desirable features are not handed down in strict Mendelian fashion and one cannot pair up a bird with a big head with one with a small head and get young which have special head quality. This is where in-breeding steps in, and in-breeding upsets all theories when applied to pure colour varieties.

"I once had a Green cock which stamped his type on every hen I mated with him. All his young were similar, from several different hens, and we must recognise this bird as being prepotent simply because he was the result of in-breeding and he was homozygous not only for colour but for certain desirable features. His young one year were identical in type with those of another, though he had different wives. The value of such young stock is very great and when one pairs, as I did, a cock like this, with a 'buff' for the first round and a 'yellow' for the second round, the material available is the foundation of some good stuff next year."

JUSTIFICATION FOR VIEWS EXPRESSED

After he had written the exposition which I have quoted above, Dr. Armour expressed to me his opinion that far too many "buffs" were being bred and exhibited.

I believe that Dr. Armour was theoretically correct, and yet I am of the opinion that the views he expressed, and which I have quoted above, are more academic than practical, although Canary breeders do apply the "yellow" and "buff" theory when they are mating their birds; and as they do so, it might be asked why cannot we Budgerigar fanciers do the same. I think the answer is the difficulty presented to us in distinguishing "yellows" from "buffs."

If I go through the birds at a show or those in our own aviaries, I am sure I can in many cases say with accuracy "That is a 'buff' " and "that is a 'yellow' ", but in numerous other instances I cannot tell one from another. It will be noted that the Doctor himself admitted that this was the difficulty. I agree with his description of the difference between a "buff" and "yellow." It is the border line cases which get me puzzled.

And if we cannot always tell one from another how can we make use of the principle when we are selecting mates? I think the wise breeder subconsciously applies the theory when he is selecting his pairs. He won't continuously continue to "double buff" (mating "buff" to "buff" generation after generation) and, similarly, he will not pair "yellow" to "yellow" season after season without any "buff" crossing, because he will realise that he is putting together birds which are not suited to each other.

A fancier using a breeding team consisting of all "buffs" would not go far and neither would a fancier using nothing but "yellows."

CHAPTER 16

MENDELISM AND COLOUR INHERITANCE

COLOUR EXPECTATIONS

This book aims to be classified as a practical treatise on Budgerigar culture and not as a scientific work. Therefore, I do not intend to write at great length on the subject of genetics. Nevertheless, I should not have completed my task if I were not to devote some space to the mechanism of inheritance and to Mendelism, which has rendered invaluable service to colour production generally and to the correct development of new colour varieties in particular.

There is a mistaken idea in the minds of many people that the Mendelians put forward Mendel's principles of inheritance as an alternative and superior method of breeding high-class exhibition stock to the practical livestock breeders' systems described by such terms as "selection," "elimination," "in-breeding," "line-breeding," and "out-crossing." Actually the scientists do not make any such claims. They simply show us by means of Mendelism how characters are inherited, and they provide us with formulae which enable fanciers to mate their birds together in such a way that they will produce the colour results desired. They enable us to eliminate all that wastage of good material which would occur if breeders had to rely solely on their own intuition, haphazard experiment and a process of trial and error instead of the accurate data which the labours of the biologists have produced.

I repeat that Mendelism is an *aid* to the old breeding methods and not an alternative to them. In the case of Budgerigars, Mendelism, so ably applied in the first place many years ago to colour production by Dr. H. Duncker and General Consul Cremer, made it possible for the Budgerigar Society to issue several editions of Dr. H. Duncker's *Book of Budgerigar Matings.*

Later editions of this magnificent work were revised and brought up to date by the late E. W. Brooks and the late F.S. Elliott. The ninth edition of this book, now entitled *Budgerigar Matings and Colour Expectations,* is now out of print. This provided breeders with a perfect guide as to what colours to expect in the chicks from given matings.

Because of the existence of the expectation tables and other information contained in its pages it is unnecessary for Mendelism to be studied by any fancier unless she or he desires to delve into the fascinating though at times complex subject of genetics. I will not attempt in these pages to give more than an outline of the Mendelian principles of inheritance as applied to Budgerigars. Those who desire to go further into Mendelism for their own interest and edification have the opportunity of reading a number of scientific works written by authorities of international renown.

Mendelism is no mere unproven theory. It is indeed the true story of inheritance, and as such it is now universally accepted by biologists and by all practical livestock keepers who have made themselves acquainted with the principles originally evolved by Gregor Mendel, Monk and Abbot of Brünn.

Before it is feasible to understand Mendelism, it is necessary to know how properties are actually transmitted from parents to their offspring. And although, as I say, it is not possible in one chapter of a book to cover the vast field of genetics, I think it is desirable that I should briefly describe how characters both visible and concealed are passed along from one generation to another.

In the first place every young Budgerigar born is the outcome of the union of a minute body called the spermatozoon supplied by the cock with the ovum supplied by the hen. This brings together germ or reproductive cells which are known by the general term of gamete or marrying cells. The new cell resulting from the fusion of the two gametes is described as a zygote. Within the gametes there are the chromosomes and within the chromosomes there are genes — or characters as we commonly call them — which govern the visible and invisible characteristics of the offspring.

In Budgerigars the effects of the Mendelian principles are only well understood in so far as the operation of colour characters is concerned.

Now for the production of any colour it is necessary that either (1) both cock and hen should apply what we may call a *main* character for that colour or (2) that one of the parents should supply such a main character whilst the other supplies a sister character.

In the first case the chick (zygote), since it gets the main character from both sides, will be "pure-bred" for the colour in question. In the second case, since it gets the main character from one side only and the sister character from the other, the chick will be of a mixed nature.

What will such a chick look like? The answer is that occasionally (as for example where only the shade of any given colour is concerned) an effect somewhat intermediate between that of the parent which supplies the main and the parent which supplies the sister character is produced. But much more often the main character completely overpowers its sister, the chick's colour being that of the parent which supplies the main character. When this happens, the main character is termed the *dominant* character, whilst its sister is termed the *recessive*. The discovery of dominants and recessives in this way is of great importance. I will take a simple example in Budgerigars.

A pure Light Green is mated to a Skyblue. Light Green is dominant to Skyblue. Therefore all the youngsters in the first generation will be Light Green in appearance, but they will *all* have the ability to breed Skyblues, and will be described as Light Green split blues (written Light Green/blues).

If you mate two of these Light Green/blues together you will then breed Skyblues in addition to birds Light Green in appearance, because in some cases when the gametes combine to form a zygote two Skyblue characters will be brought together; they will be present in double dose. If, on the other hand, one of these Light Green/blues were mated to a pure Light Green there would be no Blues, because in no case would there be the recessive Skyblue character carried by both the cock and the hen. When a Light Green/blue is mated to a Skyblue, the expectation is fifty per cent Light Green/blues and fifty per cent Skyblues.

DETERMINATION OF SEX

The sex of offspring is controlled in this way:-

The hen has two sex chromosomes — one an X or male chromosome, the other a Y or female chromosome. The cock has two X (or male) chromosomes.

If an X chromosome from the cock meets an X chromosome from the hen the youngster will be a male; if it meets a Y chromosome the offspring will be a female. Therefore sex can be said in birds to be controlled by the hen.

Now I have only scratched with a pin on the surface of the wonderful story of inheritance, merely with the object of giving to my readers a simple lesson in elementary Mendelism, which subject, as I have previously said, they can study more deeply or not according to their inclinations.

Since the days of Cremer and Duncker other eminent geneticists have discovered in the Budgerigar a remarkable subject for genetical research.

When referring elsewhere to Opalines, Lutinos, Albinos, Slates, Lacewings and Cinnamons, I have stated that they are sex-linked varieties, which will naturally have caused the uninformed reader to remark "What does 'sex-linked' mean?". I will endeavour to explain.

I have stated above that the sex chromosomes in the cock are two X-chromosomes, whereas in the hen there is one X chromosome paired with a Y chromosome.

Now if there is what is known as a mutant gene (a colour gene) — say Opaline — on the X chromosome of the hen, only half her chicks, on average, can carry this gene. Her Y-chromosome cannot carry it.

Still using the Opaline by way of example, although the same remarks apply to all the sex-linked varieties, a cock may have two X-chromosomes, neither carrying the gene for Opaline; one may carry the gene for Opaline, but not the other; or both may bear the Opaline gene.

If neither X chromosome carries the Opaline gene the bird will be an ordinary Normal. If only one possesses the gene for Opaline, the cock will be a Normal/Opaline. If there is an Opaline gene on both X chromosomes it will be an Opaline.

If a hen has an Opaline gene on her X chromosome, she will be an Opaline. If she has not this gene she will be a Normal. There is no such bird as a hen split for Opaline; she is either an Opaline or a Normal.

The essential difference between a sex-linked variety and a non-sex-linked variety is that in a bird of the former kind the mutant colour gene is on the sex chromosome; in the latter it is on a different chromosome. Here is a table to make the position clear.

1. OPALINE COCK X^0 X^0 $-$OPALINE HEN X^0 Y
   Expectation: X^0 X^0 $-$Opaline cocks
   X^0 Y$-$Opaline hens

2. OPALINE COCK X^0 X^0 $-$ORDINARY* HEN XY
   Expectation: X^0 X$-$Ordinary*/Opaline cocks
   X^0 Y$-$Opaline hens

3. ORDINARY* COCK XX$-$OPALINE HEN X^0 Y
   Expectation: X^0 X$-$Ordinary*/Opaline cocks
   XY Ordinary hens

4. ORDINARY*/OPALINE COCK X^0 X$-$ ORDINARY* HEN XY
   Expectation: XX Ordinary* cocks
   X^0 X$-$Ordinary*/Opaline cocks
   X^0 Y$-$Opaline hens
   XY$-$Ordinary* hens

5. ORDINARY*/OPALINE COCK XX^0 $-$OPALINE HEN X^0 Y
   Expectation: X^0 X Ordinary*/Opaline cocks
   X^0 X^0 Opaline cocks
   XY Ordinary* hens
   X^0 Y Opaline hens

* "Ordinary" refers to birds of colour varieties other than sex-linked.

It will be noted that some of the matings described above produce Normal/opaline cocks and also ordinary cocks. Generally speaking these matings should be avoided because it is not usually possible to tell from their external appearance which are split and which are non-split. This can only be proved by test matings, which entail much waste of time — possibly a whole breeding season.

My readers must understand that whilst I have used the Opaline as my example, the story of the sex-linked Lutino, the sex-linked Albino and the Cinnamon, Slate and Lacewing is exactly the same.

Fanciers who have not studied Budgerigar genetics are sometimes confused by the terms Type I and Type II appearing against the names of birds carrying a single dark character. The following explanation makes clear the difference between the two types:-

Type I are produced by crossing a Skyblue with an Olive, resulting in Dark Green/blue *with the dark character from the Olive.* Type II are produced by crossing Light Green with Mauve resulting in Dark Greens/blue *with the dark character from the Mauve.* The distribution of the shades of colour when dealing with expectations of crosses when one parent is a Dark Green/Blue Type I or a Dark Green/Blue Type II differs from the usual Mendelian percentages of each colour. The knowledge of this will help the breeder to match the breeding pairs so as to raise as many of the desired shade of colour as possible.

A Dark Green/Blue Type I of any variety paired to a Sky Blue of any variety will give the theoretical expectation of 43% Sky Blue, 7% Cobalt, 43% Dark Green/Blue Type I and 7% Light Green/Blue. When a Dark Green/Blue Type II is used instead of a Type I then the expectation is 43% Cobalt, 7% Sky Blue, 43% Light Green/Blue and 7% Dark Green/Blue Type II. It will be observed that both pairings however give 50% blue coloured and 50% green coloured young and it is only the shade of colour that varies. The dark character in any bird described as Type I had its origin in a bird which was Olive, and in Type II in a bird which was Mauve.

Figure 16-1   Washing a Bird with a Shaving Brush

CHAPTER 17

PREPARING FOR EXHIBITION

BIRDS MUST BE IN CONDITION

A Budgerigar is in ideal show condition when it fulfils all those requirements described by me in my concluding paragraphs to Chapter 3. The acquiring of such a desired appearance is primarily a matter of health, but a course of preparation in the bird room is also essential to success, because we have to put our exhibits down spotlessly clean, perfectly steady, and, therefore, able to display to the fullest possible advantage all their good points when they stand before the judge.

Although actually, as I have indicated above, the most important factor in show preparation is the maintaining of the bird's health, having achieved that, certain processes have to be carried out by the owner, and to which this chapter is devoted.

Having postulated the perfect physical state of those specimens which are to constitute an owner's show team, I will now describe methods which will enable the exhibitor to stage his good exhibition birds so that it will be no fault of his if they do not secure a reasonable share of the honours which it is within the judges' power to bestow upon them.

In so far as Budgerigars are concerned, and in which respect they differ greatly from many other birds which are exhibited, the irregularity of their moulting often upsets all our calculations.

We have a bird all spick and span, in perfect health and absolutely ready to fight for his life at a show on the following morning. Alas, with the dawn our hopes are shattered because he has during the night dropped two feathers of his mask and with them two spots. Or he may have suddenly begun to cast feathers on his body, or dropped his tail, and we know that he has not the slightest chance of doing justice to himself when the eyes of the judge are upon him.

If one of these misfortunes occurs before the bird has left home for the show, it must not be sent. And unless one has a substitute better far have an absent entry than send an inferior or ill-conditioned specimen.

This fluctuation in feather condition has something to do with the variation in awards, and it is one reason why we sometimes find an exhibitor after a period of high success suddenly finding himself with few, if any, birds which he is able to exhibit, not because he does not own high-class Budgerigars, but because nearly all his show specimens have gone into a partial moult.

There is no known method of controlling the moult, although experiments have been conducted, and we are to a great extent in the hands of Dame Fortune in regard to it. The irregularity of this natural process in Budgerigars is a factor which does give a certain advantage to those who own large teams of show specimens. They are the more likely to be able to find at least a few birds in good feather condition, even if the majority of their team are casting feathers, whereas the smaller owner may have all his exhibition birds moulting simultaneously. But even large-scale breeders are sometimes embarrassed by wholesale moulting.

POSSIBLE METHOD OF APPROACH

The show preparation methods of different fanciers doubtless differ in detail, but I do not think they differ in principle. I will describe that system which I know most about, viz., the one which we employ at Lintonholme.

As the show season closely approaches we go round the aviaries and spot those birds which are, in our opinion, worthy of being sent out in competition. These eventually are put into the training cages.

Very suitable cages are sold in various sizes by the appliance makers.

The inside of our training cages and the wire fronts, which are cellulosed, are thoroughly washed several times weekly.

The importance of this cleanliness cannot be over-stressed. For instance, the perches and wires must be rubbed thoroughly because a bird when it is preening itself whilst drying after spraying is continually rubbing its head against them, and if they are the least bit dirty the mask will be soiled.

Several weeks before the date of the first show, the birds are transferred from the flights to the training cages. Potential exhibition specimens must also be put frequently into a show cage for a few hours at a time to ensure that they will comport themselves gracefully when the day of trial arrives. This is particularly important in the case of inexperienced youngsters.

Between Shows

When the first part of the show season is over and the general moult of October has commenced our show birds are taken from the training cages and placed in the enclosed aviaries until their moulting is nearly complete and the second phase of the show season has come in sight (early November), when they are returned to the training cages, there to remain

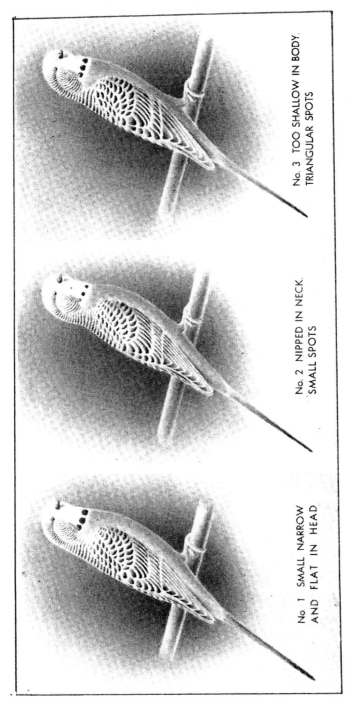

Figure 17-1   Show Faults in the Budgerigar I

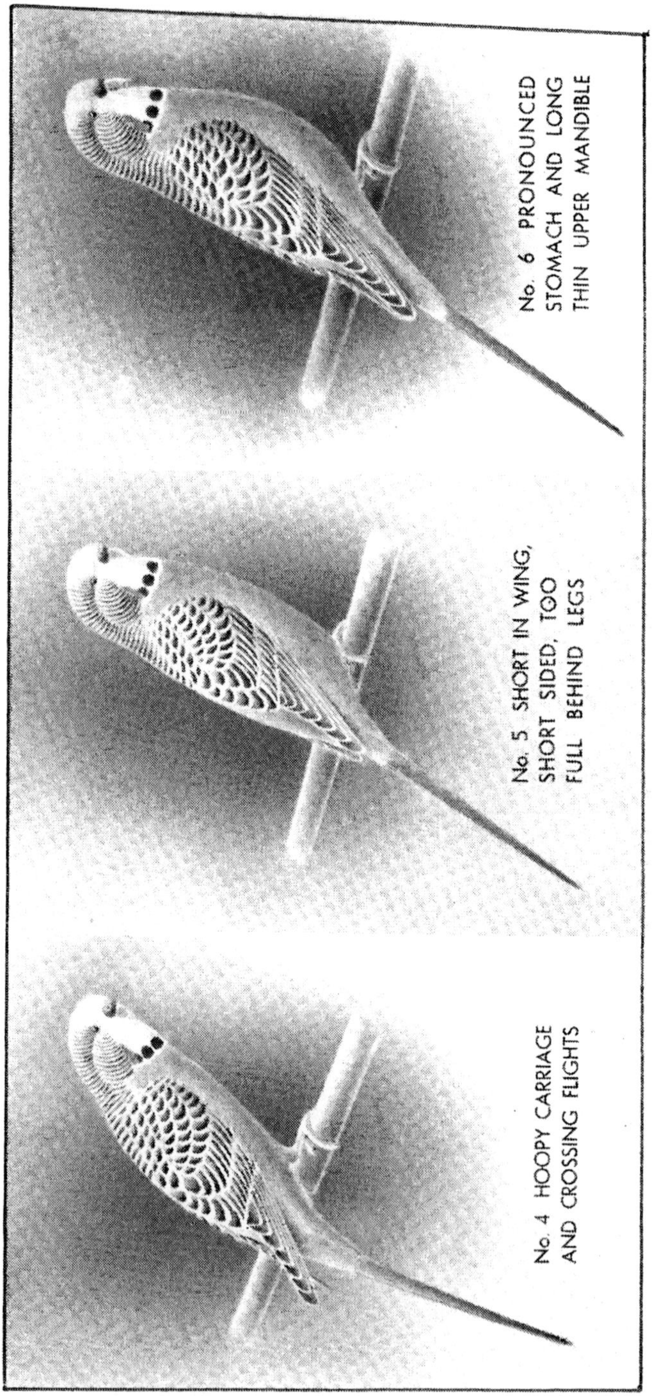

Figure 17-2   Show Faults in the Budgerigar II

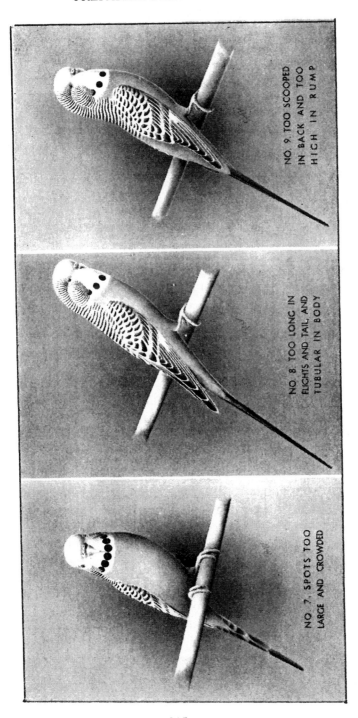

Figure 17-3 Show Faults in the Budgerigar III

215

until exhibiting is over. This procedure ensures that all the new feathers keep clean, and show preparation can be continuous.

Spraying

Let us imagine that a show at which we have decided to enter is in six weeks' time. We have in our bird room a number of candidates for competition at that event.

In a cage of the dimensions described in Chapter 6 we keep about ten birds. Cocks and hens occupy separate cages.

Twice or three times per week the birds are sprayed with cold water. We use an automatic spray, one of that type which is operated by air pressure. Having filled the spray with water the air is compressed by a pumping action, after which the mere turning of the handle liberates a fine spray through the nozzle, and continuous pumping with the hand, as demanded by some sprays, is avoided. Where only a small number of birds have to be sprayed one of the cheaper sprays fulfils the purpose.

We do not spray the birds when they are standing in the training cage. They are transferred therefrom to a Yorkshire Canary show cage which is placed on a zinc tray on a table. A hole is bored in the bottom of the cage so that the water can pass away through a rubber pipe to a drain. The use of this type of cage for spraying ensures a bird being properly sprayed all over its body, whereas if it were sprayed when standing in the training cage, in many instances one side would receive practically all the water and the other side virtually none. You know how some Budgerigars when standing will persist in facing in one direction.

The cage can be turned round to suit the convenience of the person who is doing the spraying. Two Budgerigars can be sprayed in one of these cages simultaneously.

In our bird room we use three Yorkshire show cages at the same time, and have one or two birds in each cage. In the first place, all are given a light spray to soften any dust that may be attached to their feathers. After the last three of the nine birds have received this, the first three are given a thorough soaking, then the second three, and lastly the third three. After the three birds in the first cage have had their full spraying, they are returned to the training cage and replaced by three new birds, which are at once lightly sprayed and left to take their turn for the heavier spraying. And so the process goes on in this processional manner.

The birds receive a very thorough spraying on each occasion up to within a few days of the show being held. Then, if quite clean, they are sprayed a little more lightly. They are never sprayed the day before a show, for the reason that we desire to give them an ample opportunity to recover any natural oil which the water may have taken from their feathers. There is on the market an excellent solution to add to the spray water which gives an extra sheen to the plumage.

The great object of the frequent cleaning of the training cages, and the spraying is to secure perfect cleanliness of plumage.

If not the slightest trace of soiling is to be observable when the exhibits stand in front of the white background of the show cage, continuous application of the methods which I have above described is absolutely essential. Many a Budgerigar looks somewhat unclean at a show, whereas if one observed it in ordinary circumstances it would appear to the casual observer to be as clean as needs be. It is the white background which does it. It is a case of the distinction between cleanliness and super-cleanliness; and it is super-cleanliness we want. It is not altogether easy to keep Budgies—particularly hens—in this condition. If there is a speck of dust anywhere they are prone to find it.

I am convinced that in addition to aiding cleanliness spraying with cold water is advantageous as a tonic. Just as a cold bath tones up the human system so does a cold spray have a stimulating effect on a Budgerigar.

In our rooms at Lintonholme we have electric heaters thermostatically controlled. The thermostat is never set at higher than 45 degrees, which does not suggest a room artificially heated in accordance with the normal interpretation of the term. It does, however, keep the air in the bird room at a more comfortable heat than the outside air in the coldest days of winter. Therefore, in my opinion, it aids the achievement of show condition because the birds are more comfortable and happy, and are not having to resist the normal effects of severe cold on their bodily resistance to external influences.

Aid to Quick Training

It will be remembered that in an earlier chapter I advocated putting the chicks into training cages for a few weeks after they leave their parents. If the owner has adopted this measure he will find an absence of wildness amongst his birds when he brings them in for final preparation for show, which will be most gratifying to him and will ease enormously the task of making them steady.

Individual Budgerigars vary very much as regards the time which it takes to make them stand correctly in a show cage. I find that quite a large number of them can be taken out of the training cage within a short period and placed in a show cage and they behave immediately as one would have them.

Some specimens never do really display their charms to proper advantage, particularly hens, but the majority of badly behaved Budgerigars can with patience be corrected of this offence.

Broken Feathers

The following is a procedure sometimes carried out by many exhibitors.

About eight weeks before a bird is to exhibited he catches it, spreads the wings and removes any broken flights and tail feathers, so that they will grow to their full length before the date of the show.

If a broken tail is observed it is gently removed, which is better than waiting for it to moult naturally. Within six or seven weeks it will have grown to its full length again. Likewise when the candidates are brought into training cages, if any of their tails are damaged, they are removed, in order to give them a chance of having correct tails as soon as possible.

In the marked varieties the exhibitor is permitted to trim the necklaces before his birds are sent to a show. This trimming consists simply of removing any little black specks that may surround the four throat spots which are the main attraction of the mask. The spots which are at the base of the cheek patches must not be removed. Tweezers are usually used for this purpose, though I know a few fanciers who employ fine pointed scissors.

Clean Birds — Clean Cages

Although it does not actually concern the exhibition Budgerigars themselves, there is another preparation which is of importance. It is that of sending exhibits to a show in perfectly clean cages, not only free from any sign of dirt but with their cellulose or enamel clean and bright. I appreciate that the fancier cannot be recellulosing or enamelling his cages monthly, and this is not necessary, but, on the other hand, it is often regrettable to note at a show good specimens in battered cages with much of the enamel or cellulose chipped off, often far from clean inside, and undoubtedly thereby seriously handicapped.

It is true that a judge is supposed to judge the bird not the cage, but the fact remains that first impressions to a judge are difficult to eradicate from his mind, and the sight of a cage not worthy of the Budgerigar which it contains is not calculated to make the first impression a good one.

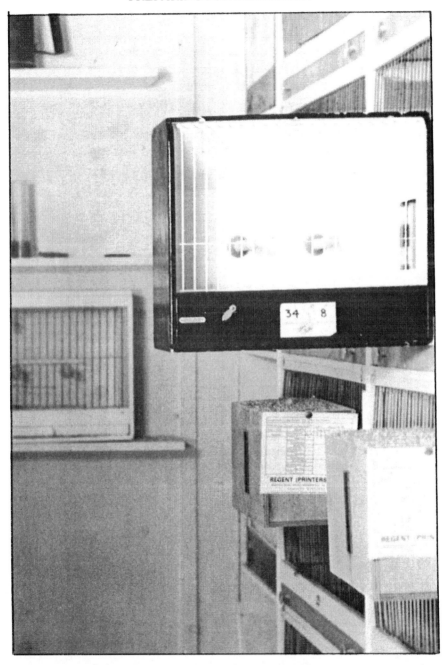

Figure 17-4 A Show Cage Hanging on a Stock Cage

THE BUDGERIGAR SOCIETY STANDARD SHOW CAGE

The implementation period to be 10 years with effect from the 1996 Show Season.

Standard Show Cage Specification

SIZE Overall measurements 355mm long x 305mm high x 165mm wide.

BOTTOM 355mm long x 162mm wide x 6mm thick with pencil round front edge. Maker's code number to be indented on the base of cage so that in no way visible when judging takes place.

SIDES 293mm high x 162mm wide x 9mm thick with pencil round front edge and 251mm radius in top front corner.

TOP 355mm long x 140mm wide x 6mm thick with pencil round front edge and 85mm x 30mm kidney shaped hand hold position centrally in length and 40mm from rear.

BACK 355mm long x 230mm high x 3mm thick.

SLOPING ROOF 9mm thick positioned 222mm from bottom of cage and 45mm from front of cage. Centre of junction between top of cage and sloping roof to be stiffened by a triangular block of wood.

FRONT RAIL 70mm high from floor of cage x 9mm thick and recessed 4mm from front of cage. Registered Trade Mark label to be fitted to front rail set in bottom left hand corner with No. 2^{38} slotted round head brass screws.

DOOR SIZE 100mm high x 90mm wide externally with sloping bevel cut to top, bottom and left hand edges. Right hand edge to be straight cut. Bottom of door to be 95mm from bottom of cage and centred on side panel. Door corners an the opposite side to the hinges can be radiused up to 5mm.

DOOR FASTENERS 1. One plain brass desk turn 25mm long fixed by brass screw to side of cage to coincide with a raised head brass screw positioned 12mm in from front left hand edge of door and 50mm from top of door.

2. One plain brass desk turn 25mm long fixed above top left hand side of door to line up with side fixing set 12mm from edge of door.

DOOR HINGES Two black painted strong hinges 25mm x 16mm fixed on right hand side of door and 10mm from top and bottom of door. **DOOR PULL** 18/25mm x 1.6mm (16 gauge) wire, black painted, S hook in centre of door.

PERCH SIZE 14/15mm diameter with both ends cut flush. **PERCH POSITION** Centre of perches and screw holes to be 140mm from bottom of cage and 112mm apart.

PERCH FIXINGS Perches to be secured to back of cage with counter sunk screws and brass cup washers and to centre crossbar on wire front of cage by 3mm deep horizontal saw cut.

WIRE FRONT Comprises of 21 wires x 2mm (14 gauge) mesh at 16mm centres. For strength, double punched set 10mm apart; curve at top, 19mm bow. Centre of middle crossbar to be 140mm above bottom of cage. Front to be fixed to cage by three extended wires at bottom and top. The centre wire at top of the cage to be cut to avoid excessive protrusion.

DRINKERS White plastic finger drawer type not to exceed 50mm in length and should be placed between the 3rd and 4th wire from left and resting on the middle bar at all times.

COLOURS Inside and wire front – White. Outside Black gloss, including top of front rail.

Preferred material for making cages is red or white deal, pine or obeche with the top and bottom a 6mm finish and the sides and false roof a 9mm finish. The back a 3mm plywood nailed outside. However cages produced in alternative materials must comply wiih all internal and external dimensions and give a similar appearance to a wooden cage when viewed from the front.

STANDARD SHOW CAGE
incorporating BS Patent No. 755106

Modern Standard Show Cage

Details kindly supplied by The Budgerigar Society

● ●

THE SCALE OF POINTS

The scale of points gives guidance to judges and fanciers on the value attached to the specified features of a bird. For the perfect bird it will be seen that *Size, shape, balance and deportment* are given 35 points and the **Head, etc,** is given 25 points. This means that 60 points go to what is loosely called '**Type**'.

Colour is 15 points for many of the varieties, but 40 points are awarded to those which require *depth of colour,* eg, Lutino, Dark Eyed (clears) and Yellows. Other variations exist for *crested birds* and for *contrast of colour or variegation.*

221

Figure 17.5 Full and Half Crested Budgerigars
Courtesy: Crested Budgerigar Club

When we resided at Idle on the edge of the industrial area of the West Riding of Yorkshire, where the air is impregnated with deposits from the belching chimneys of many mills, it was very difficult to keep our birds clean. When they were being prepared for exhibition frequent spraying did not alone suffice to rid their plumage of that soiling which, had it remained, would have robbed them of the opportunity of competing on level terms with exhibits that were as clean as new pennies.

WASHING BIRDS

Therefore there was no alternative but to resort to handwashing, and this I did. I recall that I washed every member of the teams we exhibited at the Budgerigar Society's Club show during that period.

Now at North Rigton, five miles from Harrogate, high on the hills above the valley of the Wharfe, the air is clean and pure and practically no handwashing is required, although the necessity for spraying remains. Greatly do I welcome the change, because it is certainly an advantage if handwashing can be avoided.

If one can keep a bird clean by spraying alone there is nothing to be gained by washing. On the other hand, there is nothing about washing that anyone need be afraid of, and if the requisite cleanliness cannot be achieved by any other means then I say wash without hesitation.

Many people I know are afraid to tackle the washing of a Budgerigar. It is an unwarrantable fear, quickly removed when there is obtained an understanding of the correct procedure and the fancier has had a little practice. But I advise those of my readers who have not previously carried out the operation first to wash a few birds of ordinary class not intended for exhibition in order to secure confidence in themselves.

Those who wash Budgerigars doubtless adopt methods differing somewhat in detail but not fundamentally, and therefore, I will first give a description of the usual method and then I will describe the simplified system which I adopted some years ago. The old plan, and the one still followed by most fanciers is this:-

Place the bird in a show cage and bring it into a room free from draughts and where an ample supply of hot and cold water is available. If you have not a bird room to which hot and cold water is laid on there can be nothing better than a bathroom, providing the women-folk of the house do not raise unsurmountable objections!

In addition to the cage containing the bird have at hand another perfectly clean show cage in which it will later be dried. Special drying cages for cage birds can be purchased, or as an alternative to the show cage one may use a Yorkshire Canary cage with a hot towel wrapped round three sides, though I have had no unsatisfactory results from using an ordinary Budgerigar show cage.

Before you place three deep bowls, a soft lather brush, and a bottle of liquid soap, a table or bar of an equally suitable soap—a soap of the purest quality. I use the word "soap" for the purpose of description, but as I will show later even the best toilet soap is inferior to more modern products, which cannot be classed as soaps. Soap, in fact, is outmoded for our purpose.

Into the first bowl put hot water and dissolve in it sufficient of the soap to provide an abundance of lather. Then add enough cold water to bring the mixture to the desired temperature. Until one has had enough practice to be able to know merely immersing the hands in the water whether it is too hot or not for the bird to bear, a satisfactory test is to put the elbow into the water, the elbow being more sensitive than the hand. The use of a thermometer would be a more scientific method but it is not really necessary. The water must not be so hot as to be in any way dangerous to the bird, but it must be sufficiently warm to enable the dirt to be removed with facility.

Into the second bowl pour water, several degrees cooler than the first washing water, and into bowl No. 3 water still cooler but by no means actually cold.

Now take the bird in the hollow of the right hand with the knuckles upwards and its head between the first and second fingers, which surround its neck and which, incidentally, is the correct method of holding a Budgerigar at any time.

Use no Pressure

It is not necessary—in fact it is inadvisable—to use any pressure by either hand or fingers when holding a bird, either when washing it or when it is being held for any other reason. Retain the bird in this position except when it is transferred from the right hand to the left hand.

Now place the Budgerigar into the lather in bowl No.1, spreading out the wings, the whole of the body being covered with the exception of the head.

After it has been immersed in this manner for about a minute, stroke the back, breast and wings down towards the tail with a lather brush which has been well soaked in the soapy water and which has plenty of lather attached to it.

The next step is to lay the tail down the side of the bowl and stroke it above and below with the brush, stroking, of course, in the direction of the lay of the feather and not against it—an instruction which applies throughout the whole of the brushing process.

Now spread the left wing down the side of the bowl and brush it similarly. The bird is transferred to the left hand, so that the right wing can be spread out and brushed, after which it is passed back to the right hand.

Next come the head and neck. On a dirty Budgerigar the mask is usually the dirtiest part, and it is essential to ensure that it is perfectly free from all dirt before removing the bird from the washing water to the first rinsing water. With the brush well lathered sweep somewhat vigorously, always, as I have already said, *with* the feather and not against it. Use the lather and water freely upon the head and neck but *do not push the head under the water.* When using the brush on the back of the head and neck slightly release the first and second fingers, which are surrounding the neck, so that the brush can get to the feathers underneath them.

Convinced that all dirt has been removed, transfer the bird to the first rinsing water. Without pushing the head under the surface, dip the Budgerigar well into the water, spreading out the wings. Pick up the lather brush (from which all the lather has been swilled away by its being held under a tap), saturate it with water, and with rapid strokes brush the bird from head to tail.

And now the third water, which is the second rinsing water, comes into use. Into this steep the Budgerigar as before, again not pushing its head under water, the head being rinsed with brush and sponge only. I consider it

224

to be dangerous to put the head under the water, as if this is done there is a possibility of the bird succumbing. The actual washing is now complete and the dilapidated looking object which has almost ceased to be recognisable as a Budgerigar has to be dried.

Slow Drying Preferable

With a clean, soft towel, remove all surplus water from the surface of the feather, only spending a few seconds over this part of the work. Then put the bird into the clean show cage opposite an electric stove at such a distance from it that you can place your hand on the wire without feeling any discomfort from the heat; in fact, keep it just a little bit further away than that. As drying continues remove the cage further from the stove, as reasonably slow drying is better than rapid drying.

When almost completely dry, carefully place the now more normal looking bird into a Yorkshire show cage and spray it in a similar manner to that in which birds are sprayed in the bird room as described by me earlier in this chapter. Give it a thorough soaking and return it to the show cage opposite the electric stove.

Gradually move this show cage further and further away from the stove until drying is completed. Then switch off the heat and leave the newly-washed specimen all night in the same room in which it has been washed, carefully noting that the door and window are closed. Next morning it can be taken to the bird room and placed in the training cage.

Actually it takes much less time to wash a Budgerigar than it has taken me to describe the procedure. Ten Budgerigars can easily be washed within the hour. The process is in every way more simple than my written description may convey.

It is essential in this method of washing that the soap (again I use this word only descriptively) used should be a pure soap of good quality, of which, of course, various kinds can be purchased. At one time I favoured olive oil soft soap, which was recommended to me by a very successful Yorkshire Canary breeder. And olive oil soft soap is certainly very good indeed for the purpose, but not so good as the agent I use now.

A Good Cleaner*

I gave over using olive oil soft soap when Leda was recommended to me by Mr Len Hillas, when he was aviary manager to Mr Walter Higham, and when later this was unobtainable I used a detergent. I found that these were equally good, and they removed the dirt much more quickly than did the ordinary soap. But I was ever on the look out for something even better, and

* Since this section was written new washing-up liquids have been produced.

this I found in London.

I consulted a leading Bond Street ladies' hairdresser, and he advised me to discontinue with the detergent, on no account wash with ordinary soap, but use instead Triethanolamine Lauryl Sulphate, which is the base of some of the best advertised shampoos. And this I have done ever since with complete satisfaction.

It has enabled me to eliminate the second rinsing water. That bugbear when soap is employed, slow webbing of the feather after washing, is overcome; in fact, the plumage recovers its normal appearance so rapidly that very soon after drying is complete a bird shows no signs of having been washed.

As a dirt remover T.L.S. is much superior to the best soap obtainable.

By the way, I find it desirable for the original washing water to be cooler than when soap is the cleansing agent.

Usually when washing I do not confine my attentions to one bird only but wash a number on the same late afternoon or evening; and, of course, exactly the same directions apply whether one is giving the order of the bath to two or twenty specimens. It is advisable to change the first water — the water with the soap in it — for every five birds or oftener according to your own judgement; and I always change the rinsing water after each bird is washed.

In drying arrange for the stove and drying cage to be so placed that there is no danger of a chill, and draughts must be strictly avoided. That is one reason why a show cage is satisfactory as a drying cage. No draught can come to the bird from behind and the heat is concentrated on the space within the three sides of the cage, although admittedly with a cage open on all four sides the same result can be achieved if a warm towel is placed over the half of the cage furthest away from the stove. The fancier can, therefore, use his own discretion as to which type of cage he employs for the drying process.

I favour an electric fire for drying because it maintains an even and correct temperature with greater certainty than does a coal fire.

If, however, a coal fire is the only means of heat available it should be a "red" fire, viz: one which has been sufficiently long burning for the coals to be glowing.

Never wash a Budgerigar until it has had its full evening meal. Experience has taught me that a bird with an empty or part-empty crop is likely to collapse under shock of immersion.

Budgerigars otherwise clean often have dirty masks, and spraying alone will not remove this soiling. Some fanciers unwisely wash the head only, and not the whole bird. This often leaves what the mothers of children who wash their faces and not their necks call a "tide mark." In nine cases out of ten I can detect at a show those exhibits which have had these part-washes.

Very little of the fancier's time is saved by this process. It takes only a few minutes longer to immerse the whole bird. Even if not much attention is given to the body during the process, its immersion in the water and a sweep or two with the brush will remove the possibility of a "tide mark."

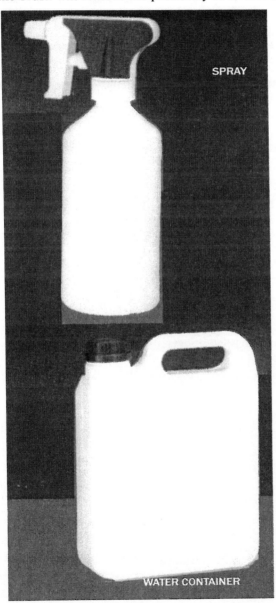

Figure 17.6 Essential Spray & Water Container
Regular spraying is recommended.

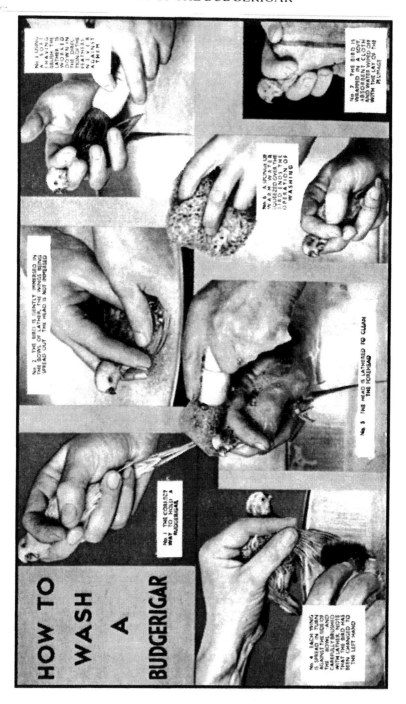

CHAPTER 18

JUDGING

POSITION THE BIRD

Because of their activity in the cage, Budgerigars are not so easy to judge as are some birds and animals. Judging something which is ever on the move, and which looks different from one minute to another owing to its change of pose, is a much more difficult task than judging (say) a series of still-life subjects, to take an extreme example.

A Budgerigar is essentially a bird of position. Let your eye rest even on one of the best exhibits when it is momentarily standing badly, and you will obtain a totally wrong impression of its merits. You must keenly watch it as it stands in its cage and as it moves, until you are able to register in your mind a portrait of that specimen as it really is. What you must actually do is to visualise it at its best, and this you will be able to do if it provides you with an appearance of its best positions more often than it does of its worst positions.

If you have followed this explanation closely you will readily understand that it is absolutely unfair to express an opinion about a Budgerigar immediately it is placed in its cage before you. You must wait until it is steady, and you must give it time to display to you its good and bad points if you are accurately to assess its qualities.

If all this is admitted, then it is, I suggest, quite clear that the speedy judging of Budgerigars can be unsatisfactory judging. In other words, a judge must give each exhibit that has any merit at all a fair opportunity of showing itself to the best advantage. And that is what any of our judges will do most willingly if the show committee has not given him too many classes on which to adjudicate in the time available. To feel rushed when judging large classes of Budgerigars is inimical to the satisfactory execution of the work, and the position is fair neither to the judge nor to the exhibitors.

And there is a moral here also for the exhibitor. No judge can be expected, in any circumstances, to wait indefinitely for a particular bird to perch and pose correctly, and, if after a reasonable lapse of time, it simply will not meet the judge's wishes, what can he do but pass along, possibly, it must be admitted, leaving out of the cards an exhibit which if it would only have shown itself to advantage might have headed the class.

So it is clear that exhibitors must so train their Budgerigars that when they are in their cages on the judging table there is little or no risk of their not making the most of themselves under the judge's critical eye.

I have dwelt on this question of position because it is one of the main causes of that inconsistency of results in Budgerigar classes which has caused many arguments at the shows and heated controversy in the Press.

MAKING AWARDS

Different judges adopt different methods when making their awards. After all, judging is not so much a matter of procedure as of the judge's ability to do the job well. I do not claim for my own *modus operandi* any special marks but it is a plan which I have found to be satisfactory in my own case, and I know it is the one which is followed by many other "wearers of the ermine" with complete satisfaction to themselves. I did not originate the system. It is as old as the hills.

The essence of the procedure I am about to describe is *elimination*. In large classes of twenty or more entries it is essential to reduce them to more reasonable proportions as soon as one can, so that there are only left on the judging table the cream of the class. This is done by selecting the *worst* and ordering the stewards to put them on one side unless they are *very* bad, in which case they are returned to the staging immediately. In fact, I frequently continue this "sending away" process until there only remain just as many exhibits as there are cards to award—usually seven.

In the beginning I have set out on the judging table every show cage in the class which I am about to judge. I walk up and down the line watching each bird intently, stopping at a cage here and there for more detailed inspection, my object being, at this stage of my work, to spot those exhibits which I do not think at that stage can possibly be "in the money," but which might be better than my first impression has led me to believe. As I pick these out I hand them to one of my stewards, who places them on an adjoining table or on the floor; but I do not allow him to take them back to their bench because I want to see them again.

Now, as I go along casting out the inferior specimens, naturally, although it may be a secondary consideration at this stage, I observe birds which I can see will be fighting for the honours at the finish. I move these along to the left-hand side of the table, so that they will be awaiting me when the elimination process is completed.

And so the work proceeds until there are, say, a dozen cages left. I may then eliminate five more, leaving the seven birds which will secure the seven prize cards to be placed in order of merit; or I may retain on the table the whole twelve and put them into what I consider to be their correct positions in accordance with their respective merits. As to which of these two courses I follow is entirely decided by the closeness of the competition—in other words, whether it is easy or difficult to carry the elimination-of-the-worst process any further when I have reduced the class to about a dozen.

But before I make my final placings of the birds remaining I always have just another look at every exhibit which previously I have put aside, perchance I have, through some oversight, missed a really good one which deserves to be amongst those still on the table and which are about to go through their final test. This second review is soon accomplished, and it is time well spent, because it saves a judge from having to admit after lunch that he has overlooked a worthy competitor.

There now remains only putting into correct order the seven or more remaining exhibits. This is the most interesting phase, and the one which demands the greater skill.

A Distinct Advantage

The cage bird judge is happily placed compared with the pigeon judge, because he can change the cages about into the birds' order of merit, gradually moving the best towards the left and the worst towards the right, altering the position of one here and another there as his impressions of the respective exhibits' merits develop into definite conclusions, until finally he has the birds remaining on the table in what he is convinced is their correct order. Then the numbers of the successful exhibits go into his judging book, the stewards put the cards on the cages, and the work commences all over again with the next class.

A good judge must in the first place thoroughly understand the Budgerigar's show properties. Continuous study, close observation, and considerable experience alone will develop that thorough understanding of the subject which is demanded of him who can adjudicate with credit to himself and satisfaction to the exhibitors. Ordinarily good eyesight, with, or without glasses, will not alone suffice; the judge must possess a thorough grasp of all that is meant by "form" and he must have a good eye for colour.

Then he must have complete confidence in his own ability. The judge who is continuously in a state of indecision is likely to make the most appalling mistakes. The confident judge will satisfy himself always, even if he displeases some of the exhibitors. The judge lacking in confidence will please neither.

Now, whilst timidity is usually born of lack of knowledge, this is not always the case. It is sometimes a question of temperament. I have known some men whose opinions on certain animals or birds, examined individually, were always reliable but who nevertheless "went all to pieces" when judging at a show, and made mistakes incomprehensible even to themselves later in the day.

This type of judge, the man who understands the show properties and could describe the ideal specimen to you with perfect accuracy, gets the exhibits into the wrong order for one of several reasons:

Firstly, he may be a highly sensitive person who is so afraid of making errors that he makes many. His intense desire to satisfy is actually his undoing. All the time he is going through the classes he is wondering what the fanciers present will think of his awards. This worries him so much that the birds begin to appear to his eyes practically all as good as each other. They all look more or less alike. Many young judges have had this dreadful experience. I had it myself when as a youth I first judged at a big show of pigeons, and I shall never forget it.

The best thing to do in these circumstances is to go away from the birds for a respite of ten minutes or so, and then return to the task. The little break often causes the relative merits of the competitors to become more apparent.

This phenomenon is usually confined to a man's initial efforts as a judge, and in most cases experience removes the possibility of its recurrence. But some fanciers never overcome it, and they should really refrain from accepting judging appointments.

Then we have that type of judge who has a sound understanding of the subject but who has no comparative sense. He, again, can criticise or praise the individual specimen, he can assess its value to a nicety, but he simply cannot place in their correct order of merit a number of birds not very unequal in exhibition requirements. For this class of fancier there is no cure; he can never become a good judge.

There is another variety of judge who, although he may be an honest man, is afraid of putting down birds which have won their classes at earlier shows. So he tries to find them. If he spots one he gives it first even though had he not known about its previous success, it would have been "down the line", because he does not consider it as good as the judge at an earlier show must have done; or perhaps competition at that event was not so strong.

Sometimes one of the unwise judges *thinks* he has given first to Mr —'s winner at — when actually it is not that bird at all. Then indeed he is in a mess! This is most unfair judging and contrary to the spirit of our hobby.

And then, of course, there is he who accepts appointments knowing full well, if he would be true to himself, that he has not as yet sufficient knowledge of the Budgerigar to enable him to appraise accurately the show properties of the exhibits and come through the task of judging with complete satisfaction to all concerned.

I have described all these possible failings in judges in order to show that the fancier who does not suffer from any of them is he who approximates to

232

the ideal judge. Fortunately in the Budgerigar Fancy we have a number in this category—men blessed with the judicial temperament, always calm and collected, confident, knowledgeable, judging neither too quickly nor too slowly, anxious to please yet not over-anxious, occasionally making mistakes—of course, there is no judge who is always right if he will but admit it—and ever willing to give the reasons for their awards after judging—in short, judges under whom exhibitors can enter with complete confidence. There is an old saying the good judges are born not made, and there is, believe me, a great deal of truth in it.

THE STANDARDS

The Budgerigar Society's Standard should be the ruling guide to all our judges. That is one of its primary purposes. Different judges will naturally, human nature being what it is, interpret that Standard somewhat differently, and this will ever be one reason why awards differ from show to show with the same exhibits in competition; and yet those who are entrusted with the placing of the cards must endeavour to follow the Standard to the very best of their ability. They must not set up standards of their own even though in some details they may disagree with the official one. The good judge ever has in his mind's eye the ideal specimen of which the Standard is a description.

The Budgerigar Society's Scale of Points, published below, is of great value to young judges, not because any judge making his awards by the comparison principle, which is the only proved sound method of judging livestock, ever actually counts points as he proceeds with his work, but because a Scale of Points shows the relative importance of the different properties. It removes from a judge's mind any doubt as, for example, whether head is more valuable than body outline, and so on.

Although I do not claim superiority of ability over other judges, I will describe the order of importance of the respective properties in the Standard as I place them when I am judging; and this order I know will be approved by many other judges, because undoubtedly a number of us hold opinions which are not at great variance.

In the first place, we will take condition as being essential in an exhibition specimen and not put it into any particular order because it is a *sine qua non,* although there are degrees even of good condition. That being accepted, the sequence in which I place the various properties is as follows:-

Type, including shape of body, shape of head, and carriage combining position of wings and tail; colour; size; throat spots and mask generally; wing markings. (Of course, throat spots and wing markings do not count at all in Whites of Light Suffusion, Yellows, and red-eyed pure Yellows and Whites, because to be ideal they should not have any). Under the general

THE MAIN FEATURES OF A BUDGERIGAR

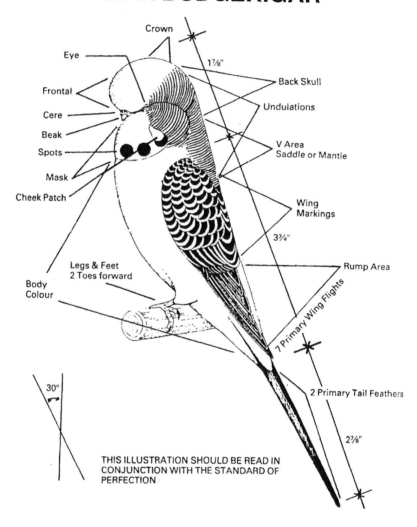

Crown

Eye

Frontal

Cere

Beak

Spots

Mask

Cheek Patch

1⅞"

Back Skull

Undulations

V Area
Saddle or Mantle

Wing
Markings

3¾"

Legs & Feet
2 Toes forward

Body
Colour

Rump Area

7 Primary Wing Flights

30°

2 Primary Tail Feathers

2⅞"

THIS ILLUSTRATION SHOULD BE READ IN
CONJUNCTION WITH THE STANDARD OF
PERFECTION

Figure 18.1

The Modern Budgerigar Standard

Issued by the Budgerigar Society

heading of Type I include symmetry and charm referred to at some length in Chapter 3.

This list is but a generalisation—it cannot be more—but maybe a description of the judging of an imaginary class of Cobalt cocks as an example will the better convey to my readers just how the different show properties appeal to me.

So here I am at the show, and on the judging table my stewards have put the twenty birds which have been entered in a class.

First of all I find three which are obviously out of condition. They are not tight in feather and they show no alertness. Out they come.

Now I spot one which is badly shown. Its mask is dirty and it looks as though it had not seen a wash or a spray for a long time. My eye strays to a bird of really commanding appearance—a smart one, and apparently good in colour. He goes along to the left for further examination. Several of these do I see as the casting out process goes along and always they go up to the left to do battle later.

So far only four birds have been taken off the table. More will have to be eliminated in order to leave me with that reasonable number for final decision as referred to earlier in this chapter. To be honest, I like to spot these faulty ones fairly quickly, because it makes my task all the easier by virtue of my very soon having comparatively few birds left to deal with.

Ah, here's a narrow shallow chested one. None of that desired curvature is there about it; in fact it is angular and it is snaky headed. I note it is quite good in colour and not faulty in markings but they cannot carry it "into the money". So that's another one handed to the steward.

I see a very small one. Is it good enough in type to make up for its lack of size? It is not. Down it goes.

Rather too Aldermanic

Here's a good bird carrying much substance. It doesn't seem very alert. It's deep in chest; in fact it is too deep in chest. The chest line fairly bulges out. It is good in colour and big in head. Can I leave it in? No, I can't—it's too ponderous; it lacks smartness.

Now I find a bird of good size, very shapely, bright and breezy, of nice colour and markings, but small in head, and yet I have only seen two better as I have gone along, so I shall have to send it up to the left perchance there are not sufficient good ones to put in front of it. (Of course, as one judges in this way one naturally forms an impression as to whether the class generally is of high, medium, or low quality, and one instinctively knows whether even only moderate birds may stand a chance of being in the prize list and should, therefore, be passed up to the left for later consideration).

Now I have before me two with that beautiful, true Cobalt colour which is so much to be preferred to the bluey Cobalt hue. They are nice in spots and wing markings, not very big but they are typical, so they must go to the left.

Here's one good in type, in rare condition, fairly good in colour, one spot is missing but the others are good. Does he stand a chance? No he doesn't. Why? Because of his hoopy carriage. It's awful. He drops his tail and bends his back and sticks his head forward. It's a pity, but his posture is the antithesis of that for which I am looking. So another one is eliminated.

The next is a good bird in every way but unfortunately he has two spots down, and although spots do not go *too* high in my order of property importance, as I said in the chapter on markings, birds with two spots missing cannot really do the trick, though it's bad luck for the owner, as probably the spots were intact when the exhibit left home. I have to hand that one to my steward also.

Bird with One Tail Feather

I come to a bird with only one tail feather, and according to the Standard there should be two. Logically, it is not fair to put birds amongst the prizes when they have only one long tail feather when one handicaps specimens because they have split tails. A Budgerigar cannot have a split tail if it has only one long tail feather left in. And while I would not necessarily, if competition were not very strong, put a bird *completely* out of the running because it had only one tail feather, in a company such as this it won't do, so I reduce the number of birds left on the table by another one.

I have now eliminated ten and I have ten left and seven prizes to award. I have the ten cages in a line in front of me. The judging is becoming less easy. My intention now is to find the three worst, and they are all rather good ones that are left in.

Those more blue in colour I move towards the right. Those of the correct Cobalt colour I move towards the left. Here's that big good one with the correct colour that I had noted particularly earlier. I still don't like his head. He will have to go down a bit and he does, to the seventh position.

Another walk down the cages and I realise that the two which are of the blue colouring must come out. I have now eight in front of me. One more to eliminate and all the rest will secure cards.

That very important property, head, begins to count. Those with the smaller heads are moved down towards the right.

Standing in positions 5 and 6 are two birds, equal in shape, equal in colour and markings; in fact there is nothing divides them except the position in which they stand. One poses beautifully; the other is "across the perch".

Standing above No. 4 is a nice all-round bird of very good colour but he is dipping his tail slightly and hasn't quite the depth and width of breast of some ahead of him, although he by no means fails in this property.

Another walk down the line, and I realise that the birds standing in positions 1,2, and 3 are the three best birds in the class, and that 4, 5, 6, and 7 are in their correct order. What now remains is to place 1, 2, and 3 accurately, and this is by a long way the most difficult part of the judging of this very strong class of Cobalt cocks.

Very little divides them. I say to myself: "Something has got to decide the issue and I have got to find it." There is no such thing as a perfect bird. To be hypercritical they all have small faults. It is a question of deciding which has the fewest of these small faults; or if they are equal in numbers of faults, which is the best in the most important properties? Most carefully have they to be examined. There doesn't seem to be anything between them as far as colour is concerned. They are all beautifully marked, all in fine condition, all full of life.

Nipped in Neck

I have observed something: Viewed from the front, one is slightly narrower in head than another, not much, but just enough to make a difference. I notice, however, just as I am about to transfer the two cages, that the bird which is slightly wider in head is also slightly nipped in neck, only very slightly or, of course, he would not be at this end of the class, as nipped necks are so undesirable. So that bird must stay where it is and the one slightly narrower in head must stand above him. Those two are in order second and third.

Let me look at No. 1. He is neither narrow in head nor nipped in neck, and he is just as good in colour, body markings, size, and carriage as 2 and 3. Now I am satisfied. The three birds are as they should be in my opinion. The job is done!

Many other points, of course, could have been the deciding factor when competition ran so close—one crossing its wings just a little more than another but not sufficient to cause it to have been eliminated earlier, as it certainly would have been by me if it had crossed its wings scissor fashion, patchiness on breast, and so on.

The judging of Any Other Colour classes is rather a vexed question. Some judges in these classes are inclined to divide the colours.

For instance they put a Cinnamon 1st, then they will not put another Cinnamon 2nd simply because it is the same colour as the winner. And if they put a Yellow-wing 2nd they won't put a Yellow-wing 3rd, because it is the same colour as the 2nd, even though apart from colour variety Cinnamons should have been 1st and 2nd, or alternatively Yellow-wings 2nd and 3rd. I have only taken these colours as examples, of course.

Personally I think judges should judge the birds as Budgerigars, ignoring what their respective colour varieties may be, and if it should happen that birds of the same colour stand 1st, 2nd, and 3rd, so be it. If, of course, the birds are of equal merit, which is virtually impossible, then there would be

THE BUDGERIGAR SOCIETY'S
SCALE OF POINTS

Variety	Size shape balance and deportment	Size & shape of head incl. mask & where applicable spots	Colour	Variety markings
Normal (Light, Dark, Olive, Grey Green)	35	25	15	25
Normal (Skyblue, Cobalt, Mauve, Violet, Grey)	35	25	15	25
Opaline (Light, Dark, Olive, Grey Green)	35	25	15	25
Opaline (Skyblue, Cobalt, Mauve, Violet, Grey)	35	25	15	25
Cinnamon (Light, Dark, Olive, Grey Green)	35	25	15	25
Cinnamon (Skyblue, Cobalt, Mauve, Violet & Grey)	35	25	15	25
Opaline Cinnamon (Light, Dark, Olive, Grey Green)	35	25	15	25
Opaline Cinnamon (Skyblue, Cobalt, Mauve, Violet, Grey)	35	25	15	25
Lutino & Albino	35	25	40*	–
Clearwings (Yellow-wings & Whitewings Light, Dark, Olive & Grey Green Skyblue, Cobalt, Mauve, Violet & Grey)	35	25	15	25
Crested or Tufted (in all shades & varieties)	35	25	15	25+
Spangles (in all shades & varieties)	35	25	15	25
Spangles Double Factor	35	25	40*	–
Pied (Dominant) (in all shades & all varieties)	35	25	15	25
Pied (Clearflighted) (in all shades & all varieties)	35	25	15	25
Pied (Recessive) (in all shades & all varieties)	35	25	15	25#
Dark-Eyed (Clear Varieties)	35	25	40*	–
Yellowface (Mutant 1, Mutant 2 and Goldenface all varieties Blue Series)	35	25	15	25
Rainbows (Opaline Whitewing Yellowface & Goldenface)	35	25	15	25
Yellow (Light, Dark, Olive) (including Opaline & Cinnamon)	35	25	40*	–
Yellow & White (Suffused) (in all shades including Opaline & Cinnamon)	35	25	15	25
Grey Yellow & Grey White (in all shades (light, medium & dark) incl Opaline & Cinnamon)	35	25	15	25
Greywing (Light, Dark, Olive, Grey Green, Skyblue, Cobalt, Mauve, Violet & Grey) (including Opaline Greywing)	35	25	15	25
Lacewings (Yellow & White) (incl. Opalines)	35	25	15	25
Fallow (Light, Dark, Olive, Grey Green, Skyblue, Cobalt, Mauve, Violet & Grey) (including Opaline Fallow)	35	25	15	25
Opaline, Cinnamon & Opal. Cin. Clearwings	35	25	15	25

* Points for depth and clarity of colour
# Points for contrast of colour and variegation and % of wing markings
+ Points included for shape and quality of Crest

Team of six birds of any colour or team of four of any one colour.
Points: General colour & variety 50; uniformity 50.

some justification for separating the colours in the manner I have described.

Another point about these Any Other Colour classes: Much as I support the encouragement of new colours and desire to see them developed, I am entirely opposed to putting a bird of very poor type in front of specimens of excellent type and colouring just because it happens to be one of the newest colours known to the Fancy. Certainly if a representative of one of the new colours approximates to a bird of the older colours in shape, markings, etc., then I think it is quite wise to encourage the newer colour by giving it the preference.

The purport of my remarks is that one must not allow any fashion for varieties to warp one's judgement as to what is required in so far as type, markings, etc. are concerned. And because I have said this I do not want anyone to get the impression that I am not amongst those who desire to see the development of new colours. I most certainly do, providing they are creatures of beauty, but I do feel that in Any Other Colour classes it is not fair to put inferior specimens — merely because they are something new — in front of high-class birds of the older colour varieties.

These remarks apply with equal force to the awarding of specials for the best Budgerigar in the show, because there again as in the Any Other Colour class one has to select the champion from competitors of different colour varieties.

"Best in Show" Awards

Referring to specials for best in show, many are the methods by which these are awarded, except, of course, where there is only one judge and then he has only himself to consult, and he picks his own best bird. The best special judging system of all at any sizable show, where several judges are employed, and where there is a rather lengthy special list, is to give one judge the sole task of awarding the specials.

Provide him with one or two good stewards and a judging table, and he will be able to make a start on his job soon after the class judges have commenced, and he will complete his awards soon after the last class slip has gone in. One of the stewards must be armed with a list containing all particulars of the specials offered, nomination, Society membership and so on.

When people argue with me about my preference for one specials judge only and contend that several judges should award the specials, I invariably answer: "If you can trust one judge to award the prizes in the separate classes, why can't you trust him to select the special winners?"

Figure 18-2 Good Utilisation of Space. The Cupboards beneath the Flights and the foldaway tables are very good space-savers.

Guidelines for Judges and Exhibitors*

Faults and/or defects which should be penalised by judges: Where the word penalised is used, it denotes that a penalty should be applied by a judge, according to his opinion, of the degree of the severity of the faults and/or defects which are before him for consideration. Where a DIRECTIVE is given it must be strictly adhered to.

COMMON TO ALL VARIETIES.

1. CONDITION IS ESSENTIAL. If a bird is not in condition it should be penalised. Perfect show condition is defined as a bird that is in complete feather. Whether it be Yellow or Buff, the feather should show the bloom of good health and good preparation.

2. LONG FLIGHTED. No bird showing long flighted characteristics is eligible to take any award. **(DIRECTIVE)**

3. Birds showing any sign of **SCALYFACE** must be removed from the show bench by the show management on the instruction of the judge. **(DIRECTIVE).** Where possible affected birds should be isolated from the show hall, as should any exhibit which shows signs of sickness and distress.

4. FLECKING is defined as any dark mark (flecks or grizzle) on the crown or frontal of the head, these markings should be penalised severely, bearing in mind that the standard for every variety denotes THE FRONTAL AND CROWN MUST BE CLEAR AND FREE FROM ALL MARKINGS

5. OPALESCENCE. This fault can occur in all varieties where the pattern and distribution of markings is as the normal light green, and is defined as being a visible overlay of body colour intruding on the cheeks, back of the head, neck and wings which detracts from the definition of markings as depicted in the pictorial ideal and described in the colour standards. The varying degree of opalescence must be penalised accordingly.

6. SPOTS. Where applicable in the standards, missing, irregular or badly shaped spots should be penalised, the size of the spots should be in proportion to the rest of the make-up of the bird as is depicted in the pictorial ideal.

7. PRIMARY FLIGHTS. Birds displaying less or more than seven primary flights should be penalised.

8. INHERENT FAULTS. eg. Dropped tail, nipped neck, poor backline, poor deportment, poor wing-carriage, beakiness, etc.... should be penalised.

9. TEMPORARY FAULTS. Missing primary flight or tail feathers, spot feathers (particularly outer spots) and the presence of pin feathers or blood quills should be assessed with due regard to the effect on the overall balance of the exhibit, and should be penalised accordingly.

*These are the rules of judging issued by The Budgerigar Society. Fanciers are advised to obtain the latest information from the Society.

10. ANY DEFORMITY.   Should be penalised.

11. BODY COLOUR. Patchiness and/or dilution of body colour above the level of that described in the colour standards and any suffusion of another colour other than that described in the colour standards should be penalised.

FAULTS AND/OR DEFECTS CONFINED TO SPECIFIC VARIETIES,

additional to those listed in guidelines 1 to 11 as above where applicable.

12. ANY VARIETY OPALINE.

WING MARKINGS: The edges of all wing feathers should be well defined and show the same colour as the body, absence of body colour on the wings, smudging or thumb marks of the pattern and distribution of the wing markings should be penalised. MANTLE/ SADDLE should be the same colour as the body and any dark markings in the 'V' area should be penalised, any very heavy dark markings within the area of undulations at the back of the head and neck should also be penalised.

TAILS: Absence of or variegation of solid colour in primary tail feathers should be penalised.

13. NORMAL and OPALINE CINNAMON, NORMAL and OPALINE GREY WING. The body colour in these four varieties should be penalised if it is below or in excess of 50% of the normal body colour in depth and intensity.

14. LUTINO AND ALBINO: The following deviations from the standard should be penalised: pale violet colour in cheek patches, cinnamon brown spots, or markings on the back, wings or tail. suffusion throughout. Albino; there throughout. wings or tail. Lutino; there should be no green Albino; there should be no blue or grey suffusion

15. CLEARWING. (Normal Yellow-wings and Whitewings). The following deviations from the standard should be penalised: dilution of body colour down from approximately the normal depth and intensity; pale violet, pale blue or pale grey cheek patches; absence of blue or grey colour in primary tail feathers; any markings on wings according to the depth of such markings; opalescence on back of head, neck or wings. N.B. Cinnamon Yellow wings and Cinnamon Whitewings must be shown in the A.O.C. classes.

16. CRESTED. An incomplete or damaged circular, half circular or tufted crest should be penalised, and the other faults listed in these guide-lines for whichever variety is carrying the crest should also be considered and penalised accordingly.

17. SPANGLE. The following deviations from the standard should, be penalised: completely black feathers on the wings; incomplete or absent throat spots. DOUBLE FACTOR SPANGLE. Any black or grizzled ticking visible anywhere on the bird, or green, blue or grey suffusion, should be penalised.

18. DOMINANT PIED. The following deviations from the standard should be penalised: an all clear yellow or white body colour: all clear yellow or white wings;   spillage of

mask colour around the neck and back of head and the absence of one or more spots.

19. CLEARFLIGHT: The absence of the head patch, broken body colour and/or the presence of dark primary wing or tail feathers should be penalised.

20. RECESSIVE PIED: Dark markings on wings if less than 10% or more than 20% of total area should be penalised. Zebra markings on the frontal should also be penalised bearing in mind that standard for every variety denotes that the FRONTAL AND CROWN SHOULD BE CLEAR AND FREE FROM ALL MARKINGS.

21. DARK-EYED CLEAR YELLOW AND DARK-EYED CLEAR WHITE. Any odd green or blue feathers or green or blue suffusion in the body, or any black or grizzled ticking or suffusion in the wings should be penalised.

22. YELLOWFACE. Mutant 1. Spillage of yellow colour from the mask into the body colour should be penalised; the exception being as described in NOTE 2 of Yellowface and Goldenface mutations Standards.

23. YELLOWFACE Mutant 2 and GOLDENFACE Mutations.
In the double factor form both may display some light spillage of yellow colour into the body colour adjacent to the bottom edge of the mask which is permissible, reference should always be made to the notes 1, 2, and 3, which accompany the written standards for these yellowface mutations

24. LACEWINGS. Incomplete patterns of normal or opaline cinnamon brown markings including primary tail feathers, or any suffusion of green or blue/grey colour into the body colour should be penalised.

25. NORMAL AND OPALINE FALLOWS. A complete absence of body colour should be penalised.

26. WRONG CLASSING OF EXHIBITS. When this is necessary Judges should indicate on the cage label the reason. Where doubt exists, wrong classing should only be carried out after consultation with fellow Judges. The only marks that Judges should make on cage labels are Class Positions, Best of Colour (BOC), Section Awards, Wrong Class (WC) and reason for removal from staging and reason for disqualification. N.B. It is not permitted to indicate the position within the colour line-up.

27. **THE STANDARD OF PERFECTION, SCALE OF POINTS, COLOUR STANDARDS AND PICTORIAL IDEALS AND THESE GUIDELINES**
should all be read in conjunction with each other, they all play a part in
serving as a guide to both Judge and Exhibitor.

28. SHOW CLASSIFICATION. Show schedules can be confusing for inexperienced fanciers, therefore it is advisable that all show promoting societies use the correct description of birds (as defined in the B.S. Colour Standards) when setting out the mandatory show classification, eg. OPALINE CINNAMON (not cinnamon opaline).

Figure 18.3 Tufted Crest Budgerigar
Courtesy: Crested Budgerigar Club

CHAPTER 19

TALKING BUDGERIGARS

SELECTION

Although *The Cult of the Budgerigar* is primarily written for those who breed these birds for exhibition purposes, I feel it would not be complete unless reference was made in its pages to a most interesting and endearing attribute of this beautiful Parakeet, viz., its ability to learn to talk in a similar manner to that of the larger Parrots.

There are today in houses all over the world Budgerigars which can talk with marked ability, perform little tricks for the enjoyment of families and visitors, and which have become so tame and friendly that no pet could be a greater source of delight.

Many thousands of chicks are now sold annually to be taught to talk. This is a phase of Budgerigar culture distinct from breeding for exhibition.

It is necessary to purchase your potential "talkie" when it is a baby only a few days out of the nest. It must then be placed in a large cage, as small cages are unsuitable for a bird of such activity.

Cocks Preferred

As cocks make the better talkers and are generally more companionable, it is desirable to purchase one of this sex. Here a little difficulty arises because it is not always easy to discover with certainty the sex of a youngster at this tender age. But some breeders become quite adept at differentiating the sex of the chicks, one method being to allow the youngster to nip one's finger, the hens even at this stage of their lives having a stronger bite than the cocks.

If you look into the nostrils there are more signs of blue in cocks than in hens, even though the wattles of both sexes are at that age blue-white. Also, the ceres of cocks are usually more rounded and the head formation is different.

When the chick is placed in the cage in the house which is to be its home, a careful watch must be kept upon it to see that it is eating properly.

245

Budgerigars will usually learn to crack the husks and feed themselves within four or five days of leaving their parents.

Generally speaking women make the best teachers, no doubt because of their lighter voices, which are easier to imitate.

Tame the Bird

Before talking lessons start Master Budgie must be tamed. He should first be taught to stand on a thin stick or a pencil and later on the finger. Soon he will become so friendly that he will allow the owner to tickle the back of his neck, a form of caress which Parrots love. Before long the young pupil will become so tame that he can be brought out of his cage and even though he may fly round the room, he will rapidly fly back to his trainer, stand on her shoulder and display his affection for her.

In order to get the chick to perch on the finger a good plan is to put the forefinger across the front of the legs and press gently against the body. The bird will then have no alternative but to step on to the finger or fall off the perch.

This taming process should be conducted calmly and with gentleness; in fact everything possible should be done to avoid scaring the pupil by your attentions. A fright of any kind in these early days of its tuition will retard progress considerably. Within a month the bird should be very tame, but the talking lessons can commence as soon as it is reasonably steady.

STARTING THE LESSONS

In the first place, it is advisable to teach one word at a time, not going on to another word until the teacher is sure that the previous word has been correctly learnt. A Budgie "learns to learn." Having taught it one sentence or phrase it is easier to teach it another, and then easier still to teach it a third; and so it goes on.

Some Budgerigars can be made into good talkers quickly; others never succeed in becoming efficient.

As I mentioned, it is generally accepted that hens cannot be taught to talk except on rare occasions. Although quite a number of hens have become talkers, nevertheless, they are not so suitable as cocks. Undoubtedly cocks are more friendly in disposition than hens, and for this reason if anyone desires to keep a few Budgerigars in a cage in the house as pets—in preference to one bird—I always advise keeping cocks and no hens. If a cock and a hen are kept in a cage their desire to breed makes them restless and unsatisfactory.

It is necessary to keep a "talkie" in a cage alone away from sight and sound of other Budgerigars so that the only voice it hears is the human voice. It is advisable also that the lessons should be given by one person; otherwise the bird will become confused.

I have heard of some hobbyists putting into the cage of a talking Budgerigar a young chick fresh from the nest with a view to the older bird acting as schoolmaster to the younger, but I have not seen reported any particular success in this direction.

A talking Budgerigar which shows signs of becoming an expert can be induced to learn verses of nursery rhymes by the use of a gramophone. This should be placed near the cage and the same record or part of the record run through many times continuously each day, until the bird does what is expected of him. It is better to do this in sections, the bird learning one sentence at a time.

Figure 19-1 Budgerigar; A good show specimen
(Courtesy: *Cage and Aviary*)

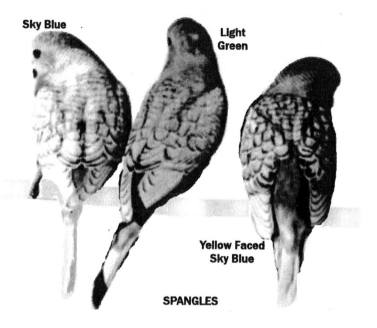

Sky Blue

Light Green

Yellow Faced Sky Blue

SPANGLES

Figure 19.2 Spangles

These are really laced birds and not Spangles at all, which should be small markings evenly spread, if the true poultry spangle definition is followed.* See page 60 for description.

---

* See *Understanding Old English Game* or *Old English Game Bantams* or *Old English Game Colour Guide*, Joseph Batty, BPH

CHAPTER 20

DISEASES

PREVENTION THE AIM

As regards disease in Budgerigars frankly I am more concerned with prevention than cure, and I do not intend to give a list of the complaints from which our birds suffer and a series of prescriptions, although there are on the market some excellent remedies which the fancier can have in his bird room in readiness. I am not a veterinary surgeon and I have not the ability always to diagnose correctly from symptoms just what a Budgerigar is suffering from when I find it huddled up, with its feathers almost assuming the perpendicular, and looking thoroughly miserable, which are invariably the signs that something is definitely wrong.

A veterinary surgeon who has knowledge of the pathology of small animals and birds (this does not apply to all vets by any means) is no doubt able to state with accuracy what is the matter with a Budgerigar if he has the opportunity of examining it, and he may effect a cure if the patient is entrusted to him sufficiently soon after the first signs of indisposition are apparent.

But this is usually beyond the layman's skill except in cases of simple ailments which can be dealt with satisfactorily if attention to the invalid is not delayed. The average fancier like myself has but small veterinary knowledge and in cases of a *serious* illness overtaking one of his birds death usually occurs.

Although Budgerigars are generally healthy and vigorous, their resistance to disease is not great and efforts to cure any major illness are usually in vain.

I am a sentimentalist in so far as animals and birds are concerned, and therefore, naturally, I do not like to see a Budgerigar die if anything which I can do can save its life, but if I could harden my heart I should never try to cure a very sick specimen but should end its sufferings by killing it, because of the strong opinion which I hold, and which I have expressed elsewhere in this book, that a bird which has ever suffered from a serious disease should never be bred from and never sold. It is the "patching up" of Budgerigars of

249

weak constitution and of those which have been very ill which is one of the major causes of the troubles which some breeders experience, particularly during the breeding season, and which I have described in Chapter 10.

I will not go over ground which I have already trodden in this work beyond emphasising the fact that it would be all to the good of the Budgerigar Fancy if the maxim of strict elimination of the unfit—in other words the old jungle law of the survival of the fittest—were applied ruthlessly on all occasions.

In previous chapters I have described those methods which other breeders and myself employ in order to retain vigour in our birds, and I contend that if this advice is taken and acted on meticulously sickness in Budgerigar establishments will cause owners little or no worry.

Although, as I have previously said, Budgerigars as a race are extraordinarily healthy and exceedingly easy to keep in good condition, there are diseases which they can contract and many of these are directly due to debility. If a bird gets into a debilitated or "run-down" state then its resistance to any kind of disease is lowered and it is liable to become seriously ill and die.

French Moult

We have read a lot about French Moult, which usually affects youngsters soon after they begin to fledge. Its symptoms are the dropping of the flight and tail feathers and the bird's inability to replace them properly, the remaining feathers appearing weak, curly and unnatural. The victims of this complaint cannot fly and they are what are known as "runners".

When I wrote the first edition of *The Cult of the Budgerigar* in 1935 the cause of French Moult was unknown and I have to confess the position is unchanged. We still don't know. Many theories have been expounded. Some consider this feather deficiency is inherited in accordance with Mendel's principles in a similar way to that in which colour is inherited. Some have ventilated the opinion that it can be attributed to improper feeding on the part of the parents. Some writers express the view that weak parents are the cause of "runners". Other reasons adduced are breeding from immature stock, over-breeding and so on.

A popular idea is that a parasite of some sort is the cause of French Moult. No very serious research in this direction was undertaken until about 1945. Then Dr M.D.S. Armour, assisted by Mr Andy Wilson, F.Z.S., and Mr John G. Campbell, F.R.C.V.S., F.R.M.S., of the Royal (Dick) Veterinary College, Edinburgh, began their investigations, the outcome of which was the publication by the Budgerigar Society in 1946 of "Report on Research into Cause, Prevention and Cure of French Moult in Budgerigars."

According to this treatise French Moult is attributable to Fodder Mites.

The authors did not claim that it was the last word on the subject. In fact, the old Scientific Committee of the Budgerigar Society, under the guidance of the ex-Chairman, the late E.W. Brooks, employed commendable endeavour in elucidating some of the questions which were not entirely settled when the above treatise was published, particularly in regard to the treatment of aviaries, nest boxes and the birds themselves with D.D.T. which had to be used strictly in accordance with the instructions given by Dr Armour, and later by Mr Brooks on behalf of the Scientific Committee.

Many fanciers were, and still are, not satisfied that the mites isolated are the cause of French Moult, and other theories have been propounded. Prominent among these is that described in the *Budgerigar Bulletin* of September, 1951, by the then Editor, the late A.V. Garnett. He attributed French Moult to red mite, and provided evidence in support of his assertion.

As stated in an earlier chapter there is now being conducted at Reading University intensive research into the cause and prevention of French Moult. This is being sponsored and financed by the National Council of Aviculture. At the time of writing no definite conclusions have been reached by those who are conducting this work.

Much research has been carried out in America, and a number of theories propounded.

Personally, I have not yet been able to subscribe to any one of the numerous theories put forward. If I were to hazard a guess I would say the idea of Prof. T.G. Taylor and others that the basic cause is malnutrition plus some perhaps as yet undiscovered agent—maybe a mite, we do not definitely know—is as near the truth as we have ever been.

The complaint is named French Moult because it is said it first made its appearance in the huge aviaries in France in which thousands of Budgerigars were bred to supply the European pet trade.

I do not wish my readers to form the opinion that French Moult is a very serious hindrance to Budgerigar culture. If it were, then, of course, there would not be reared to maturity every year so many thousands of healthy young birds. Every breeding season in many establishments no "runners" appear; in others there are very, very few; in some they are more numerous.

French Moult is not really a disease; it is a feather deficiency. There is nothing loathsome about it. In many cases the feathering becomes normal in the course of time.

I have indicated that the treatment of serious diseases in Budgerigars is usually unsuccessful and that in the majority of cases the patients die, but, on the other hand, if birds are caught and caged when they first appear to be slightly indisposed, and are properly treated immediately, they can often be put right within a few days and their becoming seriously ill can be avoided. Particularly does this refer to specimens which have caught a chill due to sudden changes in temperature, standing in draughts, and so on.

FEATHER DUSTERS: Another strange feather problem, when the feathers grow in different directions, in an untidy fashion, has become known as the 'Feather Duster'. This is the result of a rogue gene, which shows when the faulty chick gets its feathers. Besides producing this freak of nature it seems that the gene is lethal so the birds affected die fairly quickly, possibly at the first moult. If detected in a breeding pair they should be culled, or at least not bred from again.

FREQUENT CAUSE OF DEATH

Apropos, I am certain that some Budgerigars which are not very well die not because of the chill or some other trouble from which they are suffering, but because they have no appetite for food and they really succumb to starvation. I have sometimes saved the life of a bird on these occasions by giving it milk mixed with one of the suitable propriety products. Of course, forcible feeding with seed is not to be recommended because actually lack of appetite is a symptom of the complaint and ordinary food would do more harm than good.

Warmth is remarkably beneficial when a Budgerigar shows the first signs of illness, and whilst it will not alone cure anything of a serious nature, many birds will be quickly restored to normal health if they are kept in a warm place. For this purpose of great service is the hospital cage invented by Mr Andy Wilson, F.Z.S. It is an admirable contrivance. It is electrically heated, the heat can be varied in accordance with the judgement of the owner, and when a sickly specimen is placed in it there is no fear of draughts or undesirable temperature variability. This hospital cage can also be used for drying purposes after washing as described in Chapter 17.

Not only should a bird in which indisposition is detected be quickly removed for the purposes of treatment, but it should also be taken as far as possible away from other birds in order to effect isolation, because it must be agreed that the symptoms which I have described as being those of a sudden chill can also be the symptoms of one of the more serious diseases, and as most of the illnesses to which bird flesh is heir can be attributed to micro-organisms or filterable viruses there must be complete isolation in order to avoid other birds being infected.

Amongst these more serious diseases which usually end fatally, probably the most common is enteritis in one of its several forms. Septicaemia is another. Then occasionally Budgerigars suffer from those ailments which affect all living things such as asthma, paralysis, bronchitis, constipation, and pneumonia. Coccidiosis kills some Budgerigars, just as it does poultry and rabbits.

Most of the Budgerigar books which have been published give remedies for these complaints. I will be quite frank and say that I cannot advise any particular medicines in preference to others because I say to my readers that if they have any birds seriously attacked by any one of these illnesses the probability is that they will die, or their owners will humanely decide to end their sufferings.

A Budgerigar which is rickety should be destroyed. It is valueless. What the breeder has to do is to avoid as far as possible owning birds which suffer from rickets, the cause of which may be Vitamin D deficiency or a lack of calcium.

I do not want any of my readers to get the impression that disease in Budgerigars is prevalent. Actually, as I have said before, as a race they are extraordinarily healthy, but like all living things they are not immune to disease.

Believing that information about the Budgerigar's internal organs and their functions will be interesting to my readers I quote below a description which was kindly supplied to me by that eminent veterinary surgeon, the late Henry Gray, M.R.C.V.S., who wrote: –

"The alimentary canal through which the food passes to be digested and assimilated and the dregs or faeces to be discharged comprises the mouth, pharynx, oesphagus or gullet; the crop or reservoir to store the food; the proventriculus or glandular stomach which secretes mucus and other digestive juices or ferments; the gizzard or muscular stomach in which the food is triturated before it passes into the intestine to undergo further chemical changes; the rectum or straight or terminal section of the bowel; and the cloaca or vent chamber which receives the debris or faeces before they are discharged through the anus or vent into the external world.

SECRETING GLANDS

"There are various secretory or endocrine glands all along the alimentary canal which pour special secretions into it to aid in digestion and produce chemical changes in the food so as to render it assimilable and aid in keeping up the functions of the whole system. The mucus glands secrete material to make the food and faeces more able to glide along the alimentary canal. The first important gland is the pancreas situated on the duodenal loops of the small intestine into lumen of which the pancreatic duct opens, so that the pancreatic secretion can pass and convert the fats into a saponified liquid. Next the liver which pours bile through the bile duct to pass on to the duodenum.

"Just above or in front of the testicles are the suprarenal glands. They are whitish and no larger than a rape seed. Their secretion plays a great part in the circulation and they control the bloodvessels. The lobes of the kidney are hidden in the recesses under the broad sacral bone. The urinary canals which carry the more or less semi-solid whitish urine open into the cloaca.

253

The urine of birds is semi-solid and forms the white part of the faeces. There is no urinary bladder in birds. The testicles which are attached under the loin just behind the lungs secrete semen which is carried by canals opening into the cloaca. This opening is provided with a papilla or small prominence.

"There is only one active ovary and oviduct, the left. The right atrophies in early life and leaves behind it a degenerative vestige. The ovary is provided with ovisacs in which the yolks develop. When the yolk is ripe the sac bursts and the yolk enters the funnel end of the oviduct. The first part of this tube secretes the albumen which surrounds the yolk. The middle parts secrete the enveloping membrane or skin and the terminal portion secretes the material for the shell. The testes, the ovary, and the oviduct undergo involution and return to their primary state when the birds are not breeding and thus they become very small or thin.

"The cere in the male often becomes brown and it then resembles that of the female; and in the female it not rarely blue. This change of colour is usually due to degeneration of the testes or ovary. In some species such as the pheasant the hen may take on all the characters of the plumage of the cock, due to ovarian degeneration."

Figure 20.1 Mutation Known as a 'Feather Duster'

INDEX